THE BOOK OF GENESIS

the Smart Guide to the Bible™ series

BE SMART. BE INSPIRED.™

Joyce L. Gibson
Larry Richards, General Editor

NELSON BOOKS
A Division of Thomas Nelson Publishers
Since 1798

www.thomasnelson.com

The Book of Genesis
The Smart Guide to the Bible™ series

Published by Nelson Reference, a Division of Thomas Nelson, Inc., P.O. Box 141000, Nashville, Tennessee 37214.

Originally published by Starburst Publishers under the title *Genesis: God's Word for the Biblically-Inept.* Now revised and updated.

General Editor: Larry Richards
Managing Editor: Lila Empson
Associate Editor: W. Mark Whitlock
Scripture Editor: Deborah Wiseman
Assistant Editor: Amy Clark
Design: Diane Whisner

ISBN 1-4185-0993-0

Printed in the United States of America
06 07 08 09   9 8 7 6 5 4 3 2 1

Introduction

Welcome to *The Book of Genesis—The Smart Guide to the Bible*™. It is another in a series that makes the Bible enjoyable and easy to understand. This is not a traditional Bible study or commentary.

To Gain Your Confidence

The Book of Genesis—The Smart Guide to the Bible™ is for you if you are looking for an easy-to-read overview of the Bible's first book. You won't find detailed time lines or complicated explanations of words from ancient Hebrew. Instead, you'll meet fascinating Bible characters with insights into the customs of the day. Best of all, you'll read about God, the Creator of the universe, who took a personal interest in their lives. Actually, I hope this introductory study will, like an appetizer, awaken your hunger to study even more!

Let's Start with the Bible Itself

You hold a Bible in your hand and it is one book. But it's really a collection of sixty-six books written by a number of authors. You'll find a list of those books in the front of your Bible. You'll also notice that the books are listed under two headings: Old Testament (thirty-nine books) and New Testament (twenty-seven books). There's a good reason for this: the Old Testament was written before Jesus Christ was born. The New Testament was written after his birth. The Old Testament, written between 1400 BC and 400 BC, deals with events from Creation until 400 years before Jesus was born. The New Testament, written between AD 40 and AD 100, deals with Jesus' birth, life, death, resurrection, and ascension, as well as the Church, which began when people believed that Jesus was indeed the Son of God and the Savior of the world.

Many years after the Bible was written, Bible experts took the books and divided them into chapters and verses. Now when you see a reference, such as Psalm 23:6, you can find it quite easily by locating first the book, then the chapter, and then the verse.

But after all that, the Bible is still one book with one message from God to you.

Why Is the Bible So Special?

The Bible is not an ordinary book, even though it was written by ordinary people. That's because God was the source of their writings. They wrote what God inspired them to write. God himself gave them special insight and wisdom to write what he wanted. That's why we call the Bible the Word of God.

Why Study the Bible?

1. The first reason to study the Bible is that it is God's Book, his message to you. He gave you the Bible so you can know him! For more than two thousand years, God has been talking to people through the Bible. As you turn the pages of your Bible, you'll see again and again references to God speaking, telling the human writers what they were to put down. The best way you can know God is through the Bible.

2. Another reason to study the Bible is that it is truth—about God, about the world you live in, about you, and about how God wants you to live as you get to know him. Even though the Bible was written many years ago, it is God's message to you today, and its truth has power to change your life.

3. Still another reason to study the Bible is that God gives you answers to questions you have about how the world began, what makes people act the way they do, how God can give meaning and purpose to your life, what happens to people when they die, and where our world is headed.

Why Study Genesis?

Genesis is the first book of the Bible. In it you will find answers to many questions that people are asking today. Perhaps you have asked some of these questions:

- Where did the universe come from? How did it start?
- Is God a real person?
- If God is a real person, does he care about people like me?
- Can I have a worthy purpose in my life?
- Why does God allow people to act in ways that hurt themselves and others?
- Why do we have fighting and famines and other disasters? Why doesn't God do something about them?

These and many more questions are dealt with in the first book of the Bible. Now let's look more closely at who wrote Genesis and what the book is all about.

Who Wrote Genesis?

The first five books of the Bible are known as the Pentateuch. They are Genesis, Exodus, Leviticus, Numbers, and Deuteronomy. Moses wrote these books (except the part about how Moses died, which was probably written by Joshua). However, Moses could not write about the beginnings as an eyewitness. Genesis is truth through revelation. He wrote the account of beginnings as God revealed it to him.

What Is Genesis All About?

Genesis is a book of beginnings. In it God takes you back to the very beginning and tells about

- the beginning of the universe and a perfect world
- the beginning of people
- the beginning of sin and suffering
- the beginning of nations
- the beginning of rebellion against God
- the beginning of God's plan to rescue people from sin and enable them to live in harmony with him

Genesis is not a science text that gives intricate details on how God created the universe, our world, and life on Earth. It is not a history text with exact dates of when events occurred (see Appendix A for a time line). Rather, it contains all you need to know about why God created the world and placed you in it.

Why Are There Stories in Genesis?

As you turn the pages of Genesis you will find stories of people who lived long ago. Perhaps you are asking, since the Bible is the truth about God, why did he give us stories of people? Good question!

The answer is that God knows you well. He knows that you and I become acquainted with other people by seeing them in action and hearing them in conversation. Instead of giving only descriptions of his character (though he has included many verses in the Bible that do that), God also provides stories that show his interaction with humans who were just like you and me.

God has given us the stories of things that happened to people in Old Testament times as examples for us to follow, and as warnings to help us avoid the mistakes those people made long ago. "All these things happened to them as examples, and they were written for our admonition" (1 Corinthians 10:11 NKJV).

But there's even more. You are not on your own as you read the Bible. God's Holy Spirit is with you to communicate truths about God and to help you understand them in your heart. Moreover, the Holy Spirit will help you respond to the truths you discover as you read under his guidance.

A Word About Dates

One date people are especially interested in is the date when the universe began. You will not find that date in Genesis—not even a hint! What you will find is where the universe came from and who created life and made the first man and woman.

A Word About Words

There are several interchangeable terms: Scripture, Scriptures, Word, Word of God, God's Word, Book, etc. All of these mean the same thing and come under the broad heading called the Bible. I will use each one at various times, but I will use "Bible" most of the time.

The word *Lord* in the Old Testament refers to Yahweh, God, whereas in the New Testament it refers to God's Son, Jesus Christ.

One Final Tip

God, who gave us the Bible, is present whenever we read it, so it helps to read the Bible prayerfully. As you read Genesis, you'll see God's love extended to people, his desire to have them know and trust him, his warnings to help them avoid self-destructive acts, his great mercy in forgiving their wrongdoing, and his complete faithfulness in keeping his promises. He will be that way with you too, because God never changes.

When you open your heart to God and ask him to speak to you, he really does it. Ask God to speak to you as you read Genesis, and you'll be surprised how wonderfully the Bible will enrich your life!

About the Author

Joyce L. Gibson, who was born in Toronto, Ontario, spent her first four years in Nigeria with her missionary parents. When the family returned to Canada, where she grew up, she knew she wanted to write and teach the Bible. This became her passion. After attending Prairie Bible College and Wheaton College, she became a Bible curriculum editor, writing and developing curriculum, at Scripture Press publications in Wheaton, Illinois, a position she held for thirty-seven years. During that time she taught children in Sunday school, children's church, vacation Bible school, and club programs. She has edited *Anchor*, Haven Ministries monthly devotional, for thirty years. Her great love for storytelling and teacher training has taken her across the U.S. and Canada to Jamaica and Egypt.

About the General Editor

Dr. Larry Richards is a native of Michigan who now lives in Raleigh, North Carolina. He was converted while in the Navy in the 1950s. Larry has taught and written Sunday school curriculum for every age group from nursery through adult. He has published more than two hundred books, and his books have been translated into some twenty-six languages. His wife, Sue, is also an author. They both enjoy teaching Bible studies as well as fishing and playing golf.

Understanding the Bible Is Easy with These Tools

To understand God's Word you need easy-to-use study tools right where you need them—at your fingertips. The Smart Guide to the Bible™ series puts valuable resources adjacent to the text to save you both time and effort.

Every page features handy sidebars filled with icons and helpful information: cross references for additional insights, definitions of key words and concepts, brief commentaries from experts on the topic, points to ponder, evidence of God at work, the big picture of how passages fit into the context of the entire Bible, practical tips for applying biblical truths to every area of your life, and plenty of maps, charts, and illustrations. A wrap-up of each passage, combined with study questions, concludes each chapter.

These helpful tools show you what to watch for. Look them over to become familiar with them, and then turn to Chapter 1 with complete confidence: You are about to increase your knowledge of God's Word!

Study Helps

The thought-bubble icon alerts you to commentary you might find particularly thought-provoking, challenging, or encouraging. You'll want to take a moment to reflect on it and consider the implications for your life.

Don't miss this point! The exclamation-point icon draws your attention to a key point in the text and emphasizes important biblical truths and facts.

death on the cross
Colossians 1:21–22

Many see Boaz as a type of Jesus Christ. To win back what we human beings lost through sin and spiritual death, Jesus had to become human (i.e., he had to become a true kinsman), and he had to be willing to pay the penalty for our sins. With his death on the cross, Jesus paid the penalty and won freedom and eternal life for us.

The additional Bible verses add scriptural support for the passage you just read and help you better understand the underlined text. (Think of it as an instant reference resource!)

How does what you just read apply to your life? The heart icon indicates that you're about to find out! These practical tips speak to your mind, heart, body, and soul, and offer clear guidelines for living a righteous and joy-filled life, establishing priorities, maintaining healthy relationships, persevering through challenges, and more.

This icon reveals how God is truly all-knowing and all-powerful. The hourglass icon points to a specific example of the prediction of an event or the fulfillment of a prediction. See how some of what God has said would come to pass already has!

What are some of the great things God has done? The traffic-sign icon shows you how God has used miracles, special acts, promises, and covenants throughout history to draw people to him.

Does the story or event you just read about appear elsewhere in the Gospels? The cross icon points you to those instances where the same story appears in other Gospel locations—further proof of the accuracy and truth of Jesus' life, death, and resurrection.

Since God created marriage, there's no better person to turn to for advice. The double-ring icon points out biblical insights and tips for strengthening your marriage.

The Bible is filled with wisdom about raising a godly family and enjoying your spiritual family in Christ. The family icon gives you ideas for building up your home and helping your family grow close and strong.

Isle of Patmos
a small island in the Mediterranean Sea

something significant had occurred, he wrote down the substance of what he saw. This is the practice John followed when he recorded Revelation on the **Isle of Patmos.**

What does that word really mean, especially as it relates to this passage? Important, misunderstood, or infrequently used words are set in **bold type** in your text so you can immediately glance at the margin for definitions. This valuable feature lets you better understand the meaning of the entire passage without having to stop to check other references.

the big picture

Joshua

Led by Joshua, the Israelites crossed the Jordan River and invaded Canaan (see Illustration #8). In a series of military campaigns the Israelites defeated several coalition armies raised by the inhabitants of Canaan. With organized resistance put down, Joshua divided the land among the twelve Israelite

How does what you read fit in with the greater biblical story? The highlighted big picture summarizes the passage under discussion.

what others say

David Breese

Nothing is clearer in the Word of God than the fact that God wants us to understand himself and his working in the lives of men.[5]

It can be helpful to know what others say on the topic, and the highlighted quotation introduces another voice in the discussion. This resource enables you to read other opinions and perspectives.

Maps, charts, and illustrations pictorially represent ancient artifacts and show where and how stories and events took place. They enable you to better understand important empires, learn your way around villages and temples, see where major battles occurred, and follow the journeys of God's people. You'll find these graphics let you do more than study God's Word—they let you *experience* it.

Chapters at a Glance

PART TWO: God and Abraham

PART THREE: God and Isaac

PART FOUR: God and Jacob

PART FIVE: God and Joseph

Part One
God: The World and People He Created

Genesis 1 The Beginning

Chapter Highlights:
- The Heavens and the Earth
- Living Creatures
- Man and Woman
- It's Complete and It's Very Good

Let's Get Started

Try to imagine total emptiness. No sky. No land. No heat. No light. No time. No sign of life. No objects. No sounds. Total emptiness.

Genesis
the name means "beginnings, origins"

sovereign
God's right and power to govern all things

Contrast this image with our world today. Instead of emptiness, we have earth and sky, daily sunrises and sunsets, and seasons. We are living human beings—alive physically, mentally, emotionally—capable of relating to other humans socially. Around us we can see the achievements of people, some showing astounding creativity and mental ability, all developed from resources on earth.

How did emptiness become a complex, orderly universe? How did our world begin and how did it start to hum and throb with life? We would not know the answers if we did not have the book of **Genesis**.

In Genesis, God takes us back to the beginning. He pulls back the curtain to reveal how the universe began. He does not provide us with a scientific text, documented with step-by-step procedures and a rigid timetable. Rather, God reveals himself to be the **sovereign** Creator of all matter and life.

The Heavens and the Earth

Welcome to an awesome event—the beginning of time and history. God, who exists without beginning or end, acted to make a beginning point. He did this through Creation (see Appendix A).

GENESIS 1:1 ***In the beginning God created the heavens and the earth.*** **(NKJV)**

The first verse in the Bible introduces us to the key person of all Scripture—God—and takes us back to the start of our world. It doesn't define who God is, where he came from, or what he looks like. Rather, the verse offers the simple truth that God was in exis-

go to

faith
Hebrews 11:3

originated
John 1:3

Creator
one who brings something original into being

faith
belief, confidence, trust

tence even before the beginning and reveals to us how everything in the universe began. He is the **Creator** of life and matter. Whatever exists owes its origin to him.

We understand that God, as Creator, brought something out of nothing. We accept this by **faith**. But the Hebrew word for "create" is *bara*, which also means "to begin or originate a sequence of events." With this in mind, we can say that God originated all life and set in motion all natural order in the universe.

If we believe that God really did create all things, then we can also believe that he controls our lives and can accomplish his plans for us.

what others say

C. S. Lewis

No philosophical theory which I have yet come across is a radical improvement on the words of Genesis, that *in the beginning God made heaven and earth.*[1]

Anne Graham Lotz

The opening phrase of Genesis reveals the divine nature of God. It states without giving room for even reasonable doubt as to his existence, that "in the beginning *God*..."(Genesis 1:1, italics added). In this statement two attributes of God's divine glory are revealed: He is greater than Creation, and he is separate from Creation.[2]

V. Gilbert Beers

The first words of the Old Testament introduce us to the Bible's central message. In the beginning, God. Behind the physical universe is a living Person. This Person is not only powerful, but is also magnificently creative. All the wonders and beauties of our world existed first in the imagination of God. Then he spoke, and they were created...from nothing. How great this God we meet in the Bible must be![3]

There were no eyewitnesses to the beginning of the universe. Only God was there. The Genesis account was written by Moses as God revealed the truth to him. Moses was uniquely qualified to receive and record God's revelation. As an infant born to Israelite parents in

Egypt, he came into the world under a death warrant. Pharaoh, ruler in Egypt, had made the Israelites his slaves and had commanded that all their male babies must be drowned in the Nile River. Moses' life was miraculously spared. More amazingly, he was then secretly adopted into Pharaoh's royal family and was educated in the palace, receiving the best training available in the world. God chose Moses to lead the slaves out of Egypt and through the wilderness to the land he had promised to give them.

Trinity
union of three persons in one Godhead

At Mount Sinai, God called Moses to climb up the mountain. Moses stayed alone with God for forty days. During that time God gave him the Ten Commandments. Moses became a prophet. God spoke through him to the Israelites and guided him to write the account in roughly 1450–1400 BC. God revealed information about himself and his actions on earth, information that Moses could not possibly have had apart from God's revelation.

Bringing Order Out of Chaos

GENESIS 1:2 ***The earth was without form, and void; and darkness was on the face of the deep. And the Spirit of God was hovering over the face of the waters.*** *(NKJV)*

Chaos. That was the condition when God began to form something new and so pleasing that he could pronounce it as good.

We learn from science that there is a law of entropy (known as the Second Law of Thermodynamics), which states that when left alone, any system will decline, fall into disorder, and decay. We see this when heat is lost, when metal rusts, and when wrinkles form on our faces. God's Spirit, the third Person of the **Trinity**, hovered over what was empty and without form and decided to reverse what we know as the natural workings of thermodynamics.

How did the universe begin? For ages people have raised this question and have come up with a variety of answers from colorful myths to scientific theory. There are three prevalent theories about the origin of the universe:

1. ***The "Big Bang":*** the belief that the universe began to exist at a specific time—somewhere between 10 and 20 billion years ago—and formed as a result of a spontaneous explosion. This is the dominant scientific theory about the origin of the universe, and is based on math, chemistry, physics, and biology.

what others say

Bruce Malone

Even the simplest living cell is an incredibly complex machine. It must be capable of detecting malfunctions, repairing itself, and making copies of itself. Man has never succeeded in building a machine capable of these same functions. Yet most scientists accept the belief that life arose from non-life (in spite of the evidence clearly indicating that it did not and could not happen).[4]

Dr. Larry Richards

But what caused the Big Bang? No scientist has an answer. One science book calls this the "ultimate mystery" and says "there is no scientific answer to what happened before the Big Bang." Then the writer goes on to say that "we must accept that the universe did begin." For Christians, this is no surprise at all. The Bible tells us that "in the beginning God created" (Genesis 1:1). We already knew that the universe was created from nothing—by our God.[5]

2. ***Intelligent Design:*** the belief that the universe began to exist as the intended result of an intelligent cause. Instead of earth and its processes just happening by chance or coincidence, Intelligent Design suggests that they happen on purpose. Critics of this theory charge that the theory is a thinly veiled reference to God; supporters of the theory say that's not so. They say detecting the presence of an intelligent designer doesn't require identifying the designer.

what others say

Michael Behe

A Christian should feel confident, because in my opinion, the great untold story of the past 50 years in science has been how much science is pointing beyond nature, showing that the universe is not self-explanatory, but requires something beyond itself to explain it.[6]

3. ***Creation:*** the belief that the universe began to exist exactly as described in the book of Genesis and in other places in the Bible. While faith is a key component of this belief, creationists point out that science provides ample proof of this theory.

what others say

David Hall

If Genesis does not mean what it says, then other passages are equally questionable.[7]

Arno Froese

Religion is based on faith and science on substance. When it comes to creation, we have the words of Hebrews 11:3: "Through faith we understand that the worlds were framed by the word of God, so that things which are seen were not made of things which do appear." We don't need anyone to tell us if, how and when the earth was created because we understand it through faith.[8]

Darwin's Monkey Business

It's nearly impossible to discuss these three theories without bringing up Charles Darwin's theory of evolution. The theory focuses not on the origin of the universe but on the origin of the species. In his 1859 book entitled *On the Origin of the Species*, Darwin asserted that all species of living things have descended from a common ancestor and that they develop through a series of small, inherited changes. Those changes are said to increase the living thing's ability to compete, survive, and reproduce. Opponents of Darwinism point out numerous flawed areas of this theory. For example, read below what journalist Lee Strobel states.

what others say

Lee Strobel

Darwin's theory predicted a long history of gradual change, with the differences slowly becoming bigger and bigger until you get the major differences we have now. But the fossil record, even in Darwin's day, showed the opposite.[9]

spoke
Psalm 33:9

What Are They Teaching in School These Days?

What to teach students about the beginning of the universe and the origin of life has touched off heated controversy and fierce courtroom battles ever since the Scopes "monkey" trial of 1924, when John T. Scopes was found guilty of breaking Tennessee law by teaching evolution. The Supreme Court didn't get involved in the debate, however, until 1968, when it ruled in Epperson v. Arkansas that evolution can be taught in public schools because it is a science. Creationism was legally declared off-limits since it is considered to be based on religion, not on scientific facts. Many people continue to wage legal battles to secure equal classroom time for teaching all three of the leading origin theories: evolution, creation, and intelligent design.

Play Nice, or I'll Separate You Two

> **Genesis 1:3–5** ***Then God said, "Let there be light"; and there was light. And God saw the light, that it was good; and God divided the light from the darkness. God called the light Day, and the darkness He called Night. So the evening and the morning were the first day. (NKJV)***

God spoke a word with creative power and light was produced which removed the darkness that had blanketed the surface of the deep (Genesis 1:2). Some scholars believe this light was not the sun, whose creation is not mentioned until Genesis 1:16, but some fixed light source. Other scholars believe the sun should be included in the meaning of the phrase "the heavens and the earth," in which case the sun was created in verse 1. Either way, God separated light from the darkness, naming them day and night. As the earth rotated, there would be periods of light and darkness. This act of Creation came on the first day with other days of Creation following. God created the universe by speaking. His words have power to create.

On this first day God began a pattern that follows throughout Creation:

1. God spoke a creative word.
2. The creative word brought visible results.

3. God was pleased with the results and pronounced them good.

4. God designated what number that day of Creation was.

A Day? What Kind of Day?

The short little word *day* has caused much heated discussion when connected with the Creation account. When we speak of a day, we usually refer to a twenty-four-hour time span. Other times, we speak of a day as a general period of time, such as "the day of the Roman Empire," or even as a longer period of time, such as "prehistoric days." Were the six days of Creation twenty-four-hour periods or longer? Many Bible-believing people believe that the days of Creation were literal twenty-four-hour days. Other Bible-believing people point out that "with the Lord one day is as a thousand years, and a thousand years as one day" (2 Peter 3:8 NKJV). They say that the six days of Creation could have spanned many, many years.

People who are interested in the origin of the universe have speculated how the word *day* should be interpreted. They have developed the following theories.

1. ***The gap theory, also called the ruin and reconstruction theory:*** According to this theory, God's creation, stated in verse 1, was perfect. It was ruined, however, by Satan, an angelic being who attempted to overthrow God. When he was cast out of heaven, he caused the chaos described in verse 2. According to the gap theory, the account of God's creation, beginning in verse 3, is God's act of reconstructing and restoring his Creation. The gap between verses 1 and 2 is thought to be ages long. That interlude, some scholars believe, brings the Biblical account of Creation into harmony with accepted geology and its billions of years of fossil records. Other scholars point to the following possible inconsistencies between the gap theory and the Biblical creation account.

Possible Gaps in the Gap Theory

The Gap Theory	The Bible
God created everything over a period of millions or billions of years.	God created everything in six days, according to Genesis 1 and Exodus 20:11.
Many creatures lived and died before Adam was created.	Adam was given dominion over every living thing. (Genesis 1:28)
The fossil record was established when living things died during the gap.	Death, disease and suffering came after, not before, the Fall (Genesis 3 and Romans 5:12). The fossil record was established during the Flood.

2. ***The geological ages theory:*** According to this theory, ***day*** is considered to be a figurative term for a geological age. These ages occurred before human life was found on earth, and the process is continuing. According to this theory, the geological ages span millions of years and are named Precambrian, Paleozoic, Mesozoic, and Cenozoic.

3. ***The twenty-four-hour–period theory:*** According to this theory, each day indicated in the Creation account was an actual day in Moses' life in which God revealed to him what he had created.

4. ***The literal twenty-four-hour-day theory:*** This theory suggests that the days described in Genesis 1 are literal twenty-four-hour periods in which God performed the acts of creation.

5. ***The literary framework theory:*** According to this theory, days are used as an outline for the Creation account. While the facts of Creation are accurate, the framework is simply a literary device.

6. ***The myth theory:*** This theory views the account in Genesis 1 as being only symbolic. While accepting that God created, it does not accept the account as being historically accurate.

what others say

Anne Graham Lotz

Through the centuries there has been much discussion as to whether the days of Genesis 1 are literal, 24-hour days or longer periods of time. If you believe that each day of Creation represents a longer period of time such as a geological age, consider the following: On the third day, fruit trees were made. On the fifth day the insects necessary to pollinate the fruit trees were made. If each day was longer than a 24-hour period, perhaps even millions of years, how did the fruit trees survive without the necessary insects?

On the other hand, if you believe the days were literal 24-hour periods, consider this: Genesis 1 says that both Adam and Eve were created on the sixth day. Yet Genesis 2 describes God's creation of Adam as being followed by a longer period of time during which he gave Adam the desire for a wife. Then he created Eve.[10]

Is It an Old Earth or a Young Earth?

Just how old is our world? Lodged within the debate over the origin of life and the definition of the word *day* as it relates to Creation is a separate debate over the age of the earth. Some Christians feel the answer is a trivial point of Scriptural doctrine. Others believe it is a critical issue because they say the answer hinges on whether a person believes the Bible to be without error.

As Bible-believing people looked at the Bible, they found genealogical records, some of which could be matched to dates that were historically accepted. They thought that by counting the generations, they could work backward to Adam and thereby come up with a reliable date of Creation. Back in the 1600s, Archbishop James Ussher did this. According to his calculations, the date of Creation was 4004 BC. Was Earth really created only four thousand years before Jesus was born? That would be a young earth.

Many people accepted Ussher's word, and Bibles were printed showing his dates for the various generations. Unfortunately, Bible experts did not understand that the genealogical lists in Scripture included only important people whose names would be recognized. In these lists, the word "son" meant "descendant." Several generations could have been skipped over.

Other people believe the world began billions of years ago and that through the process of evolution it became habitable to humans. They think that ours is a very, very "old Earth."

go to

tent
Psalm 104:3

palace
Amos 9:6

what others say

Todd Strandberg

> To be able to say that the earth is only a few thousand years old, we would have to greatly abbreviate the historical evidence found in the fossil records. The earth contains countless layers of sedimentary fossils that reveal a vast wealth of geological and organic activity.[11]

something to ponder

Are we living on an old Earth or a young Earth? No matter how we answer the question, we have to base our answer on incomplete information in the Bible. God has chosen not to give us the date.

This Might Cloud the Issue

GENESIS 1:6–8 ***Then God said, "Let there be a firmament in the midst of the waters, and let it divide the waters from the waters." Thus God made the firmament, and divided the waters which were under the firmament from the waters which were above the firmament; and it was so. And God called the firmament Heaven. So the evening and the morning were the second day. (NKJV)***

GOD AT WORK

Water covered everything. On the second day God separated the water, placing some in the atmosphere above, leaving air space between. The water in the atmosphere is in the form of clouds in the sky. The act of separating the water to make the sky (the atmosphere) happened on the second day of Creation.

The word *sky* refers not only to the phase of the sun, moon, and stars (Genesis 1:14) but also to where birds fly (Genesis 1:20).

The atmosphere is not an expanse of emptiness. God stretches out the heavens like a tent and dwells in a lofty palace there. He has not abandoned his Creation, but is available when people call on him with trusting hearts.

On Which Day Did God Create Fertilizer?

GENESIS 1:9–13 ***Then God said, "Let the waters under the heavens be gathered together into one place, and let the dry land appear"; and it was so. And God called the dry land Earth, and the gathering together of the waters He called Seas. And God***

saw that it was good. Then God said, "Let the earth bring forth grass, the herb that yields seed, and the fruit tree that yields fruit according to its kind, whose seed is in itself, on the earth"; and it was so. And the earth brought forth grass, the herb that yields seed according to its kind, and the tree that yields fruit, whose seed is in itself according to its kind. And God saw that it was good. So the evening and the morning were the third day. (NKJV)

God moved the water to form seas, draining areas of land that lay under the water. God set boundaries for the seas and established large land masses which would support vegetation. Under the land, which he called earth, he provided rich resources of minerals, and on the surface he made a carpet of fertile soil.

He then made vegetation, grass, herbs, and trees that would cover the ground and be suitable food for animals and humans. He also provided for the vegetation to reproduce itself.

God at Work

God created vegetation with the provision for it to continue. He created each plant with seed, according to its kind. Throughout the centuries varieties in vegetation have been developed—but each within its kind. We have varieties of apples, for example, but an apple has not naturally evolved into a cucumber.

what others say

Henry M. Morris

Implanted in each created organism was a "seed," programmed to enable the continuing replication of that type of organism. The modern understanding of the extreme complexities of the so-called DNA molecule and the genetic code contained in it has reinforced the biblical teaching of the stability of kinds. Each type of organism has its own unique structure of the DNA and can only specify the reproduction of that same kind. There is a tremendous amount of variational potential within each kind, facilitating the generation of distinct individuals and even of many varieties within the kind, but nevertheless precluding the evolution of new kinds![12]

Light, Lights—and How Many More Lights?

GENESIS 1:14–19 ***Then God said, "Let there be lights in the firmament of the heavens to divide the day from the night; and let them be for signs and seasons, and for days and years; and let***

inhabited
Isaiah 45:18

them be for lights in the firmament of the heavens to give light on the earth"; and it was so. Then God made two great lights: the greater light to rule the day, and the lesser light to rule the night. He made the stars also. God set them in the firmament of the heavens to give light on the earth, and to rule over the day and over the night, and to divide the light from the darkness. And God saw that it was good. So the evening and the morning were the fourth day. *(NKJV)*

How far? We can't measure. How many? We can't count. In fact, it's not possible to know. We don't need to know the exact number of stars in the sky, but God wants us to know why the stars are there. He tells us "The heavens declare the glory of God; and the firmament shows His handiwork" (Psalm 19:1 NKJV).

what others say

Henry Hengeveld

Astronaut Buzz Aldrin got it right when he became one of the first humans to witness an earthrise from the vantage point of the moon. He was so moved that he recited the familiar words from Genesis: "In the beginning, God created the heavens and the earth."[13]

George Will said, "Hubble recently sent back to earth—to this strangely lush speck in one of perhaps 50 billion galaxies—infrared images of the faintest, most distant galaxies ever seen. They could be more than 12 billion times 6 trillion miles away. (That is, 12 billion light-years away, a lightyear being the distance light travels in a year—approximately 6 trillion miles, at 186 miles per second.)"[14]

Living Creatures

God had provided everything needed for living creatures. He created life-giving light, pure air, and abundant water, fertile soil, minerals, and lush vegetation. He was not done, for he had planned for earth to be inhabited. Now that he had provided everything needed for living creatures, all was ready for the fifth day.

GENESIS 1:20–23 ***Then God said, "Let the waters abound with an abundance of living creatures, and let birds fly above the earth across the face of the firmament of the heavens." So God created great sea creatures and every living thing that moves,***

with which the waters abounded, according to their kind, and every winged bird according to its kind. And God saw that it was good. And God blessed them, saying, "Be fruitful and multiply, and fill the waters in the seas, and let birds multiply on the earth." So the evening and the morning were the fifth day. *(NKJV)*

go to

birds
Matthew 6:26

flying creatures
Matthew 10:29

No Shortage of Fish or Fowl

We hear about endangered species, about fish that are dying in our polluted rivers, and that there is such a dangerous shortage from over-fishing that some ocean fishermen are restricted in their trade. Imagine a world with water actually teeming with many kinds of marine creatures from whales to microscopic organisms. Imagine a sky alive with colorful birds that fly and feed without fear of any danger.

God gave these creatures the capacity to reproduce after their own kind. Both plants and animals had the original code for the many breeds and varieties now on earth.

something to ponder

God cared so much about them that he blessed them and told them to multiply and expand so they could occupy other parts of earth. And he continues his care. Jesus, the Son of God, spoke of his Father's concern for the well-being of birds by providing for birds and watching over all his flying creatures.

Much More Than a Pet Parade

GENESIS 1:24–25 ***Then God said, "Let the earth bring forth the living creature according to its kind: cattle and creeping thing and beast of the earth, each according to its kind"; and it was so. And God made the beast of the earth according to its kind, cattle according to its kind, and everything that creeps on the earth according to its kind. And God saw that it was good.*** *(NKJV)*

God provided an abundance of creatures of the land, not only in number but also in variety. He created animals that can be domesticated (livestock), creatures that move along the ground, and wild animals that most of us see only in zoos, photographs, or movies.

This was the sixth day, but God was not through. The best was yet to come.

go to

dominion
Psalm 8:6–8

Man and Woman

GENESIS 1:26–27 ***Then God said, "Let Us make man in Our image, according to Our likeness; let them have dominion over the fish of the sea, over the birds of the air, and over the cattle, over all the earth and over every creeping thing that creeps on the earth." So God created man in His own image; in the image of God He created him; male and female He created them. (NKJV)***

We come now to a sharp departure from the pattern we have seen in the account of Creation. Up to this point, God has simply spoken a creative word, and that word has brought visible results. Now God speaks, giving four astounding revelations:

1. He said, "Let Us." When God used the plural pronoun "Us," we got the first glimpse in Scripture of God, who is one person, yet is more than one in his unity. We have the suggestion of distinct persons. From other parts of the Bible, we know that Creation is attributed to three persons:

    - Father (God)—Acts 4:24
    - Son (Jesus Christ)—John 1:1–2; Colossians 1:15–17
    - Holy Spirit—Psalm 104:30

2. God had spoken a creative word to bring forth the parts of Creation. Now he says he will "make" the man and woman. Clearly, the creative process for people is different. When God created other living creatures, he made them in great numbers, but now he made only one man and one woman.

3. God created man and woman in his image, in his likeness, bestowing on them the unique quality of personhood—a spirit, something not given to any other part of Creation.

4. God separated man and woman from other parts of Creation by assigning them the role of ruling (having dominion) over all creatures.

key point

God created man and woman in an act of creation separate from other parts. He assigned them the role of ruling over all creatures.

what others say

Dr. Larry Richards

We know from the Bible that God has emotions and values, appreciates beauty, demonstrates creativity, makes distinctions between right and wrong, loves and even sacrifices himself for the sake of others. We know from the Bible that God is a Person, with identity and individuality.

These attributes constituting personhood mark humanity from the rest of creation. In fact, all those elements of good which are found in man must have their source in likeness to the divine.[15]

Rick Warren

God did not *need* to create you, but he *chose* to create you for his own enjoyment. You exist for his benefit, his glory, his purpose, and his delight. Bringing enjoyment to God, living for his pleasure, is the first purpose of your life. When you fully understand this truth, you will never again have a problem with feeling insignificant. It proves your worth.[16]

It's All Yours!

GENESIS 1:28 ***Then God blessed them, and God said to them, "Be fruitful and multiply; fill the earth and subdue it; have dominion over the fish of the sea, over the birds of the air, and over every living thing that moves on the earth."*** *(NKJV)*

God gave the first man and woman freedom, responsibility, and authority. He gave his blessing on the roles they were to assume: reproducing themselves and ruling (having dominion) over all living creatures in the water, in the air, and on the land.

Nobody needs to worry about having worth. Every person has worth because God loves and cares for each one. God places his value on every human because he has given each one dignity and a responsibility to fulfill.

The See-Food Diet

GENESIS 1:29–30 ***And God said, "See, I have given you every herb that yields seed which is on the face of all the earth, and every tree whose fruit yields seed; to you it shall be for food. Also, to every beast of the earth, to every bird of the air, and to everything that creeps on the earth, in which there is life, I have given every green herb for food"; and it was so.*** *(NKJV)*

Flood
a catastrophic flood, described in Genesis 6–8

Sermon on the Mount
Jesus' first and longest discourse, given in Matthew 5–7

In his day-by-day acts of Creation, God prepared earth to produce just the right kinds of vegetation that would meet the nutritional needs of all creatures. The man and woman could eat whatever appealed to them. Marine creatures, birds and other flying creatures, and land creatures could all find abundant food to sustain life and give enjoyment.

There would never be a shortage of food, because God had built into all forms of vegetation the capacity to reproduce itself.

what others say

J. Vernon McGee

I assume that man was a vegetarian at first, and not until after the **Flood** did man become a meat eater.[17]

James Montgomery Boice

God cares for nature, in spite of its abuse through man's sin. But if he cares for nature, then he also obviously cares for us and may be trusted to do so. This argument occurs in the midst of Christ's **Sermon on the Mount** in which he draws our attention to God's care of the birds (animal life) and lilies (plant life) and then asks, "Are you not much more valuable than they?...If...God clothes the grass of the field, which is here today and tomorrow is thrown into the fire, will he not much more clothe you, O you of little faith?" (Matthew 6:26, 30).[18]

It's Complete—and It's Very Good

GENESIS 1:31 *Then God saw everything that He had made, and indeed it was very good. So the evening and the morning were the sixth day.* (NKJV)

Six days of Creation—and what God had made was very good. What God had created was beautiful, abundant, completely useful, capable of continuity and expansion, and more important, designed to display the glory of God and accomplish all that he had planned. God created humans in his image and gave them the capacity to know him. He loved them and planned for them. In this first chapter of Genesis, we have God communicating the amazing theme that runs through all of Scripture—his revelation of who he is, who we humans are, and how God and humans can relate.

The account of Creation given in Genesis 1 is succinct. God reserves some details for the account given in Genesis 2.

God created the first man and woman "in his image," with the capacity to know him and communicate with him. He gave them gifts—the ability to think, to feel, to choose—to be used in ways that would bring him pleasure.

something to ponder

In the book of Revelation, God gives us a picture of heaven when human history is wrapped up. The Lord God Almighty will be seated on a throne. Twenty-four elders will bow before him in worship and lay their crowns before the throne. They will say: "You are worthy, O Lord, to receive glory and honor and power; for You created all things, and by Your will they exist and were created" (Revelation 4:11 NKJV).

Every day we are helping fill the pages of human history. As people made in God's image, we have the privilege of honoring him in the way we choose to live.

Before we leave the Bible account of Creation, let's look at various views of how the universe began.

Beliefs About the Beginning

Modern Beliefs	Secular	Judeo-Christian	Islam	Hindu	Buddhism
Source	Evolutionary theory	The Bible	Qur'an	Veda	Numerous sacred texts
Origin of Universe	Universe began in an unexplained "Big Bang" 15 million years ago.	God spoke and caused the universe to come into existence.	Allah created the universe.	Brahma, the creator god, created seven great sages to help him create the universe.	No attempt to explain the origin of the universe.
Origin of Life	Humans evolved with other animals from spontaneously generated single-cell life.	God created all animal life and created humans in a separate, special act of creation.	Allah created life.	Brahma created 10 fathers of the human race.	No attempt to explain the origin of life.
View of Deity(ies)	God is unknown and unknowable.	One personal and knowable God exists.	One god, Allah, is powerful, personal, and compassionate; justice, however, is his most important trait.	Many gods manifested by the one supreme being, Brahman.	There is no absolute God; Gautama, called the Buddha, is founder and teacher.
Relation of Deity(ies) to Universe	God is irrelevant as the universe is subject only to natural law.	God is beyond the universe, but sustains it and can act upon it and within it.	The presence of God in the world is seen not through supernatural signs but through the order of nature.	Some consider Brahman to be personal and loving; others describe him as impersonal and uninvolved with life on earth.	There is none; many Buddhists believe pain and suffering in the world are proof that God does not exist.
Relation of Man to Deity(ies)	Has no statement to make about man's relationship to the supernatural.	God created humans in his own image and granted them dominion over the earth. God loves humans actively.	Man is to be in charge of creation under the authority of God with the goal of bringing it into complete moral order.	One can acquire spiritual "points" through contact with holy objects and holy people.	Those seeking enlightment must follow their own spiritual path.
Destiny of Man and the Universe	Second law of thermodynamics indicates that the universe will cool and die. Death is extinction for every individual.	God will destroy this universe; create a new and righteous one. Human beings will be raised to blessedness or punishment.	Salvation depends on man's actions and attitudes; each person will be judged and either admitted to heaven, a place filled with worldly delights, or condemned to hell, a place of indescribable torment.	Salvation is the escape from the endless cycle of birth, death, and rebirth either in the arms of a loving, personal god or by dissolving into the abyss of Brahman.	Salvation lies in losing one's sense of self in order to reach nirvana, a transcendent, permanent state of existence.

Chapter Wrap-Up

- "In the beginning God created . . ." (Genesis 1:1 NKJV). The opening words of Genesis 1:1 establish that God was in existence even before the beginning of our universe. He is the Creator. Without him there would be no world and there would be no people on earth today. God created the heavens and the earth, bringing order out of what was waste and void. (Genesis 1:1–2)

- God made light and separated light from darkness. He called the light "day" and the darkness "night." This was the first day of Creation. (Genesis 1:3–5)

- God made the sky and sea. He separated the water, placing some in the atmosphere above. The act of separating the water to make the sky was the second day of Creation. (Genesis 1:6–8)

- God made land and plants. He moved the water to form seas and then established land masses which would support vegetation. This was the third day of Creation. (Genesis 1:9–13)

- God made the sun, moon, and stars. He made light not only to provide beauty but also to make growth possible for vegetation and to schedule time and seasons. This was the fourth day of Creation. (Genesis 1:14–19)

- God made birds and fish. He created creatures of the sea and every kind of winged bird. He gave these creatures the capacity to reproduce after their own kind. This was the fifth day of Creation. (Genesis 1:20–23)

- God made land animals and man. He provided an abundance of creatures of the land, a variety of animals that can be domesticated as well as wild creatures. And he made man and woman in his own image to rule over all that he had made. This was the sixth day of Creation. (Genesis 1:24–31)

Study Questions

1. What insights into God's character do you get from Genesis 1?
2. What do the heavens reveal about God?
3. In what ways did God's creation of man and woman differ from his creation of other parts of the universe?
4. What responsibility did God give to the man and the woman?

Genesis 2 The Crown of Creation

Chapter Highlights:
- God's Day of Rest
- The Man
- The Garden
- The Woman
- No Embarrassment, No Shame

Let's Get Started

In Genesis 1 we saw the panoramic view of God's Creation. Now in chapter 2, we move in for a close-up look at God's creation of humans, the crown of his Creation. Here we discover details that supplement, but do not contradict, what was revealed in the first chapter.

go to

name
Isaiah 40:25–26

Again, God did not give a science text report. Instead, he gave us something far better. In this close-up view we discover more insights into who he is, how special we humans are to him, the place of significance and dignity he has planned for us, and how he planned for us to give him pleasure as we enjoy relating to him.

We see God providing in Eden an ideal environment to inhabit. He gave the first man and woman challenging work, the opportunity to choose to obey him, companionship with each other, and best of all the privilege of having fellowship with their Creator.

Grand Opening Earns Rave Reviews

GENESIS 2:1 ***Thus the heavens and the earth, and all the host of them, were finished.*** *(NKJV)*

What a report! God's Creation was a complete success! All goals were accomplished, not just for the initial launching of Creation, but with all systems on "go" for hundreds and thousands of years.

God created the heavens and the earth in all its complex design, with incredible variety of size, color, and purpose. From galaxies of 100 billion stars to a gentle snowfall on a winter's morning, God's Creation displays his love of beauty and detail.

what others say

John Piper

Every one of the billions of stars in the universe is there by God's specific appointment. He knows their number. And, most astonishing of all, he knows them by name. They do his

weary
Isaiah 40:28

omnipotent
unlimited authority and power

sanctified
set apart for God's purposes

> bidding as his personal agents. When we feel the weight of this grandeur in the heavens, we have only touched the hem of his garment.[1]

Tom Skilling reports, "The vast majority of snowflakes—perhaps 95 percent or more—fall at speeds of 1–6 feet per second, says snow expert and Colorado assistant state climatologist Nolan Doesken. A snowflake's surface area and its mass are the most important factors. Large flakes act like parachutes and often slow down while kernel-like snow pellets known as 'grapple' can fall much faster. Tiny ice prisms, like those that give the sun its hazy appearance in bitterly cold, subzero air, fall at much lower speeds.

"Doesken . . . is based at Colorado State University at Ft. Collins and tells me that a cubic foot of snow (12" on a side) may contain 1,728,000 individual snowflakes."[2]

Finally, a Breather!

> GENESIS 2:2 ***And on the seventh day God ended His work which He had done, and He rested on the seventh day from all His work which He had done.*** *(NKJV)*

The **omnipotent** God resting? The God who spoke a creative word and the sun, moon, and billions of stars appeared and took their places precisely where God had planned? The God who spoke a creative word and the sequoia trees and delicate ferns appeared? The God who spoke a creative word and then came huge lumbering animals and tiny ladybugs—and then the amazing human? Yes, God had finished what he began, and it was time to rest.

God was not weary from the immense creative activity. It was time to rest because everything had been completed exactly as planned.

I Get Six and You Get the Rest

> GENESIS 2:3 ***Then God blessed the seventh day and sanctified it, because in it He rested from all His work which God had created and made.*** *(NKJV)*

Looking closely at Genesis 2, we find that several significant things stand out on the seventh day:

1. God blessed this day. On the first through the sixth days, God was pleased with Creation, but he had not blessed the day. The seventh day was special in that he made it holy.

2. There is no mention of morning and evening, as there was for previous days. God's work of creating was complete.

3. The seventh day was a day of rest, the **Sabbath**. This is the first mention of a theme that runs throughout the Bible. The Sabbath was meant to be such a significant part of our lives that God included it in the **Ten Commandments** and reinforced its importance in other parts of Scripture.

go to

Sabbath
Exodus 20:8–11

Genesis was written in the Hebrew language. In Hebrew, Sabbath is *shabat*, which means "rest," "cessation of activity." Throughout Scripture we find that in planning the Sabbath, God was providing for our physical and spiritual welfare.

something to ponder

1. The Sabbath, the seventh day of Creation, was the day God rested (Genesis 2:2–3).

2. The seventh day of the Hebrew week was a day set aside to honor the Lord and to rest from regular work (Exodus 16:23).

3. The Sabbath became a symbol of God's special **covenant** with the nation of Israel. As God's people observed the Sabbath, they demonstrated their heart commitment to God (Exodus 31:12–17; Isaiah 58:13–14).

4. Over the years, the Israelites developed a number of laws that restricted activities on the Sabbath. **Pharisees** criticized Jesus for permitting his disciples to pick some heads of grain and eat them as they went through grain fields on the Sabbath (Matthew 12:1–14). They also became indignant when they observed Jesus healing on the Sabbath (Luke 13:10–17). Jesus corrected them by pointing out that God had provided the day for rest and refreshment. It was appropriate to do good to others on that day.

5. In the days of the **early church**, Christians began to meet on the first day of the week, the day that Jesus was raised from the

Sabbath
seventh day of the Hebrew week

Ten Commandments
ten rules given by God

covenant
an agreement between two or more parties defining relationships and responsibilities

Pharisees
Jews who strictly observed oral laws and traditions

early church
the first believers in Jesus Christ in the years immediately following Jesus' return to his Father in heaven

dead (John 20:1; Acts 20:7). They used the day for worship and rest. This tradition is why today we have church services on Sunday rather than Saturday.

go to

peace
John 14:27

rest of heart
Matthew 11:28–30

6. God promises a spiritual Sabbath rest to us (Hebrews 4:5–11). We can experience this peace and rest of heart when we place our faith in him, respond to his love with obedience, and commit our lives to his care and direction.

what others say

Bill Hybels

God wants us to honor the Sabbath by refraining from work, focusing on worship, and engaging in activities that contribute to our physical, emotional, and spiritual renewal.[3]

Ron Mehl

Exodus 20:11 says that in six days the Lord made the heaven and earth, the sea, and all that is in them, and rested on the seventh day. Do you think the Lord might have some insights into his own creation? Do you think he might know something about you and me that we tend to forget? The Lord knows us so well, doesn't he? And in his deep love for us, he knows how much we need to rest. To lie down. To reflect. To reconnect with him, the very author of life. He has built this need within us as surely as our need for water and food and oxygen.[4]

apply it

God designed the concept of Sabbath rest for our good. We can enjoy true rest—physical, mental, emotional, and spiritual—when our faith rests in God.

ISAIAH 58:13–14 ***If you turn away your foot from the Sabbath, from doing your pleasure on My holy day, and call the Sabbath a delight, the holy day of the LORD honorable, and shall honor Him, not doing your own ways, nor finding your own pleasure, nor speaking your own words, then you shall delight yourself in the LORD; and I will cause you to ride on the high hills of the earth, and feed you with the heritage of Jacob your father. The mouth of the LORD has spoken.*** *(NKJV)*

Creation 2.0?

GENESIS 2:4–6 *This is the history of the heavens and the earth when they were created, in the day that the LORD God made the*

earth and the heavens, before any plant of the field was in the earth and before any herb of the field had grown. For the LORD God had not caused it to rain on the earth, and there was no man to till the ground; but a mist went up from the earth and watered the whole face of the ground. (NKJV)

earth
1 Corinthians 15:47

Here Moses gives a fresh introduction to the Creation account. He does not repeat information given in Genesis 1, but will add significant details that had not been included in that account. Moses briefly describes the scene on earth just before God created man. God had created the heavens and the earth, but had not yet created vegetation, since there was no one to "till the ground" (Genesis 2:5 NKJV). There was no rainfall, but mists or water vapors from underground "watered the whole face of the ground" (verse 6 NKJV).

psalmist
author of a song in the book of Psalms

You Da Man!

GENESIS 2:7 ***And the LORD God formed man of the dust of the ground, and breathed into his nostrils the breath of life; and man became a living being.*** (NKJV)

What an awesome account we are given. God, whose creative word had brought the universe into being, took the dust of the earth that he had created and formed the body of man. He then breathed into man's nostrils "the breath of life" (Genesis 2:7 NKJV), thus energizing man. He became "a living being" (verse 7 NKJV), an incredibly complex person—an outer body with amazing physical and mental capacities and possessing an inner personality, with a spirit that could communicate with his Creator.

God made man "in His own image" (Genesis 1:27 NKJV). He formed him from the dust of earth, breathed into him the breath of life, and made him a person capable of interacting with his Creator. Man was unique in all creation. Considering the vastness of the universe, however, man may have seemed insignificant. But he wasn't.

The **psalmist** wrote about his sense of awe when he looked at the night sky and the glorious display of moon and stars. Awed by the immensity of what he could see with the naked eye, he asked,

PSALM 8:3—9 ***When I consider Your heavens, the work of Your fingers,***
The moon and the stars, which You have ordained,
What is man that You are mindful of him,

And the son of man that You visit him?
For You have made him a little lower than the angels,
And You have crowned him with glory and honor.
You have made him to have dominion over the works of Your hands;
You have put all things under his feet,
All sheep and oxen—
Even the beasts of the field,
The birds of the air,
And the fish of the sea
That pass through the paths of the seas.
O LORD, our Lord,
How excellent is Your name in all the earth! (NKJV)

what others say

Ronald B. Allen

Man is the apex of the creative works of God. As male and female, man was made in majesty to reflect the glory of God on earth. Man is the bearer of the very image of God; this is his differentia—that which marks him out from all other created things.[5]

Isaac Newton

In the absence of any other proof, the thumb alone would convince me of God's existence.[6]

Dr. Paul Brand notes, "Take a model of the human skeleton and look at the size of the tiny bones in the fingers and toes. Those bones in the toes support all your weight. If they were larger and thicker, many athletic events would be impossible. If fingers were thicker, so many human activities—such as playing stringed instruments—would be impossible. The Creator had to make those difficult choices between strength and mobility and weight and volume."[7]

The Garden

God dwells in heaven, where everything is perfect. He created earth and made everything perfect for the well-being of the living creatures he placed there.

GENESIS 2:8 *The LORD God planted a garden eastward in Eden, and there He put the man whom He had formed.* (NKJV)

A Delight-Filled Home

allegorical
not real, but containing spiritual meaning

Someone plans a dream home. No detail is overlooked and no expense is spared in designing a living environment that is comfortable, efficient, and aesthetically pleasing. God was the architect, designer, and landscaper of a perfect home for the first man. God planted a garden that would anticipate and provide for the first human's needs.

The location of the garden was in Eden, which means "delight."

what others say

Spirit-Filled Life Bible

"A Garden" describes a real place, not an **allegorical** image. It was apparently a reserve, or enclosed, park-like area.[8]

Warren Wiersbe

"Eden" means either "delight" or "place of much water" and suggests that this garden was a paradise from the hand of God. Bible history begins with a beautiful garden in which man sinned, but the story ends with a glorious "garden city" (Revelation 21–22) in which there will be no sin.[9]

An Orchard with Two Unique Trees

GENESIS 2:9 ***And out of the ground the LORD God made every tree grow that is pleasant to the sight and good for food. The tree of life was also in the midst of the garden, and the tree of the knowledge of good and evil.*** *(NKJV)*

Trees for beauty, trees for shade, trees for food—they were all there, planned by the Creator for the health and enjoyment of man.

God placed two trees in the garden that were unique to that time and place. The first tree was the Tree of Life, a special gift from God to assure the man and woman that they would live forever in a joyous relationship with their Creator. This was theirs so long as they chose to trust him and follow his directions for their well-being.

The second tree, the Tree of the Knowledge of Good and Evil, was, in a sense, a testing tree. The fruit on the tree would not itself give knowledge of good or knowledge of evil. Instead, if the man and woman obeyed God's command not to eat of it, they would know in personal experience what is good. However, if they disobeyed and ate of it, they would know in their personal experience what is evil.

East of Where, Exactly?

GENESIS 2:10–14 ***Now a river went out of Eden to water the garden, and from there it parted and became four riverheads. The name of the first is Pishon; it is the one which skirts the whole land of Havilah, where there is gold. And the gold of that land is good. Bdellium and the onyx stone are there. The name of the second river is Gihon; it is the one which goes around the whole land of Cush. The name of the third river is Hiddekel; it is the one which goes toward the east of Assyria. The fourth river is the Euphrates. (NKJV)***

A question that has intrigued people for centuries still persists: Just exactly where was Eden? Ancient maps do not show the location. Nor do the latest computer-generated maps. However, we do have a general idea where Eden was (see Illustration #1). Moses, writing from the area of Mount Sinai, states that Eden lay to the east (Genesis 2:8). This would place it across the Arabian desert (see Appendix B). Of the four rivers mentioned, we can identify only two today, but with this information we can assume Eden was located somewhere in the valleys of the Tigris and Euphrates Rivers, in the area of modern Iraq and Iran.

what others say

Henry M. Morris

The garden of Eden was, of course, also destroyed in the Flood, so that it is quite impossible to locate it now in terms of modern geography.[10]

J. Vernon McGee

I cannot tell you where the Garden of Eden is. I am sure it is somewhere in the Tigris-Euphrates Valley; in fact it may be the entire valley. Originally, that valley was a very fertile place... At one time, the peoples inhabiting that region did not even plant grain there; they simply harvested it, for it grew by itself. It is probable that this area will someday become the very center of the earth again.[11]

Meaningful Work

GENESIS 2:15 ***Then the LORD God took the man and put him in the garden of Eden to tend and keep it.*** *(NKJV)*

While many people crave a life of leisure with no responsibilities, God knows that we actually need meaningful work.

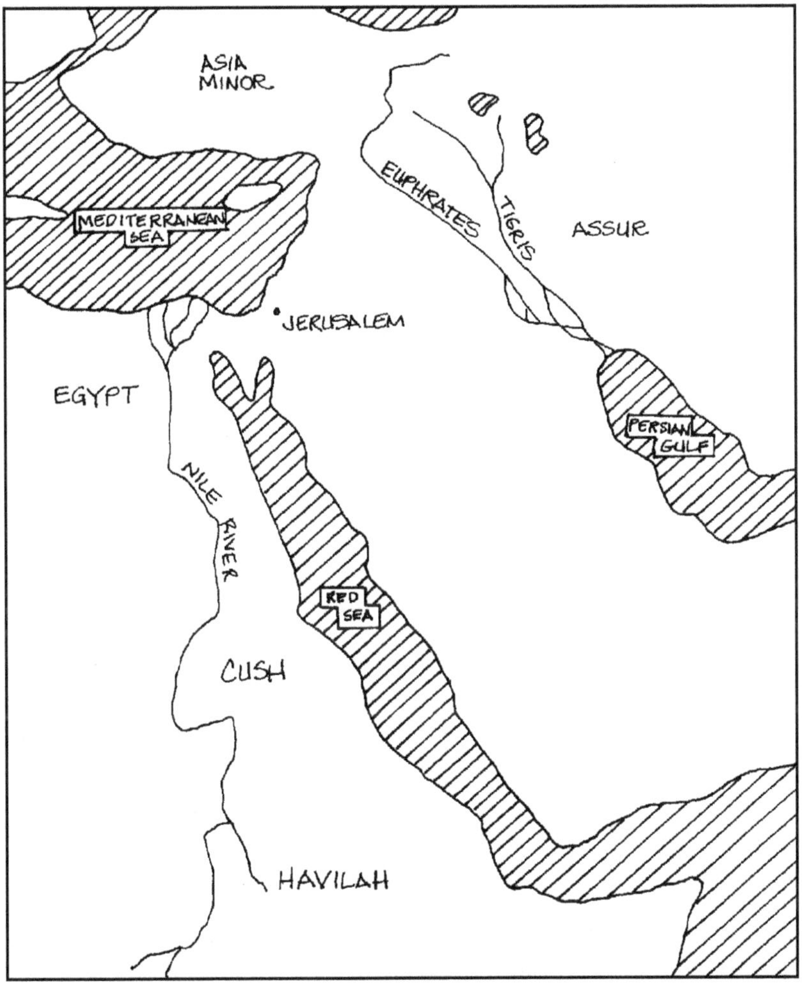

Illustration #1
Map of Eden—The first human civilizations developed in the Mesopotamian valley (modern Irac [Iraq] and Iran). Genesis places Eden in this area, listing four streams as Eden's boundaries. The only two known today are the Tigris and the Euphrates.

The Garden of Eden was in pristine condition when God placed Adam there, for God had pronounced that all his Creation was good. Adam was given an assignment of honor to cooperate with God by faithfully tending the Garden. The work would be enjoyable in that there were no weeds to contend with. His job would be to control the natural, luxurious growth.

GOD AT WORK

go to

service
Revelation 22:3

work
Deuteronomy 15:10

activity
1 Corinthians 10:31

rejoicing
Deuteronomy 12:7

As man maintained the Garden and cared for it, he would bring pleasure to his Creator while he had pleasure in the work. His work, then, would be service for the One who had made him. In this way, God would bless his work and he would participate in a God-glorifying activity.

what others say

Warren Wiersbe

Work isn't a curse; it's an opportunity to use our abilities and opportunities in cooperating with God and being faithful stewards of his creation.[12]

Carl F. H. Henry

Through his work, man shares the creation-purpose of God in subduing nature, whether he be a miner with dirty hands, a mechanic with greasy face, or a stenographer with stencil-smudged fingers. Work is permeated by purpose; it is intended to serve God and to benefit mankind.[13]

The First Rule Ever Made

GENESIS 2:16–17 ***And the LORD God commanded the man, saying, "Of every tree of the garden you may freely eat; but of the tree of the knowledge of good and evil you shall not eat, for in the day that you eat of it you shall surely die."*** *(NKJV)*

While it is true that the man was to work faithfully in the Garden, it is also true that God intended him to enjoy the fruit of his labors. Work was intended to bring pleasure and rejoicing. In the Garden were fruit-bearing trees that were pleasing to the eye and good for food (Genesis 2:9). Man was free to take from these for his own enjoyment—with one exception.

We find here the first command God gave. Yes, man had freedom to eat whatever appealed to him—and we know that the trees were "pleasant to the sight and good for food" (Genesis 2:9 NKJV). But one tree was strictly forbidden. As with all of God's commands throughout Scripture, this command was for the well-being of man, for if he ate of that tree, he would die.

something to ponder

Man, who had received the breath of life from his Creator, was given a choice. Herein we find a significant confirmation that man had been made in the image of God. Unlike anything else in God's Creation, man alone had the capacity to make a deliberate choice to obey God or to disobey him.

If he obeyed God's command and did not eat of the Tree of the Knowledge of Good and Evil, he would continue to enjoy the life God had breathed into him. If, on the other hand, he chose to disobey the command and actually eat the fruit of that tree, he would die. This is the first mention of death in Genesis. Disobedience may bring temporary pleasure, but ultimately brings dire consequences.

go to

not good
Genesis 2:18

But I Thought Dogs Were Man's Best Friend

GENESIS 2:18 ***And the LORD God said, "It is not good that man should be alone; I will make him a helper comparable to him."*** *(NKJV)*

God had prepared a perfect environment for man's health and happiness. He had created man with amazing abilities to enjoy the world around him and to communicate with his Creator. But something was missing—someone was missing. Man needed a person, another human, to be a companion to him, and God took the initiative to meet that need.

> what others say
>
> **Victor P. Hamilton**
>
> Everything thus far in Genesis that has been scrutinized by God has been given a positive assessment. Every situation has come through as either good or very good. For the first time we encounter something that is not good: man's lack of a corresponding companion.[14]

Roll Call

GENESIS 2:19 ***Out of the ground the LORD God formed every beast of the field and every bird of the air, and brought them to Adam to see what he would call them. And whatever Adam called each living creature, that was its name.*** *(NKJV)*

First, God gave man the opportunity to meet other living creatures with whom he shared life on earth. God somehow alerted the animals and the birds to go to man so that he could have the pleasure of observing them and assigning them appropriate names. God was selective in this roll call, choosing those creatures that man would most likely find companionship with—birds, cattle, and beasts of the field. No fish or creeping animals were involved.

The First Man to Have All His Ducks in a Row

> GENESIS 2:20 ***So Adam gave names to all cattle, to the birds of the air, and to every beast of the field. But for Adam there was not found a helper comparable to him.*** *(NKJV)*

This process of having the animals pass in review had a divine purpose. God had formed man's body (Genesis 2:7) and the bodies of all these animals (2:19) out of the ground. They had the basic physical components in common, but man was unique and set apart from the animals. He had the intelligence and insight to assign the names appropriately.

The process of becoming acquainted with the birds and animals brought something important to light. Not one of them could be a suitable helper to man. No animal had been made in God's image, and therefore they lacked the qualities that would make them real companions. Man was complete, yet incomplete.

what others say

Anne Graham Lotz

Whatever Adam called them "that was the name," indicating he named them correctly the first time and did not have to change the name later. It seems like a fun, simple exercise, but in the beginning when everything was newly created, it would have required extensive wisdom and intellectual knowledge of the various species and individual animals in order to name them accurately. And because there would have been hundreds if not thousands of species, it would have required enormous commitment to finish the task.[15]

The Woman

GOD AT WORK

God moved in to complete his creation of the universe. He fulfilled man's need for a companion, someone far different from any living creature already made. Creating the woman was God's final act. And it was a grand climax to all he had made!

GENESIS 2:21 ***And the LORD God caused a deep sleep to fall on Adam, and he slept; and He took one of his ribs, and closed up the flesh in its place. (NKJV)***

This Guy Really Can Take a Ribbing

In making a helper-companion for man, God moved to a different creative act. He caused Adam to go into such a deep sleep that he would not be aware of any discomfort. God removed one of the man's ribs from his side and then closed up the opening. It should be noted that the Hebrew word *tsela*, translated here as "rib," is more often translated "side." If that is the meaning here, then we see God removing one of the man's sides—bone, flesh, and blood— and then closing up the opening.

what others say

Henry M. Morris

The thought evidently is to stress that woman was made neither from Adam's head (suggesting superiority to him) nor from his feet (suggesting inferiority), but from his side, indicating equality and companionship.[16]

An Arranged Marriage

GENESIS 2:22 ***Then the rib which the LORD God had taken from man He made into a woman, and He brought her to the man. (NKJV)***

In an act of creation, God formed a woman from the rib (or part of the side) he had removed from the man. Like the man, she was made in God's own image (Genesis 1:27). What were the man's thoughts as God presented the woman to him? He had reviewed the birds and animals, naming them all but not finding the companion he needed. Now here was a woman.

what others say

Richard J. Foster

Our human sexuality, our maleness and femaleness, is not just an accidental arrangement of the human species, not just a convenient way to keep the human race going. No, it is at the center of our true humanity. We exist as male and female in relationship. Our sexualness, our capacity to love and be loved, is intimately related to our creation in the image of God. What a high view of human sexuality![17]

You're a Part of Me!

GENESIS 2:23 *And Adam said:*
"This is now bone of my bones
And flesh of my flesh;
She shall be called Woman,
Because she was taken out of Man." (NKJV)

Man, who had looked over each living creature and assigned each an appropriate name, looked at woman. What crossed his mind? Instant identification—something he had not sensed while naming the animals.

something to ponder

Here was a person made in the image of God as he was, someone who was a human, as he was, someone who would be the helper-companion that God knew he needed. She was, in the most significant sense, a part of him. They alone in all Creation shared the same substance, the same image. As the crown of God's creation, they could relate to each other physically, intellectually, and spiritually. God, who made us, knows best what will meet our physical, mental, emotional, and spiritual needs.

what others say

Elisabeth Elliot

When God created the world he saw each thing that he made as good. But when he made man, he saw that it was not good that man should be alone. Man is a social creature like the animals. They move in pairs or flocks or herds. God designed the answer to Adam's aloneness: a woman. They were a couple, meant to answer to each other.

Each, however, was still alone in a profound sense—in a separate body, alone before God, bearing his image, answering to him, responsible. This aloneness was a good thing, for everything in the Garden was perfect.[18]

Though We Appear to Be Two, We're Really One

GENESIS 2:24 ***Therefore a man shall leave his father and mother and be joined to his wife, and they shall become one flesh.*** *(NKJV)*

Here God offers a principle that began that day and continues still. When a man and a woman unite in marriage, they enter a relationship that goes beyond every other family relationship. A man will leave his parents and begin such an intimate relationship that the two become one.

Many centuries later, Jesus spoke of God's view of marriage, adding that what God joins together, people outside the marriage relationship must not separate.

go to

marriage
Matthew 19:1–12

walking and talking
Genesis 3:8–9

what others say

Edith Schaeffer

God had created people, male and female, with a capacity for oneness with each other, a fruitful physical oneness that would bring forth another generation of people. God created people with a capacity for oneness in working together, communicating verbally, exchanging ideas, doing creative works, eating together and "walking and talking with God in the cool of the evening."[19]

No Embarrassment, No Shame

GENESIS 2:25 ***And they were both naked, the man and his wife, and were not ashamed.*** *(NKJV)*

Marriage was God's institution, not something invented by humans for their convenience. This divine origin brings dignity and transparency to an institution based on the relationship of one man and one woman that was designed by God and still has his blessing.

key point

In the serene atmosphere of the Garden, the man, the woman, and their Creator could freely communicate with one another. The man and woman were naked because they could be transparent, having nothing to hide. They could share their thoughts and feelings without hesitation. They were innocent and enjoyed complete openness with each other and with God. God created man and woman to be recipients of his love and delight.

what others say

Lloyd Ogilvie

> The secret of enjoying God is discovering that what provides him with enjoyment in us is also what produces lasting enjoyment for us. There's no greater enjoyment in life than bringing delight to our Father. And his delight is that we understand and know Him.[20]

God created us for his enjoyment. He also built into us the capacity to enjoy him. The greatest pleasure in life is in knowing God and having complete confidence that he knows us intimately and is pleased in that knowledge.

Chapter Wrap-Up

- God completed Creation in six days, then rested on the seventh day, blessing and "sancitifying" it. (Genesis 2:1–3)
- God created man, breathing life into him, making him different from all the rest of Creation. (Genesis 2:4–7)
- God prepared a Garden and put man in it to care for it. (Genesis 2:8–15)
- God gave man his first command—not to eat of the "tree of the knowledge of good and evil"—showing that man had freedom of choice. (Genesis 2:16–17)
- Since none of the animals were suitable to be man's helper, God created woman from man's rib to be his wife. (Genesis 2:18–25)

Study Questions

1. How does Creation show that God is concerned about details?
2. How does the seventh day of the week differ from the other six?
3. How does our attitude toward the Sabbath today compare with God's original intent?
4. What does Adam's experience in the Garden teach us about work?
5. What does Genesis 2 teach us about marriage?

Genesis 3 Trouble in the Garden

Chapter Highlights:
- Temptation and Sin
- Consequences of a Wrong Choice
- God's Gracious Provision

Let's Get Started

We can't imagine a more idyllic setting for the first man and woman than what they were given in the Garden of Eden. God had created the universe with gem-like Planet Earth, then filled Earth with lush vegetation and living creatures. Finally he created the man and woman in his own image. The world was filled with peace and harmony, everything fulfilling the purpose for which it had been created. God's evaluation: it was good, very good.

This, however, is not the picture of our world today. What happened? The answer lies in a choice made by the first man and woman. God had given them **moral** responsibility, the freedom to choose to do right or to do wrong. Genesis 3 records the account and the consequences of their choice, and the loving provision God made in response.

moral
doing, as well as knowing, what is right

Temptation and Sin

All was well in the Garden of Eden. The man and woman basked in the beauty of their world. All their needs were met in their physical surroundings, in their enjoyment with each other, and, best of all, in their relationship with their Creator. Enter the villain who had a strategy to bring ruin to God's perfect world.

Never Talk to Strangers (Especially Serpents)

GENESIS 3:1 ***Now the serpent was more cunning than any beast of the field which the LORD God had made. And he said to the woman, "Has God indeed said, 'You shall not eat of every tree of the garden'?"*** *(NKJV)*

The man and woman lived in the Garden where vegetation was lush and animals moved freely. One day, when the woman was alone, perhaps enjoying a walk among the bountiful fruit trees, she met an

Satan
an angelic being who is the enemy of God

temptation
an inward pull to do wrong

commandment
God's instruction for human beings

Tree of the Knowledge of Good and Evil
its fruits signified the ability to know good and evil by personal experience

test
a way of revealing who a person really is

tempt
to arouse a desire to do wrong by seeming to offer a benefit

unexpected visitor: a serpent who spoke to her. Now the serpent was one of God's created animals, thought to be both exceptionally beautiful and graceful.

We know from other parts of Scripture that **Satan** was acting and speaking through the serpent, and his motivation was to deceive the woman. Then she would yield to **temptation** and break God's **commandment**.

He approached her and asked, "Has God indeed said, 'You shall not eat of every tree of the garden'?" (Genesis 3:1 NKJV). His approach was designed to shock her and to arouse doubt about God's goodness.

> what others say
>
> **Warren Wiersbe**
>
> Satan isn't an originator; he's a clever imitator who disguises his true character. If necessary, he can even masquerade as an angel of light. When he came into the Garden, Satan used the body of a serpent, one of God's creatures that he had pronounced "good" (Genesis 1:31).[1]

something to ponder

God placed the **"Tree of the Knowledge of Good and Evil"** in the Garden as a **test**, a way the man and woman could reveal their love for him by obeying his command. It was the only thing forbidden to them. The serpent used that tree for a different purpose: to **tempt** the woman to fail the test by disobeying God's command.

There is a lesson to be learned here, for God places "trees of testing" in our lives, too. We can either delight in their presence, viewing them as symbols of God's refining love and knowing he will provide for all our needs, or we can agonize about what we don't have. When you look at things this way, you begin to see how foolish it is to disobey God. To disobey God is to defy the only Being who knows inside and out what we need the most.

go to

deceive
2 Corinthians 11:3; Revelation 12:9; 20:2–3

angel of light
2 Corinthians 11:14

Close, but No Cigar

GENESIS 3:2–3 ***And the woman said to the serpent, "We may eat the fruit of the trees of the garden; but of the fruit of the tree which is in the midst of the garden, God has said, 'You shall not eat it, nor shall you touch it, lest you die.'"*** *(NKJV)*

The woman corrected the serpent's insinuation that God had denied her something that she should have had the right to enjoy. She said that God had told them they could eat fruit from the trees in the Garden—with one exception (Genesis 2:16). She pointed out that she and her husband were not to eat fruit from one tree, the Tree of the Knowledge of Good and Evil (verse 17). Then she showed that Satan's subtle insinuation about God's goodness was taking effect. She added something that was not true by misquoting God as saying, "Nor shall you touch it, lest you die" (3:3 NKJV). God had not said that they could not touch the tree.

The woman fell into the trap of altering what God had said. Because God is totally wise, what he says is exactly what he means. He tells us that we are not to add to his words or take away from them.

go to

not to add to his words or take away from them
Deuteronomy 4:2; Revelation 22:18–19

something to ponder

Bald-Faced Lie

GENESIS 3:4–5 ***Then the serpent said to the woman, "You will not surely die. For God knows that in the day you eat of it your eyes will be opened, and you will be like God, knowing good and evil." (NKJV)***

Satan boldly denied God's warning, "for in the day that you eat of it you shall surely die" (Genesis 2:17 NKJV). He called God a liar and then said falsely that the reason God had warned them was because God was afraid that if they ate the fruit, they would become as wise as he is in knowing both good and evil.

Satan tried to get the woman to exert her will in opposition to God's.

what others say

Victor P. Hamilton

Whenever one makes his own will crucial and God's revealed will irrelevant, whenever autonomy displaces submission and obedience in a person, that finite individual attempts to rise above the limitations imposed on him by his Creator.[2]

A Shared Choice

GENESIS 3:6 ***So when the woman saw that the tree was good for food, that it was pleasant to the eyes, and a tree desirable to make***

go to

deceived
1 Timothy 2:14

one wise, she took of its fruit and ate. She also gave to her husband with her, and he ate. *(NKJV)*

The woman was deceived by the serpent so that she believed his lies. She looked at the fruit and was tempted to reach for it. First, it looked good for eating. It also pleased her aesthetically—appealing to her sense of beauty. But more, the thought of what it might do for her was compelling. She wanted the wisdom. She wanted to be like God. So she reached out to take some of the fruit and she chose to eat it. Then she gave some of the fruit to Adam, who apparently had not been part of the conversation with the serpent. He took the fruit from her and made a deliberate choice: he ate it.

what others say

David A. Seamands

Humans, created to live over and above all other creatures, but under God, listened to the voice of the Evil One.... [Satan] sowed the deadly seeds of temptation in Adam's and Eve's minds until they began to question the goodness of God's character. They no longer saw God's loving limitation, "You must not eat from the (one) tree" as the Father's gracious provision for his children to enjoy even more fully all the other trees in the garden.[3]

Elisabeth Elliot

When we begin to doubt [God's] love and imagine that he is cheating us of something we have a right to, we are guilty as Adam and Eve were guilty. They took the snake at his word rather than [taking] God [at his word]. The same snake comes to us repeatedly with the same suggestions: Does God love you? Does he really want the best for you? Is his word trustworthy? Isn't he cheating you? Forget his promises. You'd be better off if you do it your way.[4]

something to ponder

The woman's response to temptation was not an isolated incident. We respond in similar ways even today. We learn from 1 John 2:15–17 that the temptations we face today parallel those that the woman faced.

We are warned: "Do not love the world or the things in the world. If anyone loves the world, the love of the Father is not in him. For all that is in the world—the lust of the flesh, the lust of the eyes, and the pride of life—is not of the Father but is of the world. And the world is passing away, and the lust of it; but he who does the will of God abides forever" (1 John 2:15–17 NKJV).

Temptation, Then and Now

The Woman's Temptation (Genesis 3:6–7)	Today's Temptations (1 John 2:16)
The fruit was good for food.	People want things for pleasure, not necessity.
The fruit was pleasant for her eyes.	People desire things they see that are physically attractive or that appeal to the other senses.
The fruit was desirable for gaining wisdom.	People take pride in what they have instead of giving God—the giver of all things—the credit for providing those blessings.

Satan has continued his practice of tempting people to disobey God. Many people in the Bible yielded to that temptation:

- Esau was tempted to sell his birthright (Genesis 25:29–34).
- The Israelites were tempted to worship a golden calf (Exodus 32:1–8).
- Achan was tempted to take forbidden items from Jericho (Joshua 7:21).
- Samson was tempted to reveal the secret of his unusual physical strength (Judges 14:16–17).
- David was tempted to commit adultery with Bathsheba (2 Samuel 11:2–4).
- Solomon was tempted to marry godless foreign women, who in turn tempted him to worship their false gods (1 Kings 11:1–4).
- Gehazi was tempted to deceive Naaman and take a gift that the prophet Elisha had refused (2 Kings 5:20–23).
- Jonah was tempted to disobey God's direction to preach to the people of Nineveh (Jonah 1:1–3).
- Peter was tempted to deny even knowing Jesus (Matthew 26:69–75).
- Ananias and Sapphira were tempted to deceive Peter by keeping for themselves some of the money from the sale of property (Acts 5:1–4).

The Bible also includes examples of those who resisted temptation:

- Joseph resisted the persistent appeals of Potiphar's wife (Genesis 39:1–10).

go to

tempted
James 1:14

- Job resisted the temptation to accuse God of doing wrong to him, even though he suffered extreme losses (Job 1:21).
- Daniel and his friends resisted the temptation to eat royal food and wine God had forbidden (Daniel 1:1–16).
- Jesus resisted temptation after forty days of **fasting** (Matthew 4:1–11).

We are all tempted, but God has provided us with all we need to resist temptation. We are promised, "No temptation has overtaken you except such as is common to man; but God is faithful, who will not allow you to be tempted beyond what you are able, but with the temptation will also make the way of escape, that you may be able to bear it" (1 Corinthians 10:13 NKJV).

something to ponder

fasting
choosing to go without food and/or drink

shame
a sense of humiliation for having done wrong

conscience
an inner sense of what is right and wrong

Shame on Me

GENESIS 3:7 ***Then the eyes of both of them were opened, and they knew that they were naked; and they sewed fig leaves together and made themselves coverings. (NKJV)***

It only took a moment. Suddenly everything changed. The man and woman were overcome with a feeling they had never experienced: **shame**. The man and woman had been deceived. Their eyes were opened, not to the wisdom of God, as the serpent had promised, but to their own nakedness.

Gone was the openness they had enjoyed as husband and wife. Their guilt made them want to conceal themselves. So they found fig leaves, perhaps the largest leaves in the Garden, and made garments to cover their bodies.

what others say

Warren Wiersbe

Sin ought to make us ashamed of ourselves. God has given us an inner judge called "**conscience**" that accuses when we do wrong and approves when we do right.[5]

Gilbert Bilezikian

Before their downfall, the humans' nobility as God's image-bearers shielded them from the frailty of their humanity. Once the protection was removed, their eyes were opened to each other's exposure in weakness, one miserable sinner gazing at

> the misery of another sinner. The pain of exposure was so intolerable that they sought the pitiful cover of fig leaves as a substitute for the glory of the innocence that had clothed them.[6]

go to

hiding
Psalm 139:7–12

light
1 Timothy 6:16

fellowship
mutual sharing

The Saddest Walk in History

> GENESIS 3:8 ***And they heard the sound of the LORD God walking in the garden in the cool of the day, and Adam and his wife hid themselves from the presence of the LORD God among the trees of the garden.*** *(NKJV)*

In the cool of the evening, as the sun set, God strolled through the Garden. When the man and woman heard his approach, they were overcome with shame and fear. They were afraid to see God and to have him see them. The **fellowship** they had enjoyed with God no longer appealed to them. They avoided spending time with the one who loved them, for they knew he would see their guilt. They hid among the trees.

A Call That Chilled the Heart

> GENESIS 3:9–10 ***Then the LORD God called to Adam and said to him, "Where are you?" So he said, "I heard Your voice in the garden, and I was afraid because I was naked; and I hid myself."*** *(NKJV)*

God, knowing all things, knew exactly where the man and woman were hiding. He also knew why they were hiding. He knew they had made a moral choice to disobey his command, a command he had given them for their own good. He called out, "Where are you?" He waited.

The man and woman came out from hiding. The man admitted he had heard God approaching, was afraid because he was naked, and therefore hid.

God is light. His holiness and purity are complete. In contrast, sin brings darkness. When the man and woman sinned, they did not want to face the light. Jesus says, "This is the condemnation, that the light has come into the world, and men loved darkness rather than light, because their deeds were evil" (John 3:19 NKJV).

something to ponder

Inescapable Questions

repent
turn from disobedience and desire to obey

GENESIS 3:11 ***And He said, "Who told you that you were naked? Have you eaten from the tree of which I commanded you that you should not eat?"*** *(NKJV)*

God already knew the answers to the questions he asked. But the man and woman needed to admit what they had done. Actually, no one had told them they were naked. The conscience within had shouted that. Adam's reply exposed his great wrongdoing. He would not have known he was naked if he had not sinned. How the man and woman answered God's questions would reveal if they understood the terrible gravity of their choices and whether they were ready to **repent**.

Our human tendency is to hide sin and shrink from even admitting its presence in our lives. By covering it over, we allow a spiritual wound to fester. As the Master Surgeon, God knows that the only way to get rid of sin is to expose it and deal with it.

Blameshifting 101

GENESIS 3:12–13 ***Then the man said, "The woman whom You gave to be with me, she gave me of the tree, and I ate." And the LORD God said to the woman, "What is this you have done?" The woman said, "The serpent deceived me, and I ate."*** *(NKJV)*

Instead of confessing their sin, the man blamed his wife and she in turn blamed the serpent. Adam even implied that God was at fault, since he had given the woman to Adam.

what others say

R. C. Sproul

Temptation is something that rises from within the evil inclinations of our own hearts. We can't excuse our sin by saying that the devil made us do it or, worse, that God has provoked us or inclined us to sin.[7]

Liz Curtis Higgs

Shifting blame is practically an American pastime. So whom shall we blame for our proclivity to sin? Our mothers? Our grandmothers? Wanna go all the way back to Eve? Or take a page from Adam's diary and blame God—"It's your fault,

Lord. You made me this way!" No. God gave us his Spirit to empower us, his Word to strengthen us, and his Son to catch us when we fall. We have no one to blame but ourselves when we choose to sin. And no one to thank but our Creator when he chooses to save us from our sins...again.[8]

From the earliest days of life on earth sin has brought consequences. People may deny it, forget it, or ridicule it, but the fact remains.

Still, They Both Admitted, "I Ate"

GENESIS 3:14–15 *So the LORD God said to the serpent:*
"Because you have done this,
You are cursed more than all cattle,
And more than every beast of the field;
On your belly you shall go,
And you shall eat dust
All the days of your life.
And I will put enmity
Between you and the woman,
And between your seed and her Seed;
He shall bruise your head,
And you shall bruise His heel." (NKJV)

Consequences for the Serpent

First, God addressed the serpent that had provided the physical body through which Satan had tempted the woman—he would be punished. Instead of being exceptionally attractive, and possibly standing upright, he would crawl on the ground and "eat dust" (Genesis 3:14 NKJV). There would be enmity between humans and the serpent, reminding them always of the consequences of the choice the first man and woman had made.

But there was more. God spoke to Satan, who had spoken through the serpent. While Satan would cripple (or "bruise [the] heel") of the descendants of the woman, her offspring would crush Satan's head.

Scholars interpret God's statement about the woman's offspring, or seed, to be the first **Messianic Promise**, that is, the first time God promised that from the descendants of the woman someone would come who would deliver the final blow to Satan. While Satan would bruise the heel of the woman, the Messiah would crush his head. This was a word of hope. Ultimately, the consequences for Satan will climax when he is defeated by God and consigned to eternal punishment.

Consequences for the Woman

GENESIS 3:16 *To the woman He said:*
"I will greatly multiply your sorrow
and your conception;
In pain you shall bring forth children;
Your desire shall be for your husband,
And he shall rule over you." (NKJV)

God then turned to the woman and told her the consequences of her choice to disobey his command. She would have increased pain when bearing children. She would also have disequilibrium in her relationship with her husband. She would have an inner need to win his approval while he would attempt to rule over her. Of the eighty times the Old Testament speaks of childbirth, in sixty it mentions the pain. The prophets refer to childbirth pain to emphasize the seriousness of the coming divine judgment.

eternal punishment
Revelation 20:7–10

Messianic Promise
God's promise to send an **anointed one**

anointed one
one chosen by God to be the Messiah, the Savior and Ruler over all

salvation
God's action through Jesus Christ in delivering believers from the power of Satan, sin, and death

what others say

Elisabeth Elliot

The spirit of godly obedience is not in us; our wills have not been unconditionally turned over to the Master, as long as we determine our own action by what others do. To husbands God says (unconditionally), "Love your wives." To wives he says (unconditionally), "Submit to your husbands." If each lets his obedience be contingent upon the other's, there is a standoff. The command to husbands is the business of husbands. The command to wives is the business of wives. Let each "mind his own"—direct his attention to the thing required of him—and harmony will be the result.[9]

Consequences for the Man

GENESIS 3:17–20 *Then to Adam He said, "Because you have heeded the voice of your wife, and have eaten from the tree of which I commanded you, saying, 'You shall not eat of it':*
"Cursed is the ground for your sake;
In toil you shall eat of it
All the days of your life.
Both thorns and thistles it shall bring forth for you,
And you shall eat the herb of the field.
In the sweat of your face you shall eat bread
Till you return to the ground,
For out of it you were taken;
For dust you are,
And to dust you shall return."
And Adam called his wife's name Eve, because she was the mother of all living. (NKJV)

ground would be cursed
fertility diminished; introduction of thorns and thistles

innocent
knowing only what is good and right

alienated
separated from another because of hostility

reconciliation
to be restored to a right relationship

God then told Adam the consequences of his rebellion against his command. The **ground would be cursed**, and man would have pain and sweat in his work of cultivating it. As man toiled in his constant battle with thorns and thistles, he would remember the consequences of his sin, which included physical death. Some day his body would return to the ground.

God had said, "But of the tree of the knowledge of good and evil you shall not eat, for in the day that you eat of it you shall surely die" (Genesis 2:17 NKJV). The man and woman disobeyed God's command. Though they didn't fall down dead immediately, death occurred—and we have that death with us today. What happened when they chose to disobey God?

- They were no longer **innocent**. They were now experienced in knowing and doing evil.
- They knew shame. Their guilt made them lose their transparency with each other and with God.
- They were afraid of God and wanted to hide from him.
- They were **alienated** from God and unwilling to seek **reconciliation**.
- They did not take responsibility for their sin, but shifted blame and made excuses.
- They faced physical death.

go to

son of the morning
Isaiah 14:12

perfect
Ezekiel 28:12–13

rebellion
Isaiah 14:13–15

charged
Job 4:18

thrown out of heaven
Ezekiel 28:17

destroy
1 John 3:8

greater
1 John 4:4

everlasting fire
Matthew 25:41; Revelation 20:7–10

Rebel Without a Clue

Satan did not identify himself when he approached the woman. We look to other parts of Scripture to find what God has revealed about him.

Satan is a created being, once a powerful and influential angel called Lucifer, which means "morning star" or "son of the morning." He was beautiful and occupied a place near God's throne, and he was perfect in his actions. But one day "iniquity was found" in him (Ezekiel 28:15 NKJV). He wanted to be greater than God and exalt his own throne above all other thrones. Motivated by pride, he led an angelic rebellion against God. God charged the rebels with error.

Lucifer was thrown out of heaven and given a new name, Satan, which means "adversary" or "enemy." Today Satan still leads other evil spirit beings as adversaries of God and God's followers.

Throughout Scripture Satan is described with various names that give word pictures of his evil character. Here are a few:

- Accuser (Revelation 12:10)
- Serpent of old (Revelation 12:9)
- Beelzebub, or ruler of the demons (Matthew 12:24)
- Devil, meaning "destroyer" (1 Peter 5:8)
- God of this age (2 Corinthians 4:4)
- Murderer (John 8:44)
- One who deceives the whole world (Revelation 12:9)
- Ruler of this world (John 12:31)
- Spirit at work in those who are disobedient (Ephesians 2:2)
- Tempter (Matthew 4:3)
- Wicked one (Matthew 13:19)
- Father of lies (John 8:44)

Satan is a powerful being and is active in the world. He has more power than humans have, but he is not as powerful as God is.

Christ came into the world to destroy or undo Satan's work. While Satan is active in many aspects of life on earth, Christians do not need to fear him. The one who lives within Christians is greater than Satan.

Satan's doom is already sealed. He and his angels will be cast into everlasting fire.

Was the Tree a Cruel Trick?

God pronounced as good everything he made on earth. He would not have placed the "Tree of the Knowledge of Good and Evil" in the Garden as a means of tricking the first man and woman into sin. The tree was placed in the Garden as a means of testing them. Satan, appearing as a serpent, used the tree to lead the woman to question God's love and goodness.

go to

sacrifice
Leviticus 17:11

what others say

Dr. Larry Richards

Some have seen placement of the Tree of the Knowledge of Good and Evil in Eden as some sort of trap. We need to understand it in the context of God's design of Eden. It too is an opportunity provided by God. Man's moral nature must be exercised if he is to fulfill his potential as a person. Placement of the tree is no trap, but provision of an opportunity for moral fulfillment.[10]

God's Gracious Provision

key point

God could have thrown the first man and woman into the scrap heap as a work of Creation gone wrong. But he didn't. Despite their choice to disobey his command, he reached out as a tender father would to children who had made an irreversible choice and brought sin and death into the world.

So I Won't Be Needing This Closet Full of Fig Leaves?

GENESIS 3:21 *Also for Adam and his wife the LORD God made tunics of skin, and clothed them.* (NKJV)

Adam and Eve had rebelled against God and had brought on themselves and on the whole human race terrible consequences for their sin. This chapter in their lives has been called the Fall of Man (see Appendix A), because it resembles Lucifer's fall from heaven as a consequence of his wicked rebellion against God.

However, God did not abandon Adam and Eve, nor did he leave them without hope. He provided animal skins as clothing to cover their nakedness.

something to ponder

Many Bible experts believe that in this act of taking the lives of innocent animals, God was teaching Adam and Eve the need for a blood sacrifice to remove the guilt of sin. Jesus Christ sacrificed his body so that we might be made right in God's holy eyes.

God would some day send his Son to be the ultimate sacrifice for sin, a once-for-all, perfect removal of guilt that would enable us to become righteous. In his great mercy, he provided **salvation** for all humans.

ultimate sacrifice
Hebrews 10:1–18

righteous
2 Corinthians 5:21

salvation
deliverance from the penalty of sin

cherubim
angelic beings

what others say

Ronald B. Allen

It is a mistake to regard even the most damaged of men as worthless. For despite the most awful of flaws and grievous of sins, there is still on this wretch the mark of the Master Yahweh. When we sense how terrible it is the one bearing God's image is fallen, we cannot but mourn. But we also long for a faithful restoration, knowing that in this case the restoration can be accomplished only by the original Maker himself.[11]

An Act of Mercy

Genesis 3:22–24 ***Then the LORD God said, "Behold, the man has become like one of Us, to know good and evil. And now, lest he put out his hand and take also of the tree of life, and eat, and live forever"—therefore the LORD God sent him out of the garden of Eden to till the ground from which he was taken. So He drove out the man; and He placed cherubim at the east of the garden of Eden, and a flaming sword which turned every way, to guard the way to the tree of life.*** *(NKJV)*

God banished Adam and Eve from the Garden, not as a punishment, but as an act of mercy to protect them. He knew that if they stayed in the Garden they could eat of the Tree of Life and live forever. He was sparing them the pain of living in sin themselves and in seeing the consequences of their sin continue to grow in the form of misery and evil in their descendants. To ensure their well-being, God placed "**cherubim**" and "a flaming sword which turned every way" (Genesis 3:24 NKJV) to keep Adam and Eve from returning to the Garden.

Physical death is an enemy, but it is also a mercy. We will die, but Christians will be raised up to eternal life, to sin no more and to enjoy unhindered fellowship with God.

Chapter Wrap-Up

- Satan, in the form of a beautiful serpent, approached the woman and tempted her to disobey God by eating fruit from the "tree of the knowledge of good and evil." (Genesis 3:1–5)
- The woman gave in to the temptation, disobeying God by eating the forbidden fruit, and giving some to Adam, who ate it also. (Genesis 3:6)
- Once they sinned by disobeying God, the man and woman knew shame and guilt, and their fellowship with God was ruined. (Genesis 3:7–10)
- When confronted with their sin, Adam admitted it but blamed the woman God had given him; she in turn blamed the serpent. (Genesis 3:11–13)
- God punished the serpent and Adam and Eve for their sin and sent the man and the woman out of the Garden, never to return. (Genesis 3:14–24)

Study Questions

1. How did the serpent (Satan) persuade Eve to disobey God? What methods does he use today?
2. How are the temptations we face today similar to Eve's temptation?
3. How did Adam and Eve's sin change their attitude toward God?
4. How did Jesus "bruise [the] head" (Genesis 3:15 NKJV) of Satan, as God foretold in the Garden?
5. What were the consequences of Adam and Eve's sin for them? For us?

Genesis 4–5 The First Family

Chapter Highlights:
- Cain and Abel
- A Mark of Mercy
- Getting Away with Murder
- Seth
- The Extended Family

Let's Get Started

The first couple had enjoyed life in the Garden of Eden. Now, as a consequence of their disobedience to God, they were banished from the Garden and consigned to a very different quality of life. In a real sense for them, and for us too, it was Paradise Lost.

In the first family we see the consequences of their sin in the Garden being worked out in their lives outside the Garden. All that God had foretold began to unfold. When God had spoken of death, Adam and Eve had little idea of what he meant, for they had not seen death. Now they would experience the intense pain it brings. But there was another side. There was the knowledge that while God sees all the wrong we do, he also sees when we desire to please him.

Cain and Abel

Meet the first two people to come into the world through the natural means of physical birth. (Adam and Eve had been created by God. Does that mean they had no navels?) What wonder must have filled their hearts as they discovered God's good gift of sex, the means for fulfilling his command to "be fruitful and multiply" (Genesis 1:28 NKJV).

The First Human Ever Born

GENESIS 4:1–2 ***Now Adam knew Eve his wife, and she conceived and bore Cain, and said, "I have acquired a man from the LORD." Then she bore again, this time his brother Abel. Now Abel was a keeper of sheep, but Cain was a tiller of the ground. (NKJV)***

Adam and Eve became the first parents, bringing the first baby into the world. That this was an occasion of rejoicing is clear from the name Eve gave her son. She called him Cain because with the

go to

faith
Hebrews 11:4

something to ponder

righteous
rightness with God based on one's faith in God

Lord's help she had brought a man into the world. After a time, she gave birth to another son, Abel, whose name means "vapor" or "vanity," which may indicate that by the time Abel was born Adam and Eve had seen the results of God's curse on the earth.

The two boys grew up to develop individual interests and skills. Cain became a farmer, and Abel became a shepherd.

In the birth of Adam and Eve's two sons, we see that each person born into the world has value because we are each created in God's image. God has built into each individual great potential for skills and aptitudes to be developed. To reach our fullest potential, each person needs to be linked up with God by faith. In the lives of Cain and Abel, we see a contrast between a life of trust in God and a life of self-development.

Bring Your Offering, Not Your Attitude

GENESIS 4:3–5 ***And in the process of time it came to pass that Cain brought an offering of the fruit of the ground to the LORD. Abel also brought of the firstborn of his flock and of their fat. And the LORD respected Abel and his offering, but He did not respect Cain and his offering. And Cain was very angry, and his countenance fell.*** *(NKJV)*

God no longer walked on earth in the cool of the day to fellowship with his people, but he did provide a way for them to approach him. Though we do not have God's exact instructions in this passage, it is evident that the first family understood how they were to make offerings to him.

One day Cain brought an offering of produce from his farming efforts. We can imagine that he presented the best harvest—show fruits and vegetables. Abel also brought an offering. He offered lambs from his flock.

God was pleased with Abel's offering, but not with Cain's. Why? Scholars have many speculations, but the only thing the Scripture text points us toward is the attitude behind the offering. Abel brought his offering with faith in his heart, and God viewed him as a **righteous** man. Cain, on the other hand, apparently brought his with indifference to the directions God had given. The evidence for this is the great anger he showed toward God and his brother Abel when his offering was not accepted as Abel's had been. The attitude in our hearts determines if our worship is acceptable to God.

One-Sided Conversation

GENESIS 4:6–7 *So the LORD said to Cain, "Why are you angry? And why has your countenance fallen? If you do well, will you not be accepted? And if you do not do well, sin lies at the door. And its desire is for you, but you should rule over it."* (NKJV)

God asked Cain, "Why are you angry? And why has your countenance fallen?" (Genesis 4:6 NKJV). God knew the answer, but Cain evidently chose not to reply. God went on to remind Cain that if he did what was right in making the acceptable offering, he would be accepted. But if he chose not to do what was right, sin was poised, ready to devour him. It was not too late; he could still overcome it.

Cain knew the kind of offering God wanted, but he had no intention of accepting the remedy God offered. The door to Cain's heart slammed shut to God. Evil thoughts smoldered behind that closed door.

what others say

J. Vernon McGee

When Cain brought an offering to God, he did not come by faith—he came on his own.[1]

Two Go Walking; Only One Returns

GENESIS 4:8 *Now Cain talked with Abel his brother; and it came to pass, when they were in the field, that Cain rose up against Abel his brother and killed him.* (NKJV)

First came jealousy that swept into Cain's heart. After that came anger—anger that God had accepted his younger brother's offering and not his. Then came a plan. Cain invited his brother to go out into the field with him. When he thought he was far from observation, Cain attacked his brother and killed him.

what others say

Ron Mehl

How much God loves us! He tried to reason with Cain. He tried to reassure and comfort this disappointed, angry man. And finally, he gave him a serious warning. But Cain had nurtured the anger and bitterness in his heart for so long that even God standing in the pathway before him wasn't going to stop him. He walked right around God to kill his only brother.[2]

go to

murderer
1 John 3:11–15

what others say

Edith Schaeffer

The first death was the result of a killing, a direct murder in anger. It must have come as a shock to Cain, as well as to Adam and Eve. A human being's body, not breathing, not speaking, growing cold, was something no one had seen before. Understanding must have come slowly and agonizingly, and the realization must have come back in terrible shock waves.[3]

something to ponder

Hatred and murder are so closely related, God tells us that to hate another person is to be a murderer.

- Cain murdered Abel because he was jealous of his brother's acceptance with God. Other murderers had different motives.
- David had Uriah murdered to conceal his own sin of adultery and to make a way for him to take Bathsheba, widow of Uriah, to be his wife (2 Samuel 11).
- Ehud killed Eglon, king of Moab, to launch a rebellion against Eglon's oppressive rule over the Israelites for eighteen years (Judges 3:12–30).
- Solomon ordered the death of Adonijah, who opposed God's choice of Solomon to be king of Israel (1 Kings 2:13–25).
- Absalom killed his brother Amnon to take revenge for Amnon violating his sister Tamar (2 Samuel 13).
- Stephen was murdered because of his faith in Jesus Christ (Acts 7:54–60).

An Eyewitness

GENESIS 4:9 ***Then the LORD said to Cain, "Where is Abel your brother?" He said, "I do not know. Am I my brother's keeper?" (NKJV)***

Cain thought he was alone. Did he think he would never be found out? What did he plan to tell his parents? We don't know. But there was an eyewitness to his murder. God saw it all. He asked Cain a simple question, but one Cain refused to answer. "Where is Abel your brother?" (Genesis 4:9 NKJV).

Cain's response betrayed the evil in his heart. He declared that he did not know where his brother was. Further, he denied having any responsibility for his brother. He resented that God sees everything; nothing is concealed from his eyes.

go to

evil
1 John 3:12

sees everything
Proverbs 15:3

prophet
Luke 11:49–51

Cain's Curse

GENESIS 4:10–12 ***And He said, "What have you done? The voice of your brother's blood cries out to Me from the ground. So now you are cursed from the earth, which has opened its mouth to receive your brother's blood from your hand. When you till the ground, it shall no longer yield its strength to you. A fugitive and a vagabond you shall be on the earth." (NKJV)***

God was just in delivering a punishment to Cain for his violent act. Abel's blood was on the ground. Therefore, the ground would no longer yield bountiful crops for Cain. Further, he would become a wanderer, moving restlessly from one place to another. Because Cain refused to confess his sin and seek God's forgiveness, his guilty conscience would haunt him wherever he went.

what others say

Anne Graham Lotz

Cain lost his peace. He lost real meaning to his life. His inner security and contentment. His satisfaction and sense of fulfillment. The ground would no longer produce for him, forcing him to wander from place to place as he tried to make a living in some other way. And while he wandered, the alarm of his conscience would be constantly screaming his guilt so that he could never escape what he had done.[4]

God revealed how much he values human life. It is sacred because each person bears God's image. He does not forget when his faithful followers are put to death. Many years after this incident, Jesus spoke of Abel as a prophet who had been murdered. God had not forgotten.

Too Much!

GENESIS 4:13–14 ***And Cain said to the LORD, "My punishment is greater than I can bear! Surely You have driven me out***

go to

forgiveness
Psalm 32:1–5;
1 John 1:9

something to ponder

this day from the face of the ground; I shall be hidden from Your face; I shall be a fugitive and a vagabond on the earth, and it will happen that anyone who finds me will kill me." (NKJV)

Cain does not express repentance for his great sin, but he does seem to show some regret. What was he to do? He was a farmer, and now the ground would no longer produce for him. He had lived with his godly parents and other family members. Now he was being banished from God's presence. Further, his safety was at stake. As a wanderer, he would be vulnerable to anyone who wanted to avenge Abel's blood. Those who refuse to confess and forsake their wrongdoing must suffer the consequences. God offers the way to forgiveness and cleansing, but we need to seek it.

mercy
a deeply caring response to someone who is helpless or in need

vengeance
punishing in retaliation for wrongdoing

A Mark of Mercy

GENESIS 4:15 ***And the LORD said to him, "Therefore, whoever kills Cain, vengeance shall be taken on him sevenfold." And the LORD set a mark on Cain, lest anyone finding him should kill him. (NKJV)***

Cain didn't deserve **mercy**, but God gave it. God promised **vengeance** on anyone who would take Cain's life. God also gave Cain a sign or mark that would protect him from avengers.

> what others say
>
> **Warren Wiersbe**
>
> God did a strange thing: He put a mark on Cain that would protect him from the assaults of people who wanted to kill him. We don't know what this mark was or why people would recognize it as God's protective seal; but it worked. This was purely an act of mercy on God's part.[5]

The Rest of the Story

GENESIS 4:16–18 ***Then Cain went out from the presence of the LORD and dwelt in the land of Nod on the east of Eden. And Cain knew his wife, and she conceived and bore Enoch. And he built a city, and called the name of the city after the name of his son—Enoch. To Enoch was born Irad; and Irad begot Mehujael, and Mehujael begot Methushael, and Methushael begot Lamech. (NKJV)***

Cain left the Lord's presence and moved to the east. He became a father and eventually began to build a city, which he named after his son Enoch. This may indicate that he moved on before the city was complete and let his son carry on.

The question arises: Where did Cain get his wife? The Bible account tells us about Adam and Eve; Cain, their firstborn; and then Abel, now deceased. We know, however, that Adam and Eve had many children. Even after he was over 130 years old, Adam had other sons and daughters (Genesis 5:4). There was no prohibition against marrying siblings until later. Cain would have married a sister or perhaps a niece.

go to

prohibition
Leviticus 18:9; 20:17

death
James 1:13–15

Fall
Adam and Eve's first disobedience to God

what others say

Norman Geisler and Thomas A. Howe

There were no genetic imperfections at the beginning of the human race. God created a genetically perfect Adam (Genesis 1:27). Genetic defects resulted from the **Fall** and only occurred gradually over long periods of time. Further, there was no command in Cain's day not to marry a close relative.[6]

In the New Testament, James warns us about temptation. He wrote that we are tempted when our evil desires drag us away from what God wants and entice us to do what we find appealing. He wrote that when wrong desire is conceived, it gives birth to sin, and when sin is full grown, it gives birth to death.

When is sin full grown? Where does sin lead us? For Cain, it started with feelings of jealousy and resentment, which grew to anger and matured in murder. But it didn't stop even there. As we'll see in Cain's family, that sin spread through generation after generation.

Getting Away with Murder?

GENESIS 4:19–24 *Then Lamech took for himself two wives: the name of one was Adah, and the name of the second was Zillah. And Adah bore Jabal. He was the father of those who dwell in tents and have livestock. His brother's name was Jubal. He was the father of all those who play the harp and flute. And as for Zillah, she also bore Tubal-Cain, an instructor of every craftsman in bronze and iron. And the sister of Tubal-Cain was Naamah. Then Lamech said to his wives:*

"Adah and Zillah, hear my voice;
Wives of Lamech, listen to my speech!
For I have killed a man for wounding me,
Even a young man for hurting me.
If Cain shall be avenged sevenfold,
Then Lamech seventy-sevenfold." (NKJV)

It would seem that Cain and his descendants did not suffer from Cain murdering his brother Abel. In Genesis 4:17–24, six generations are named for Cain. God gives an overview of their records:

- Lamech is the first bigamist.
- Jabal is remembered for living in tents and raising livestock.
- Jubal was accomplished in music, playing the harp and flute (string and wind instruments).
- Tubal-Cain forged a variety of tools out of "bronze and iron."
- Lamech was a boastful egotist.
- Lamech was also a killer.
- Lamech boasts that he will take care of any avenger.

Cain raised a family that became highly accomplished, but we do not read that they worshiped God. Their achievements were self-serving, not intended to honor God their Creator.

Seth

Though the Bible is silent about this, Adam and Eve must have grieved deeply over the death of Abel and the departure of Cain, who, refusing to repent of murder, became a fugitive. Their empty nest was a continual and painful reminder of their disobedience in the Garden of Eden, which had introduced sin into the world. God stepped in to show his kindness and love by giving them another son who would love and obey him.

GENESIS 4:25–26 ***And Adam knew his wife again, and she bore a son and named him Seth, "For God has appointed another seed for me instead of Abel, whom Cain killed." And as for Seth, to him also a son was born; and he named him Enosh. Then men began to call on the name of the LORD.*** (NKJV)

The First Long-Distance Call

Eve longed for a son to replace godly Abel, and at last God gave her Seth. Cain developed an ungodly community. But Seth began one that was characterized by faith. In the days of his son Enosh, "men began to call on the name of the LORD" (Genesis 4:26 NKJV). Faith counts with God more than human achievement does.

God's Hall of Faith is found in Hebrews 11. Here we find the claim to fame of Old Testament heroes. Their achievements are not in building cities, exploring new continents, or becoming accomplished artists. God rewarded them for their faith in him.

- By faith Abel offered a better sacrifice than Cain (Hebrews 11:4).
- By faith Enoch pleased God so much that he was spared death (verses 5–6).
- By faith Noah believed God's warning and built an Ark (verse 7).
- By faith Abraham made his pilgrimage to a land of promise (verses 8–10).
- By faith Abraham and Sarah believed God's promise for a son, even though they were far past child-bearing age (verse 10).
- By faith Abraham offered his son Isaac as a sacrifice, believing that God would raise him from the dead (verses 17–19).
- By faith Isaac gave his blessing to Jacob, believing that God's promises to Abraham would be fulfilled through Jacob (verse 20).
- By faith Jacob blessed Joseph's two sons (verse 21).
- By faith Joseph, Abraham's great-grandson, gave instructions that after his death his bones should be moved from Egypt to the land God had promised to Abraham's descendants (verse 22).
- By faith Moses' parents hid him to save him from Pharaoh's command that baby boys must be killed (verse 23).
- By faith Moses refused life in Pharaoh's palace and identified himself with Abraham's descendants who were enslaved in Egypt (verses 24–28).
- By faith Moses led the Israelite slaves in keeping the **Passover** (verse 28).
- By faith the Israelite slaves crossed the Red Sea safely and escaped Pharaoh's pursuing army (verse 29).

go to

Abel
Genesis 4:4

Enoch
Genesis 5:21–24

Noah
Genesis 6:13–22

Abraham
Genesis 12:1–7

Abraham and Sarah
Genesis 17:17–22

Abraham offered his son Isaac
Genesis 22:1–10

Isaac
Genesis 27:25–29, 37

Jacob
Genesis 48:10–22

Joseph
Genesis 50:22–26

Moses' parents
Exodus 2:1–2

Moses
Exodus 2:11–3:22

Passover
Exodus 12:1–30

the Red Sea
Exodus 13:17–14:31

Passover
the meal shared by Jewish families on the night God passed over the Israelite slaves and killed the firstborn of Egypt, commemorated annually

go to

Jericho
Joshua 6

Rahab
Joshua 6:22–25

Barak
Judges 4–5

Samson
Judges 13–16

Jephthah
Judges 11–12

David
1 Samuel 16:1–13

Samuel
1 Samuel 1–3

death
Romans 5:12–14

faith
Hebrews 11:5–6

- By faith the Israelites marched around Jericho until God caused the walls to fall (verse 30).
- By faith Rahab protected the Israelite spies and thus her life was spared (verse 31).

Others whose faith God recognized: Barak, Samson, Jephthah, David, Samuel, and prophets who were not listed by name (verse 32). They achieved much for God in spite of being ridiculed and persecuted for their trust in God.

Walk Through the Cemetery

the big picture

Genesis 5

Here is a genealogy from Adam via Seth to Noah, ten generations. It begins with Adam and Eve, created by God in his likeness. They brought other people into the world to live and die, one generation after another.

Reading Genesis 5 is somewhat like reading tombstones in a cemetery. It may seem depressing, but it is far from boring. Some interesting facts emerge from the genealogy:

- ***Longevity:*** Adam, for example, lived 930 years, Seth 912, Methuselah 969. Earth's environment before the Flood (Genesis 6) was conducive to longevity. This enabled parents to have large families and thus fulfill God's command to "be fruitful and multiply" (Genesis 1:28 NKJV).

- ***Death:*** God had warned that death would be the consequence of disobedience (Genesis 2:16–17). This consequence was passed on from Adam and Eve to their descendants—with one exception.

- ***Walk with God:*** Enoch had faith and walked with God and was spared death. He simply disappeared because God took him. Enoch's life shines like a light in an otherwise dark world. But Enoch's walk with God was not literal and physical. Adam and Eve had that privilege and lost it for themselves and for their descendants when they sinned. Rather, Enoch's walk was spiritual companionship with God, based on his faith. Like Enoch, we have the privilege of walking with God.

- *Toil:* When God cursed the earth, he assigned painful toil to man. Lamech (Genesis 5:29) hoped his son Noah would bring comfort to their family because of the hard work required to cultivate the land.

There were two men named Lamech.

1. ***Lamech, a descendant of Cain*** (Genesis 4:19–24), was significant because his children introduced progress in music and ironworks, but he was an ungodly man. Though people gained materially through Lamech, their morals fell sadly.
2. ***Lamech, a descendant of Seth*** (Genesis 5:3–32), was significant because he was the father of Noah, who was a just man (6:9).

what others say

W. Glyn Evans

Faith pleases God when it is a way of life with us. It was Enoch's life of faith, not his spasmodic trust, which delighted the Lord. "Enoch walked with God" (Genesis 5:22, 24). His long life of 365 years was one of trusting confidence in the Almighty.[7]

J. I. Packer

[God] made us with the intention that He and we might walk together forever in a love-relationship. But such a relationship can only exist when the parties involved know something of each other. God, our Maker, knows all about us before we say anything (Psalm 139:1–4); but we can know nothing about him unless he tells us. Here, therefore, is a further reason why God speaks to us: not only to move us to do what he wants, but to enable us to know him so that we may love him. Therefore God sends his word to us in the character of both information and invitation. It comes to woo us as well as to instruct us; it not merely puts us in the picture of what God has done and is doing, but also calls us into personal communion with the loving Lord himself.[8]

Chapter Wrap-Up

- Adam and Eve had the first children born on earth, Cain and Abel. Cain became a farmer and Abel became a shepherd. (Genesis 4:1–2)
- When God accepted an offering from Abel but rejected Cain's offering, Cain became angry. (Genesis 4:3–7)
- Cain killed his brother Abel, then denied any responsibility for him. God punished Cain by making his crops fail and causing him to become a restless wanderer. (Genesis 4:8–12)
- God showed mercy to Cain by promising vengeance on anyone who took his life and by giving him a mark of protection. (Genesis 4:13–15)
- Cain moved east and started a family. Most of his descendants apparently did not worship God. (Genesis 4:16–24)
- Adam and Eve had another son, Seth, who began a family characterized by faith. (Genesis 4:25–26)
- Adam's genealogy includes men noted for their long lives and Enoch, who never died because he walked with God. (Genesis 5)

Study Questions

1. What can we learn from Cain and Abel about the importance of our heart attitude in worshiping God?
2. How did God show mercy to Cain?
3. How were Cain and his younger brother Seth different?
4. How do the lives of Adam and Eve and, later, Enoch teach us about walking with God?

Genesis 6–7 Noah and the Flood

Chapter Highlights:
- Evil Everywhere
- Noah, a Man Who Stood Alone
- The Ark
- The Flood

Let's Get Started

What happens when a group of people are left on their own, without laws to govern their actions and leadership to guide them in making right choices? Do they work to improve moral and ethical standards? Do they organize community policing to rid their area of problems? Do they seek ways to express their worship of their Creator? Do they spur each other on to become more like God?

In this chapter we discover what happened in Noah's generation, the tenth generation from Adam. In those days people lived hundreds of years and were capable of producing many children. The population on planet Earth was multiplying, and so was the capacity for great wickedness. God saw that of all the people on earth, only one man, Noah, was righteous and blameless. It was time to cleanse the earth of the evil that was an offense to God, who is holy.

God told Noah to build an Ark, which would save him and his family during a great Flood. Noah believed God and followed his instructions. The lives of Noah and his family were saved because of God's protection.

Evil Everywhere All the Time

GENESIS 6:1–4 ***Now it came to pass, when men began to multiply on the face of the earth, and daughters were born to them, that the sons of God saw the daughters of men, that they were beautiful; and they took wives for themselves of all whom they chose. And the LORD said, "My Spirit shall not strive with man forever, for he is indeed flesh; yet his days shall be one hundred and twenty years." There were giants on the earth in those days, and also afterward, when the sons of God came in to the daughters of men and they bore children to them. Those were the mighty men who were of old, men of renown.*** *(NKJV)*

go to

angels
Matthew 22:30

fallen angels
evil angels who followed Satan in his rebellion against God

Hey Babe, You Come Here Often?

The purity of God's Creation had been turned into a moral cesspool. As the population grew, a trend began. The sons of God were marrying as many women as they desired. This led to moral decay that God abhorred. But who were the sons of God? Bible experts offer the view that they were men from the line of godly Seth who married the daughters of ungodly Cain. Or they could have been aggressive men who were influenced for evil by **fallen angels**.

We may wonder who the sons of God were, but one fact is certain: They contributed greatly to the corruption that ran rampant throughout the earth.

God then said that the days of man would be 120 years. He allowed that span of time for people to turn from their wickedness before he would send judgment.

Some believe that Nephilim were produced by sexual union between women and fallen angels living on earth. However, Jesus said that angels do not marry.

How Corrupt Can People Be?

> GENESIS 6:5 ***Then the LORD saw that the wickedness of man was great in the earth, and that every intent of the thoughts of his heart was only evil continually.*** *(NKJV)*

God had created people in such a way that their greatest pleasure and fulfillment would come from a personal relationship with him. But the world had become filled with people who had no place for him. Following the example of Cain and Lamech (Genesis 4:19–24), they pursued evil so that it filled the earth. Every inclination of their hearts and minds was bent on rebellion. They were alienated from their Creator and were destroying themselves by living in ways that opposed all the good God had planned for them. No matter what the social pressures are, each person chooses how to respond. Every individual is responsible to God.

what others say

Victor P. Hamilton

What God saw was both the extensiveness of sin and the intensiveness of sin. Geographically, the problem is an infested earth.... The situation is further aggravated because such depravity controls not only man's actions but also his thoughts: every scheme in man's imagination was nothing but evil.[1]

From Very Good to No Good

GENESIS 6:6–7 *And the LORD was sorry that He had made man on the earth, and He was grieved in His heart. So the LORD said, "I will destroy man whom I have created from the face of the earth, both man and beast, creeping thing and birds of the air, for I am sorry that I have made them."* (NKJV)

go to

patient
2 Peter 3:9

At Creation, "God saw everything that He had made, and indeed it was very good" (Genesis 1:31 NKJV). Now what he saw brought grief and filled his heart with pain. He was grieved over the terrible choices people had made and over the judgment he must give. God could not overlook the sin of the people who had been made in his image.

God never acts arbitrarily, nor does he punish people without reason. He is patient with even those who defy him. He does not want anyone to be judged, but desires everyone to repent of sin and turn to him.

Noah, a Man Who Stood Alone

GENESIS 6:8–10 *But Noah found grace in the eyes of the LORD. This is the genealogy of Noah. Noah was a just man, perfect in his generations. Noah walked with God. And Noah begot three sons: Shem, Ham, and Japheth.* (NKJV)

One man stood apart from the rest of the human race. He had responded to God's grace and God saw him as righteous and blameless. Of all people on earth, Noah had chosen to withstand the tremendous pressure to fit in with wickedness in society around him. Only Noah and his family walked in fellowship with God.

something to ponder

Noah found favor with God, not because he did anything to earn it, but because God offered his love and grace and Noah responded. He proved his heart response by walking with God—listening to his voice and following his instructions.

Sneak Preview

GENESIS 6:11–13 *The earth also was corrupt before God, and the earth was filled with violence. So God looked upon the earth, and indeed it was corrupt; for all flesh had corrupted their way on the earth. And God said to Noah, "The end of all flesh has come before Me, for the earth is filled with violence through them; and behold, I will destroy them with the earth.* (NKJV)

There was no turning back. God had shown humankind his ways, but they had chosen to follow their own ways. God spoke to the one man who had not joined them in their determined pursuit of corruption. He told Noah that a terrible event was coming. God would surely destroy the evil people and the earth—not immediately, though. He would give them time to turn from their evil ways—120 years, as it turned out.

what others say

R. C. Sproul

History is not like some fill-in-the-blank story, in which the story changes tracks every time a human makes a decision. God, assessing his creation at the time of Noah, was not surprised. He did not frantically search for some worthy family to save. He did not go back to his drawing board and strain his brain until the idea of a flood came upon him. He not only knew of the condition of man at the time, he not only planned that it would be such, he also made sure it was such.[2]

The Ark—An Astonishing Assignment

GENESIS 6:14–16 *"Make yourself an ark of gopherwood; make rooms in the ark, and cover it inside and outside with pitch. And this is how you shall make it: The length of the ark shall be three hundred cubits, its width fifty cubits, and its height thirty cubits. You shall make a window for the ark, and you shall finish it to a cubit from above; and set the door of the ark in its side. You shall make it with lower, second, and third decks.* (NKJV)

Noah was to build an Ark, or vessel that floats, from planks of cypress—a light, durable hardwood (see Illustration #2). He was to make rooms in it and cover the inner and outer surfaces with pitch, a thick, sticky substance like asphalt used to seal and waterproof. God also gave directions for the roof and for an 18-inch window that would provide ventilation. He also said there should be a door on the side of the Ark, and the Ark should have three levels of decks.

Unimaginable Punishment

GENESIS 6:17 *And behold, I Myself am bringing floodwaters on the earth, to destroy from under heaven all flesh in which is the breath of life; everything that is on the earth shall die.* (NKJV)

The punishment God predicted must have struck fear in Noah's heart. God had to cleanse the earth of its corruption, and he would do it with awesome power. Nobody who had ever lived on earth had seen a flood, so Noah could hardly have taken in the cataclysmic event that was impending. How could he even imagine a world purged of every living thing?

Up until this time it had never even rained. God watered the earth by means of underground irrigation with streams coming up from the earth which provided the moisture needed.

streams
Genesis 2:6

covenant
contract, oath, promise, or binding agreement

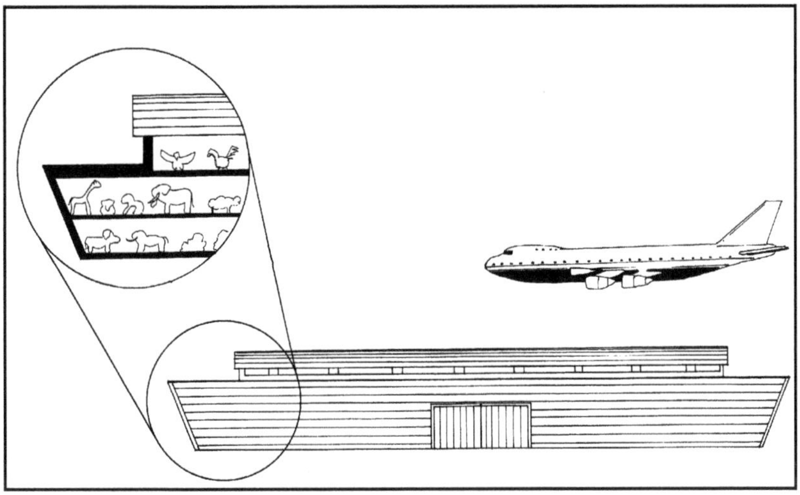

Illustration #2
The Ark—Noah's Ark was a wooden boat that was 450 feet long, 75 feet wide, and 45 feet high. It took Noah and his sons 120 years to build, but when finished, the Ark was roomy enough for Noah's family, all the animals, and food for everyone. This floating zoo would be home to Noah's family for over a year.

Unbreakable Promise

> GENESIS 6:18 ***But I will establish My covenant with you; and you shall go into the ark—you, your sons, your wife, and your sons' wives with you.*** (NKJV)

God set Noah's fears to rest when he said he would establish his **covenant** with Noah and his family. He would protect him from the punishment that would come on earth.

what others say

Victor P. Hamilton

This announcement of the covenant, even before the Flood commences, is interesting. It shows us that God's covenant with Noah in chapter 9 is no *ad hoc* arrangement, hatched in God's mind once the floodwaters had disappeared. Even before he unleashes his anger God announced his intention to save at least one human being.[3]

Unprecedented Provision

GENESIS 6:19–21 *And of every living thing of all flesh you shall bring two of every sort into the ark, to keep them alive with you; they shall be male and female. Of the birds after their kind, of animals after their kind, and of every creeping thing of the earth after its kind, two of every kind will come to you to keep them alive. And you shall take for yourself of all food that is eaten, and you shall gather it to yourself; and it shall be food for you and for them."* (NKJV)

The reason for the large size of the Ark became clear to Noah as God told him what it would contain. In addition to carrying Noah and his family, it would carry two of all living creatures and food for all.

what others say

James Montgomery Boice

What about the "millions and millions" of species? There is some difficulty in determining what is meant by the biblical word *kind*, as in "of the birds after their kind, of animals after their kind, and of every creeping thing of the earth after its kind, two of every kind will come to you to keep them alive" (Genesis 6:20 NKJV). If this corresponds to our modern classification of "family," the maximum number of families represented on the Ark would be about 700. But suppose the word actually corresponds to our word *species*? In that case, the number would be much higher—but not beyond the Ark's capacity.[4]

The size of the Ark was far greater than normal ancient sailing vessels. In fact, it was not until 1858 that a vessel of greater length was constructed: the Great Eastern (692 by 83 by 30 feet).[5]

What Do You Want on Your Tombstone?

GENESIS 6:22 *Thus Noah did; according to all that God commanded him, so he did.* (NKJV)

key point

God showed his grace to Noah when he spared him from the coming judgment. Noah's response is stated so simply that it could be placed on his grave marker. He did everything exactly as God directed him. It would have been easy to doubt God, but he trusted God enough to do everything "according to all that God commanded him." Noah did not ask questions or argue. He simply obeyed God.

What Holy Fear Built

We turn to the New Testament to get a sense of what transpired as Noah built the Ark.

Noah was known as a preacher of righteousness, but no one seems to have heeded his message. He disregarded the evil attitudes around him.

Instead, we read, "By faith Noah, being devinely warned of things not yet seen, moved with godly fear, prepared an ark for the saving of his household, by which he condemned the world and became heir of the righteousness which is according to faith" (Hebrews 11:7 NKJV).

Noah expressed his faith in hard manual labor for 120 years. He and his sons made uncounted planks of cypress beams for the Ark, lifting, sawing, hammering. Then there was the preparation of food: planting, harvesting, storing food for several people and a large animal population. In the last analysis, we will be measured by our love for God and our obedience to his Word, not by our accomplishments.

go to

preacher
2 Peter 2:5

words
Matthew 11:6

what others say

V. Gilbert Beers

If you were asked to work for 120 years to make a great boat in a desert, what would your reaction be? How would you react if all your friends and neighbors ridiculed the work? The test of obedience is not always related to how clearly we understand God's instructions, but often to how comfortable we feel in carrying out those instructions. True obedience is doing anything God wants.[6]

Amy Carmichael

Faith is not "trusting God when we understand his ways"—there is no need for faith then. Faith is trusting when nothing is explained. Faith rests under the Unexplained. Faith enters into the deep places of our Lord's words, "And blessed is he, whosoever shall not be offended in Me." Faith, having entered into those deep places, stays there in peace.[7]

And You Thought Your Neighbors Were Bad

Noah and his sons were building the Ark, and as opportunities came, Noah spoke to people about righteousness. We can be sure they heaped on ridicule and mockery as Noah warned them of the

go to

carrying on life
Matthew 24:37–39;
Luke 17:26–27

judgment seat
2 Corinthians 5:10

vertebrate
creature having a segmented backbone

coming judgment. So far as change of heart, they responded with complete indifference.

Jesus told the people of his day that while Noah was acting in obedience to God, his neighbors were carrying on life as it had been and assuming it would continue to go on generation after generation. They ate, drank, married, and gave their children in marriage without a thought that they would ever have to be accountable to God. As far as the people were concerned, God had no part in their lives. Wrongdoers may seem to prosper, but their success is only temporary. The future is safe for those who are upright.

Only with the eye of faith can we see beyond this life to the reality that some day we will each have to account for ourselves to God and receive the reward for faithful service to him.

The apostle Paul tells us that some day we must each appear before the judgment seat of Christ. The judgment seat, as Paul knew it, was a raised platform from which winners of athletic events were announced, where officials pronounced both sentences and commendations of subjects.

What Did the Ark Look Like?

Regardless of the architectural accomplishments of the descendants of Cain, the Ark must have been an amazing structure, completely unthought of in its time. Following the directions God had given, Noah began to build a huge boat far from a body of water.

The Ark was a flat-bottomed boat 450 feet long, 75 feet wide, and 45 feet high (140 by 23 by 13.5 meters). It had three decks and plenty of rooms of various sizes to accommodate animals, with additional space to store food. A window ran around the Ark just under the roof, designed to provide light and ventilation. The Ark was never intended to navigate, but only to float.

what others say

Dr. Larry Richards

Assuming that the animals hibernated, the Ark could easily have accommodated as many as 35,000 different **vertebrate** "kinds" along with Noah and his family.[8]

The Favor of Your Presence Is Requested

GENESIS 7:1 ***Then the LORD said to Noah, "Come into the ark, you and all your household, because I have seen that you are righteous before Me in this generation.*** (NKJV)

After 120 years of hard work, Noah and his sons had completed building the Ark. God issued the invitation for Noah and his whole family to go on board. The reason that Noah was singled out of all the earth's population is that God had found him righteous. God's favor had been extended to him, he had responded with faith, and Noah proved his faith by 120 years of continual loving obedience to God.

go to

food
Leviticus 11:2–23

clean animal
an animal designated by God as acceptable for eating

what others say

Elisabeth Elliot

Love and obedience are the secrets of true joy. "Joy," wrote C. S. Lewis, "is the serious business of heaven." I love that, and I am sure it must be true, for heaven is peopled with those who want no other business but to love God and to manifest that love, perfectly and continuously, by a glad obedience. Jesus said, "If you obey my commands, you will remain in my love, just as I have obeyed my Father's commands and remain in his love. I have told you this so that my joy may be in you and that your joy may be complete" (John 15:10–11).[9]

Last Minute Instructions

GENESIS 7:2–5 ***You shall take with you seven each of every clean animal, a male and his female; two each of animals that are unclean, a male and his female; also seven each of birds of the air, male and female, to keep the species alive on the face of all the earth. For after seven more days I will cause it to rain on the earth forty days and forty nights, and I will destroy from the face of the earth all living things that I have made." And Noah did according to all that the LORD commanded him.*** (NKJV)

God planned for the Ark to carry breeding pairs of animal kinds to preserve life. He was also to bring seven pairs of each kind of **clean animal**. These were for sacrificing to God and possibly for food after the Flood. Again we read that Noah meticulously followed the Lord's directions. He obeyed God because he believed God.

go to

animals
Genesis 6:20; 7:8, 15

what others say

Victor P. Hamilton

Presumably the writer could have supplied myriads of details about Noah's erection of the Ark and the assembling of the animals, but he did not. Noah's rather long and complicated exploits are condensed into these words: *he did it!* Not a note about his expertise in construction and zoology. By condensing Noah's considerable achievements into an unbelievably skeletal statement, the author concentrates on one fact only, Noah's obedience to and successful completion of the divine mandate.[10]

The Flood

GENESIS 7:6–16 ***Noah was six hundred years old when the floodwaters were on the earth.***

So Noah, with his sons, his wife, and his sons' wives, went into the ark because of the waters of the flood. Of clean animals, of animals that are unclean, of birds, and of everything that creeps on the earth, two by two they went into the ark to Noah, male and female, as God had commanded Noah. And it came to pass after seven days that the waters of the flood were on the earth. In the six hundredth year of Noah's life, in the second month, the seventeenth day of the month, on that day all the fountains of the great deep were broken up, and the windows of heaven were opened. And the rain was on the earth forty days and forty nights.

On the very same day Noah and Noah's sons, Shem, Ham, and Japheth, and Noah's wife and the three wives of his sons with them, entered the ark—they and every beast after its kind, all cattle after their kind, every creeping thing that creeps on the earth after its kind, and every bird after its kind, every bird of every sort. And they went into the ark to Noah, two by two, of all flesh in which is the breath of life. So those that entered, male and female of all flesh, went in as God had commanded him; and the Lord shut him in. *(NKJV)*

Noah did exactly as God had commanded him. God had directed him to take animals into the Ark, but did not specify how Noah was to go about the task. The Scripture reads simply that the animals "went into the ark to Noah" (Genesis 7:9 NKJV). There was no massive roundup with Noah and his sons compelling reluctant animals to go into the Ark.

The crew and passengers were on board seven days before the Lord shut the door. We can only imagine the reaction of Noah's neighbors as they observed the drama being performed in broad daylight. Inside the Ark, Noah and his family were probably getting the animals settled in their places. Outside the Ark, was God perhaps giving people one last opportunity to heed the warnings Noah had been giving for the past 120 years? What, then, was their reaction when the door was closed without any visible hand moving it?

what others say

J. Vernon McGee

For seven days the world could have knocked at the door of the Ark, and frankly, they could have come in—God would have saved them. All they had to do was to believe God.[11]

Five-Day Forecast: Rain, Rain, Rain, Rain, Rain

GENESIS 7:17–20 ***Now the flood was on the earth forty days. The waters increased and lifted up the ark, and it rose high above the earth. The waters prevailed and greatly increased on the earth, and the ark moved about on the surface of the waters. And the waters prevailed exceedingly on the earth, and all the high hills under the whole heaven were covered. The waters prevailed fifteen cubits upward, and the mountains were covered. (NKJV)***

Exactly as God had said, the rain came—forty days and forty nights of it. Subterranean fountains opened to add to the massive downpour from above. As the waters rose, the Ark gradually began to float.

Before he sent the Flood, God gave people 120 years of warning. During this time the people carried on the business of daily living without a thought of impending judgment. The parallels to society today are obvious.

what others say

Daymond R. Duck

Today, God is unimportant in the lives of multitudes, but the Bible teaches that the day is coming when every individual will spend some time in God's court. Some may never bow their knee on earth, but every knee will bow in heaven.[12]

promises
Joshua 23:14–16

As will be covered in the next chapter, we do not have to worry about God flooding the earth again. This does not mean, however, that there will be no earthly or eternal consequences for those who disobey God. God is just and holy, and therefore he will not allow disobedience to go unnoticed. That's why we all are in desperate need of Jesus: because we all disobey God and because only when we place our faith in Jesus will God see us as holy.

Only Noah Was Left

GENESIS 7:21–24 ***And all flesh died that moved on the earth: birds and cattle and beasts and every creeping thing that creeps on the earth, and every man. All in whose nostrils was the breath of the spirit of life, all that was on the dry land, died. So He destroyed all living things which were on the face of the ground: both man and cattle, creeping thing and bird of the air. They were destroyed from the earth. Only Noah and those who were with him in the ark remained alive. And the waters prevailed on the earth one hundred and fifty days.*** *(NKJV)*

What God had promised, he fulfilled. Outside the Ark every living thing on earth was destroyed, except for marine life. Sin had covered the earth. Now it was cleansed.

God always keeps his word. His promises never fail—whether the promise is of salvation or of judgment. A person may make a promise and be sincere when he makes it, but for reasons beyond his control, he may not be able to keep his word. God is not a frail human. He is totally able to fulfill every promise he makes.

A flood, an unheard-of cataclysmic event in ancient times, has been included in the oral traditions of literally hundreds of civilizations from Babylon to Papua New Guinea to Native Americans, to tribes in Peru, Mexico, Greenland, Wales, India, China, and many, many others. In more than half of the traditions, the disastrous event was caused by the evil acts of people.

It is apparent that the accounts come from one source. Though the details of the Flood accounts have been adapted to the local culture, what is consistent is some historical accuracy and the moral implications.

Since an account of the Flood is so widespread, one would think people of all cultures would order their lives in the light of the potential for God's judgment. But as we look around the world, we know this is not so. People live now much as they did in the days before the Flood: eating and drinking, marrying and giving in marriage—without a thought of coming judgment.

something to ponder

Fertile Crescent
a crescent-shaped region of the Near East stretching from the Persian Gulf to the Mediterranean Sea (see Illustration #5)

what others say

John H. Sailhamer

No other biblical passage has so many extrabiblical parallels as does the Genesis account of the Flood. More than 300 "flood texts" from around the world have been collected and published. Those texts record ancient and primitive accounts of a worldwide flood and the survival of a single man and his family. There are many other similarities, both among these documents and with the biblical story of the Flood.[13]

Was the Flood worldwide? Or was it confined to the **Fertile Crescent**, where the descendants of Adam probably lived? Here is how two theories compare:

- ***"Limited" Flood:*** Some people think there was a "limited" flood because they believe it fits the views of modern science, pointing out that rock strata and fossil records do not seem to support a worldwide flood. They say that if the purpose of the Flood was to destroy evil people, they were all living in the area known as the Fertile Crescent.
- ***Worldwide Flood:*** Other people point to the Scripture statements that "all the high hills under the whole heaven were covered" (Genesis 7:19 NKJV) and that "He destroyed all living things which were on the face of the ground" (Genesis 7:23 NKJV).

key point

While the debate continues, it is easy to overlook the one great lesson to be learned from the Flood: that God accomplished his will in the Flood, that he will indeed judge all people some day. In the Flood, God revealed his hatred for sin.

what others say

Dr. Larry Richards

Those who argue for a worldwide Flood believe that the cataclysm reshaped the surface of our planet. The mountains that were covered to a depth of 20 feet (Genesis 7:20) were not earth's present mountains. These were thrust up by the weight of the Flood waters as earth's present sea beds were depressed. Support for this view comes mainly from the language of Genesis itself, although some attempt to prove a universal flood from geologic and other scientific data.[14]

God did not delight in sending the Flood which destroyed life. He, who never changes, says,

Indeed My hand has laid the foundation of the earth,
And My right hand has stretched out the heavens;
When I call to them,
They stand up together…
Thus says the LORD, your Redeemer,
The Holy One of Israel:
"I am the LORD your God,
Who teaches you to profit,
Who leads you by the way you should go.
Oh, that you had heeded My commandments!
Then your peace would have been like a river,
And your righteousness like the waves of the sea.
Your descendants also would have been like the sand,
And the offspring of your body like the grains of sand;
His name would not have been cut off
Nor destroyed from before Me"…
"There is no peace," says the LORD, "for the wicked."
(Isaiah 48:13, 17–19, 22 NKJV)

Though these words were directed to descendants of Abraham, Isaac, and Jacob, God extends his love and grace to every individual who responds to his call to repentance.

Chapter Wrap-Up

- As earth's population grew, people grew farther away from God until the whole earth was filled with man's sinfulness. (Genesis 6:1–4)
- Grieved by people's wickedness, God decided to destroy all life on earth except for Noah and his family and some animals. (Genesis 6:5–8)
- God chose Noah, a righteous man, to build an Ark to save those God chose. He gave Noah detailed instructions for building an Ark that would float on the waters God was going to send to flood the earth. (Genesis 6:9–17)
- God promised to save Noah and his family. He instructed Noah to fill the Ark with a male and female of every kind of animal as well as seven pairs of clean animals, and food for the animals and Noah's family. (Genesis 6:18–7:3)
- Noah obeyed God completely, building the Ark as well as preaching righteousness to his neighbors who ignored him. (Genesis 6:22; 2 Peter 2:5; Hebrews 11:7)
- It took 120 years for Noah to complete the Ark. When it was filled with food, animals, and Noah and his family, God himself closed the door, giving no opportunity for anyone else to seek refuge in it. Then God sent the rain. (Genesis 7:1–16)
- For forty days and nights the rains fell. Subterranean fountains added to it until the whole earth was flooded, covering the highest mountains. Every air-breathing creature on earth was wiped out except for those safe on the Ark. (Genesis 7:17–24)

Study Questions

1. How were people in Noah's time different from people today? How were they similar?
2. Of all the people on earth, why did God choose to save only Noah and his family?
3. Why do you think God gave Noah such specific details for building the Ark?
4. What can we learn from Noah about faithful obedience to God?
5. What does the story of Noah's Ark teach us about God's promises?

Genesis 8–9 A Fresh Beginning

Chapter Highlights:
- God Remembers
- A Jubilant Landing
- A Covenant Established
- Noah's Sons

Let's Get Started

God had protected Noah and his family from a judgment so cataclysmic that all life on earth outside the Ark had been destroyed. For forty days, torrential rains beat on the roof and the Ark floated on the rising floodwaters. Day after day Noah waited. God had shut him in the Ark for his safety—but for how long? And when he could finally leave the Ark, what would he find?

We now come to, as Paul Harvey says, "the rest of the story." God remembered his own and worked to lead them into a fresh beginning. Gradually the floodwaters subsided, and after one year and seventeen days in the Ark, Noah led his family and the animals out of the Ark onto dry land.

It truly was a new beginning, starting with Noah's worship and with God communicating with Noah and giving a covenant that is still in effect today.

Blow, Wind, Blow

> GENESIS 8:1–2 ***Then God remembered Noah, and every living thing, and all the animals that were with him in the ark. And God made a wind to pass over the earth, and the waters subsided. The fountains of the deep and the windows of heaven were also stopped, and the rain from heaven was restrained.*** *(NKJV)*

Noah had built the Ark because he trusted God enough to obey him completely. He continued to trust God while he stayed in the Ark.

Outside the Ark, the Flood had accomplished God's judgment. After forty days the rain stopped falling and the subterranean fountains were closed. God remembered Noah. He sent a wind to begin the process of making the water evaporate.

go to

forgot
Psalm 9:15–17

never forsakes
Psalm 9:9–10

something to ponder

what others say

Samuel J. Schultz

Whether the Flood was local or worldwide is of secondary importance to the fact that the deluge extended far enough to include all mankind.[1]

The people perished in the Flood because they forgot God. Noah was saved in the Ark because God remembered him. God never forsakes those who put their trust in him.

The Ark Decorates a Mountain

GENESIS 8:3–5 ***And the waters receded continually from the earth. At the end of the hundred and fifty days the waters decreased. Then the ark rested in the seventh month, the seventeenth day of the month, on the mountains of Ararat. And the waters decreased continually until the tenth month. In the tenth month, on the first day of the month, the tops of the mountains were seen. (NKJV)***

After 150 days, the water had receded enough so that the Ark could rest on solid ground in the area of "the mountains of Ararat" (Genesis 8:4 NKJV). The exact location has never been positively identified. The mountains in that area vary from 9,000 to nearly 17,000 feet. As Noah continued to wait, the waters receded until "the tops of the mountains were seen" (verse 5 NKJV).

While some people consider the Bible account of the Flood to be a myth, others attempt to verify its authenticity by searching for evidence that the Ark still exists.

For example, in 1943 Ed Davis, a sergeant in the U.S. Army, developed friendships with Lourd tribesmen who took him to their village near Mount Ararat. From the village he could see in the distance something which they claimed to be the Ark. Davis reported to have seen in the village items from the Ark: a cage door, a shepherd staff, a metal hammer, dried beans, etc.

In 1953 George Greene, an oil geologist, took several photographs from a helicopter of what appeared to be the Ark. Though he has died and his photos are not available, more than thirty people have given sworn, written testimony that they saw his photos that showed the Ark protruding from ice on Mount Ararat.

In the late 1950s Gregor Schwinghammer claimed he saw the Ark from an F-100 aircraft. He said it resembled a huge boxcar lying high on Mount Ararat.

A Raven and a Dove

GENESIS 8:6–9 *So it came to pass, at the end of forty days, that Noah opened the window of the ark which he had made. Then he sent out a raven, which kept going to and fro until the waters had dried up from the earth. He also sent out from himself a dove, to see if the waters had receded from the face of the ground. But the dove found no resting place for the sole of her foot, and she returned into the ark to him, for the waters were on the face of the whole earth. So he put out his hand and took her, and drew her into the ark to himself.* (NKJV)

God had told Noah when to enter the Ark (Genesis 7:1), but did not speak to Noah once he was inside the Ark. Instead God used birds to show Noah when it would be safe to disembark. First, Noah sent out a raven, a bird that flew away and did not return. It evidently found food outside the Ark. Then Noah sent out a dove, which returned when it could not find a resting place. The water had not receded enough to expose surfaces to serve the dove's need.

what others say

J. Vernon McGee

Noah is engaged here in "birdwatching." He sends out the raven, and the raven does not come back. Why didn't that raven come back? You must recognize what that raven eats—it feeds on carrion. There was a whole lot of flesh of dead animals floating around after the Flood, and that was the kind of thing this old crow ate. He did not return to the Ark because he was really going to a feast, and he was having a very wonderful time.[2]

Waiting, Waiting, Waiting

GENESIS 8:10–12 *And he waited yet another seven days, and again he sent the dove out from the ark. Then the dove came to him in the evening, and behold, a freshly plucked olive leaf was in her mouth; and Noah knew that the waters had receded from the earth. So he waited yet another seven days and sent out the dove, which did not return again to him anymore.* (NKJV)

Noah waited another week and again sent the dove out the window. That evening the dove returned with an olive leaf in its beak. This was the first sign of life from outside the Ark. It was an indication that vegetation, which had been destroyed by the Flood, had begun to grow again.

A week later, Noah sent the dove out again. This time, however, the bird did not return, a sure sign that it had found a suitable place to rest.

> **what others say**
>
> **Matthew Henry**
>
> The olive-branch, which was an emblem of peace, was brought, not by the raven, a bird of prey, not by a gay and proud peacock, but by a mild, patient, humble dove. It is a dove-like disposition that brings into the world earnests of rest and joy.[3]

365 Notches in the Bulkhead

GENESIS 8:13–14 ***And it came to pass in the six hundred and first year, in the first month, the first day of the month, that the waters were dried up from the earth; and Noah removed the covering of the ark and looked, and indeed the surface of the ground was dry. And in the second month, on the twenty-seventh day of the month, the earth was dried.*** *(NKJV)*

go to

waiting
Psalms 27:13–14; 130:5–6

Waiting for God's timing is one of the most difficult things people have to do. Noah and his family had been in the Ark for about a year. They must have yearned for freedom to leave its confines, but Noah waited for God to show him when he should leave.

> **what others say**
>
> **Dr. Larry Richards**
>
> If we assume the Hebrew calendar, which took April (Abib) as the first month, but do not consider its thirty-day months, we can gain a picture of the sequence of events and the time Genesis says the Flood consumed.[4]

Itinerary for the Cataclysmic Cruise

Event	Scripture Reference	Probable Date
Ark built	Genesis 6:14	
Animals enter	Genesis 7:8–10	10 May
Flood begins	Genesis 7:11	17 May
Waters increase	Genesis 7:17	26 June
Waters prevail on inundated earth	Genesis 7:24	
Ark touches ground in mountains	Genesis 8:4	13 October
Waters recede, mountaintops seen	Genesis 8:5	1 January
Windows opened, raven sent	Genesis 8:6–7	10 February
Dove sent	Genesis 8:8	17 February
Dove sent again	Genesis 8:10	24 February
Ark door opened, Noah sees land	Genesis 8:13	1 April
Land completely dry, exit the Ark	Genesis 8:14–19	27 May

Please Do Not De-Ark Until God Gives the All-Clear Signal

> GENESIS 8:15–19 ***Then God spoke to Noah, saying, "Go out of the ark, you and your wife, and your sons and your sons' wives with you. Bring out with you every living thing of all flesh that is with you: birds and cattle and every creeping thing that creeps on the earth, so that they may abound on the earth, and be fruitful and multiply on the earth." So Noah went out, and his sons and his wife and his sons' wives with him. Every animal, every creeping thing, every bird, and whatever creeps on the earth, according to their families, went out of the ark.*** *(NKJV)*

One year and seventeen days before, God had told Noah to come into the Ark (Genesis 7:1). Now he spoke again, telling Noah to come out of the Ark. What welcome words they must have been. God also spoke of the new life that would come on earth. All the animals and birds that had been kept safe in the Ark were to come out and find places suitable for breeding so that their population would multiply rapidly.

In this new beginning of life on earth, Noah directed his heart to God.

Genesis: An Offering of Thanks

GENESIS 8:20 ***Then Noah built an altar to the LORD, and took of every clean animal and of every clean bird, and offered burnt offerings on the altar.*** *(NKJV)*

Noah and his family stepped into a world empty of other human life. It was a world stripped of all evidence of prior human accomplishments. There were no buildings, no pieces of machinery, no cultivated fields.

His first act was to build an altar and to sacrifice some of the clean animals and birds as his expression of thanks and praise to God. In this new beginning of life on earth, Noah directed his heart to God.

what others say

James Montgomery Boice

> [Noah] remembered God. He showed it by coming out of the Ark, building an altar, and then sacrificing some of all the clean animals and clean birds as sin offerings—thus coming to God once again as a sinner and in the way appointed.
>
> Why is this surprising? It is surprising because it is not our nature to remember God or God's goodness. We forget and at no time more readily than immediately after we have been delivered from some distressing situation.[5]

The Old Testament idea of cleanness is rooted in the holiness of God. Certain animals were "set apart" for worship; others were "unclean." To worship an utterly holy God properly, Noah was sure to sacrifice only those animals and birds that were clean. To sacrifice unclean animals would have been an affront to God's holiness.

What God Likes to Smell

GENESIS 8:21–22 ***And the LORD smelled a soothing aroma. Then the LORD said in His heart, "I will never again curse the ground for man's sake, although the imagination of man's heart is evil from his youth; nor will I again destroy every living thing as I have done.***

"While the earth remains,
Seedtime and harvest,
Cold and heat,
Winter and summer,

And day and night
Shall not cease." (NKJV)

God was pleased with Noah's offering. It gave evidence of Noah's faith in God throughout the Flood and his continuing need for God's favor on his life. It also proved that he was thankful and filled with praise that God had kept him alive through the Flood. God loved Noah's heart attitude and promised never again to curse the ground because of human failure. God knew that the human "heart is evil from . . . youth." Still, he promised never again to destroy the earth with a flood. He also instituted the four seasons, a sign of his faithfulness.

go to

pleased
Hebrews 13:15–16

what others say

Dallas Willard

For anyone who has a genuine knowledge of God, praise is the only appropriate attitude in which to live. It is the only sane attitude.

Only a vivid assurance of God's greatness and goodness can lay a foundation for the life of prayer, and such an assurance will certainly express itself in praise. The great "faith chapter" in the New Testament, Hebrews 11, tells us in simple words, "Those who come to God must believe that he is and that he becomes a rewarder of those who seek him out" (verse 6). Praise is the inevitable result in the heart of the person who thus understands God and is actually living interactively with him.[6]

A Covenant Established

GENESIS 9:1–7 *So God blessed Noah and his sons, and said to them: "Be fruitful and multiply, and fill the earth. And the fear of you and the dread of you shall be on every beast of the earth, on every bird of the air, on all that move on the earth, and on all the fish of the sea. They are given into your hand. Every moving thing that lives shall be food for you. I have given you all things, even as the green herbs. But you shall not eat flesh with its life, that is, its blood. Surely for your lifeblood I will demand a reckoning; from the hand of every beast I will require it, and from the hand of man. From the hand of every man's brother I will require the life of man.*

"Whoever sheds man's blood,
By man his blood shall be shed;
For in the image of God

go to

children
Psalm 127:3–5

blood
Leviticus 17:10–14

He made man.
And as for you, be fruitful and multiply;
Bring forth abundantly in the earth
And multiply in it." (NKJV)

Noah's offering had pleased the Lord. Now God spoke to Noah, making a covenant with him.

God blessed Noah and his sons and gave them specific directions:

- They were to enjoy having large families so that people would fill the earth (Genesis 9:1). God put his blessing on husbands and wives having children.
- In addition to eating green plants, people could now eat meat (Genesis 9:2–4). Now animals would be afraid of humans. By hunting them, humans would keep animals from reproducing too quickly.
- God did give one specific prohibition: they were not to "eat flesh with its life, that is, its blood" (Genesis 9:4 NKJV). God established the principle that the life of a creature is in its blood. Humans needed to be aware of this and respect all God's creatures.
- God required respect for human life. People are made in God's image and have value to God. To protect humans from the violence that corrupted the world before the Flood, God established the mandate for human government to punish the person who takes the life of another human. Ultimately, though, man is held accountable to God for the shedding of human blood.

what others say

Warren Wiersbe

To attack a human being is to attack God, and the Lord will bring judgment on the offender. All life is the gift of God, and to take away life means to take the place of God. The Lord gives life and He alone has the right to authorize taking it away (Job 1:21).[7]

A Covenant to Be Remembered

GENESIS 9:8–11 *Then God spoke to Noah and to his sons with him, saying: "And as for Me, behold, I establish My covenant with you and with your descendants after you, and with every living creature that is with you: the birds, the cattle, and every*

beast of the earth with you, of all that go out of the ark, every beast of the earth. Thus I establish My covenant with you: Never again shall all flesh be cut off by the waters of the flood; never again shall there be a flood to destroy the earth." *(NKJV)*

go to

rainbow
Ezekiel 1:25–28; Revelation 4:2–3; 10:1

God gave what has been called the Noahic Covenant. In it God shows his care for all Creation. A covenant is usually an agreement between two parties, but in this covenant, God did not have conditions for Noah or for the generations that would follow him. Instead, God gave an **unconditional promise** that he would never send another flood to purge the earth of all life. This covenant relieved Noah and his family from concern whenever it rained.

key point

A Rainbow Reminder

GENESIS 9:12–17 ***And God said: "This is the sign of the covenant which I make between Me and you, and every living creature that is with you, for perpetual generations: I set My rainbow in the cloud, and it shall be for the sign of the covenant between Me and the earth. It shall be, when I bring a cloud over the earth, that the rainbow shall be seen in the cloud; and I will remember My covenant which is between Me and you and every living creature of all flesh; the waters shall never again become a flood to destroy all flesh. The rainbow shall be in the cloud, and I will look on it to remember the everlasting covenant between God and every living creature of all flesh that is on the earth." And God said to Noah, "This is the sign of the covenant which I have established between Me and all flesh that is on the earth."*** *(NKJV)*

unconditional promise
an absolute promise, not limited by conditions

For most of God's promises, he asks the person to accept his word by faith. But in this covenant, he gave a visual sign that would confirm his promise repeatedly in every part of the world. That visual sign is a <u>rainbow</u>. People see it, and God sees it, and he and all people can remember his commitment that he will never send a flood that will destroy all life on earth. That is his word, and God never breaks a promise.

what others say

Kay Arthur

The rainbow is a sign for God, a reminder of His promise, but think of the comfort it must have brought to those eight who had lived through the Flood and to others who, generations later, were told about the worldwide deluge. There would be no need to panic the next time drops of water fell from the heavens—or even when incessant torrents of rain plummeted to the earth—for after the rain God's reminder to himself would be visible to all.[8]

David Atkinson

The Hebrew term used to describe the rainbow in Genesis 9 is the term normally used for the bow of a warrior. How pointed, then, is this particular sign from God at this particular time. "I set my bow in the cloud" (Genesis 9:13) is the sign of the covenant which God makes with Noah and with all living creatures. The hostility is over: God hangs up his bow![9]

Every time we see a rainbow we should stop and worship the God who always keeps his promises. He will never let us down. He loves us and cannot be less than perfect in all he does.

Besides the Noahic Covenant, there are four major covenants in the Bible:

1. ***Abrahamic: Made with Abraham***
   God promised to bless Abraham and his family, and through them to bless all people.
2. ***Mosaic: Made with the Israelites as their Constitution***
   God showed the nation of Israel how to live as his subjects.
3. ***Davidic: Made with David***
   God promised to provide from David's descendants the Messiah to be Ruler and Savior
4. ***New covenant: Made with Israel and Judah***
   The Israelites had failed under the "old" covenant. God promised a new covenant (Jeremiah 31:31–34; Ezekiel 36). This was fulfilled in the death of Jesus Christ and the subsequent giving of the Holy Spirit.

Noah's Nakedness

GENESIS 9:18–23 *Now the sons of Noah who went out of the ark were Shem, Ham, and Japheth. And Ham was the father of*

Canaan. These three were the sons of Noah, and from these the whole earth was populated. And Noah began to be a farmer, and he planted a vineyard. Then he drank of the wine and was drunk, and became uncovered in his tent. And Ham, the father of Canaan, saw the nakedness of his father, and told his two brothers outside. But Shem and Japheth took a garment, laid it on both their shoulders, and went backward and covered the nakedness of their father. Their faces were turned away, and they did not see their father's nakedness. (NKJV)

In the Flood, God had cleansed the earth of corruption, but he had not changed the human heart and the responsibility he had given for each person to make choices. That is part of being made in God's image.

Noah, who had walked with God, who had stood alone in a corrupt and violent society, who had trusted God enough to follow his directions in building the Ark and filling it with animals and birds even though he must have looked ridiculous to his neighbors, who had waited patiently until God's time to leave the Ark—this man who was a hero was also human.

He planted a vineyard and produced wine. He became drunk and lay naked in his tent. One of his sons, Ham, saw his father's nakedness and reported it to his brothers. It seems that he did this with mockery and derision. His brothers responded by covering their father with utmost modesty. No matter how strong we have been, we are never beyond the reach of temptation.

what others say

The Bible Knowledge Commentary

Intoxication and sexual looseness are hallmarks of pagans, and both are traced back to this event in Noah's life. Man had not changed at all; with the opportunity to start a "new creation," Noah acted like a pagan (Genesis 6:5; 8:21).[10]

Noah's Nations

GENESIS 9:24–29 *So Noah awoke from his wine, and knew what his younger son had done to him. Then he said:*

"Cursed be Canaan;
A servant of servants
He shall be to his brethren."
And he said:
"Blessed be the LORD*,*

The God of Shem,
And may Canaan be his servant.
May God enlarge Japheth,
And may he dwell in the tents of Shem;
And may Canaan be his servant."
And Noah lived after the flood three hundred and fifty years. So all the days of Noah were nine hundred and fifty years; and he died. (NKJV)

grace
Ephesians 2:8–10

curse
announcement of a punishment from God

idolatry
practices associated with the worship of objects

When Noah awoke and discovered what had occurred, he spoke to his sons, Ham, Shem, and Japheth, giving words that were prophetic.

He began with Ham, but did not address him. Instead, he gave a **curse** on Ham's son Canaan—a prediction that showed how Canaan's characteristics would be judged in the future. We do not know why Canaan was singled out, but we do know that the descendants of Canaan were a godless people, degraded in every way. Years later, they led the Israelites into **idolatry**. Noah said that "a servant of servants he shall be to his brethren" (Genesis 9:25 NKJV). Then Noah addressed Shem, saying he would be blessed by God and that Canaan would serve him. Years later, God called Abraham, a descendant of Shem, to be the father of the Jewish people, through whom the Savior of the world was born.

For Japheth, Noah said his descendants would become a large nation. Eventually the Gentile nations would come from him. They would receive salvation through Christ, who was born of Shem's descendants.

Every person is dependent on God's grace, for even in our highest moments of faith we also have low moments when we yield to temptation. God offers us "the exceeding riches of His grace, expressed in His kindness toward us in Christ Jesus" (Ephesians 2:7 NKJV).

what others say

David Atkinson

Genesis 9 is telling us in this vivid story of how the father of the Canaanites was guilty of ungodly behavior—towards his own father. It serves as a reminder to the people of God how easy it is to be led astray from the patterns of life appropriate to covenant people.[11]

Chapter Wrap-Up

- When the rain stopped, God sent a wind over the earth and the floodwaters began to go down. It took 150 days for the waters to go down enough for the Ark to come to rest on the mountains of Ararat. (Genesis 8:1–5)
- After forty days, Noah released a raven from the Ark to check the water level. The raven did not come back, so Noah sent out a dove. Its return told Noah that the earth was still covered by water. (Genesis 8:6–9)
- Seven days later, Noah sent the dove out again and it returned with an olive leaf. Noah knew that the water no longer covered the earth. Seven days later, he released the dove again, and it did not return. (Genesis 8:10–12)
- Noah looked out of the Ark and saw that the surface of the ground was dry, but he did not try to leave the Ark until God told him to go. (Genesis 8:13–14)
- God told Noah to bring his family and the animals out of the Ark so they could multiply and replenish the earth. (Genesis 8:15–19)
- The first thing Noah did was to build an altar and offer burnt sacrifices to God. The Lord was pleased with Noah's offerings and promised to never again destroy the earth with a flood. God also instituted the four seasons at this time. (Genesis 8:20–22)
- God blessed Noah and his sons and told them to have many children. He told them they could now eat meat as well as plants, and he warned them to have respect for human life. (Genesis 9:1–7)
- God repeated his promise to never flood the earth again, and he put a rainbow in the sky as a reminder of his promise. (Genesis 9:8–17)
- Soon Noah planted a vineyard and when the grapes ripened, he made wine and became drunk. His son Ham found Noah lying naked and drunk and, apparently, mocked him to his brothers. The other two sons covered their father without looking at him. As a result, Noah cursed Ham's son Canaan, but blessed Shem and Japheth. (Genesis 9:18–29)

Study Questions

1. What does the story of Noah's Ark teach us about waiting on God's timing?

2. What was God's plan for the people and animals kept safe on the Ark?

3. Why do you think Noah's first act when he got off the Ark was to build an altar and offer burnt sacrifices on it?

4. What was God's reason for giving the rainbow?

5. What does Noah's drunkenness reveal to us about the righteousness of men?

Genesis 10–11 Birth of Nations

Chapter Highlights:
- Noah's Descendants
- The Tower of Babel
- The People Scatter
- More on Noah's Descendants

Let's Get Started

What ever became of Noah's family? Look at a world map. Note today's many political divisions. Travel across these countries. Hear the many different languages and dialects spoken. Notice the different customs. Probe their history, the stories handed down from generation to generation. It's a kaleidoscopic visual aid.

In Genesis 10–11, God tells us what happened to Noah's family and why our world is broken up the way it is today.

After the Flood, God started a new beginning with the people he had lovingly created. Noah's sons, Shem, Ham, and Japheth, were the three from whom these nations would come. Shem had a special place in God's plan, for it was through him the promised Messiah would come.

God had told Noah's sons "Be fruitful and multiply, and fill the earth" (Genesis 9:1 NKJV). They fulfilled God's command, and in the years that followed, the world was populated. God tells how nations developed from this family and how they came to be scattered over the earth.

What Ever Happened to . . . ?

the big picture

Genesis 10

God gives us what we know as the table of Nations, an amazing record of Noah's descendants. It identifies the generations of Noah's sons, Japheth, Ham, and Shem, and gives a picture of how they expanded and eventually became the nations of the world. The chapter also indicates the general regions where they and their descendants lived. One descendant of Ham, Nimrod, is singled out for special mention in Genesis 10:8–12. He emerged as a powerful figure, known for his exceptional strength and skills as well as his aggressive leadership ambitions.

one man
Acts 17:26

Noah lived 350 years after the Flood and died when he was 950 years old. We see now what happened to his family. All the people of the world since Noah have descended from the three sons of <u>one man</u>.

In the listing of individuals in Genesis 10, we trace the tribal groups that came after Noah. Seventy descendants of Noah's sons are listed. This list is not exhaustive but provides general information on how these groups later developed into peoples. God's grace, offered to Adam and Eve in the Garden, and offered again later to Noah, was extended to each of these. Some responded. Some did not.

The descendants of Japheth became the Indo-European people who settled east into parts of Asia, north into Europe, and westward to Spain.

The descendants of Ham moved to what we know today as North Africa and the Far East. The descendants of Canaan settled in the area that God later promised to give to the descendants of Shem.

The descendants of Shem, Noah's firstborn son, became Hebrews and Syrians. The line of faith in God came through Shem and his descendants. While the descendants of Japheth and Ham are traced only through six generations, those of Shem are traced through ten.

what others say

David Atkinson

All human people, even of different national and cultural identities—as chapter 10 itself accepts—are of the same origin, have the same dignity, and belong in the same world. This undercuts all human divisiveness based on nationality, culture and race. However good, however rich national and cultural diversity can be, it should never be allowed to cloud the more fundamental fact that all human people share the same nature, breathe the same air, live on the same earth, and owe their life to the same God.[1]

Portrait of a Kingdom-Builder

Moses, writer of Genesis, interrupts the Table of the Nations to give a portrait of Nimrod (Genesis 10:8–12), "a mighty hunter before the LORD" (verse 9 NKJV) and a builder of cities, whose name became a proverb to the following generations. He exerted leadership and recruited men to build cities: Babylon and three others in the fertile plain of Shinar, and Nineveh (see Appendix B) and other cities in Assyria.

go to

pride
Proverbs 16:18

What motivated Nimrod? He has been described as a hunter or tyrant who hunted and conquered men, not animals, in his ambition to build an empire that would challenge God's right to rule over his Creation (more on this as we look at Genesis 11). God was not blind to what Nimrod was doing as he attempted to build a kingdom that would rival God's. God knows the hidden ambitions of those who oppose him.

Cush, as Ham's oldest son, had apparently resented this curse more and more as the years passed by. By the time Nimrod was born, the resentment had become so strong that he gave his son a name meaning "Let us rebel!" The inference is that Cush trained Nimrod from childhood to be a leader in a planned and organized rebellion against God's purposes for mankind.

The Tower of Babel

the big picture

Genesis 11:1–4

As people moved eastward, they decided to settle on a plain in the land of Shinar. Since only one language was spoken at that time, newcomers easily adapted to new locations. These newcomers developed an ambitious scheme to build a city that would include a tower which they expected would give them access to heaven [see Appendix A]. They intended to settle down and make a name for themselves.

After the Flood, God had commanded people to spread out and fill up the earth (Genesis 9:1). Nimrod, in his obsession to build his own empire, came up with a plan. With enormous self-confidence and pride, he settled in the plain of Shinar (Babylonia) and laid out his plans to build a city with a tower that would be used in a form of worship.

His objective for himself and his followers was audacious in its two purposes: (1) to make a name for themselves and (2) to disobey God's command that they be scattered over the face of the whole

key point

wickedness
Revelation 18

Babel
"confusion"; also an early name of Babylon

Babylon
both a capital city and an ancient empire

earth (Genesis 11:3). Their tower would reach up toward the heavens and challenge the living God, the Creator of heaven and earth. They rebelled against God without any effort to conceal their motives.

what others say

David Atkinson

> This tower is a sort of architectural symbol of humankind's asserted greatness. With its top in the heavens is an idiom for impregnable security. But it is another symbol and picture of a violation of the limits God sets to human life and to human behavior, for the sake of human well-being.[2]

The Bible states that tar or bitumen was used in the construction of the tower. Since this material was almost unknown in Israel, its mention in the Bible account verifies its accuracy.

The People Scatter

the big picture

Genesis 11:5–9

> God came down and scattered the people by confusing their languages so that they could not continue living in one place. He did this to prevent them from executing even more evil schemes. The name of the place was Babel, a reminder that God confused language there and caused the people to scatter.

The Lord came down to view the building project that was defying his plan for the people. Knowing the evil in their hearts, he moved to protect them from even more evil schemes. He stopped the building project and caused the people to scatter. He did this by causing them to speak different languages. When they could not understand each other, they had no choice but to abandon the tower.

The tower was called **Babel** and the site became the capital of **Babylon** (see Appendix B), which may be the oldest city in the world. The city and the empire that grew out of it are known throughout Scripture for their wickedness and defiance of God.

what others say

Eugene H. Peterson

The greatest work project of the ancient world is a story of disaster. The unexcelled organization and enormous energy that were concentrated in building the Tower of Babel resulted in such a shattered community and garbled communication that civilization is still trying to recover.[3]

The Tower of Babel was a ziggurat, a pyramid-like construction with stair-step sides common in the ancient Middle East and in South America (see Illustration #3). The tower was not tall in terms of modern buildings, but it had a temple built on its top which was intended to be the place of contact with God. The ancient builders were inventing their own religion, trying to reach God by their own efforts.

Illustration #3
Ziggurat—Towers like this were constructed by the people of Mesopotamia over five thousand years ago, and by the people of Central America two thousand years ago.

Nimrod's desire to build the tower grew out of his pride, his ambition to build a city and a tower that would make him so powerful that he would have no need for God. We need to look at the driving force, the major objective of our lives. Are we building a name for ourselves, a "tower" that will eliminate our need to depend on God? God is faithfully working out his plans even when it seems as if most people have turned away from him.

something to ponder

redeem
to free from the consequences of sin

what others say

Dr. Larry Richards

In Scripture "Babylon" refers to both the city and empire. In apocalyptic literature "Babylon the Great" represents human political, economic, and religious systems devoted to crass materialism and ungodly living in defiance of the holiness and sovereignty of God.

Ruins of the ancient city lie along the river Euphrates, about 50 miles south of Baghdad in modern Iraq. At its height, the city covered between 3.5 and 6 square miles (9 and 15.5 square kilometers). According to Herodotus, who wrote in the fifth century B.C., it was surrounded by 609 miles of walls up to 300 feet high and 87 feet wide. Archaeological expeditions between 1899 and 1917, and after 1958, have revealed much about this enormously wealthy city and its kings.[4]

A Close Look at Family History

the big picture

Genesis 11:10-32

The rest of the chapter picks up the genealogy from Noah's son Shem to Abram, who becomes a key person in God's plan to redeem people.

In Genesis 10 we saw how the families that came from Noah's three sons were scattered around the earth. Now we see the genealogy of Shem, which shows the line from Noah's son Shem, who received God's blessing, to Abram, who would receive a special blessing from God and would in God's timing bring the one who would **redeem** people. Abram was later known as Abraham (Genesis 17:5).

Illustration #4
Ages of Biblical People—Men who lived before the Flood lived about nine hundred years (Genesis 5). After the Flood, men lived significantly fewer years (Genesis 11). Some Bible experts say that this was the result of changes in the environment that occurred with the Flood.

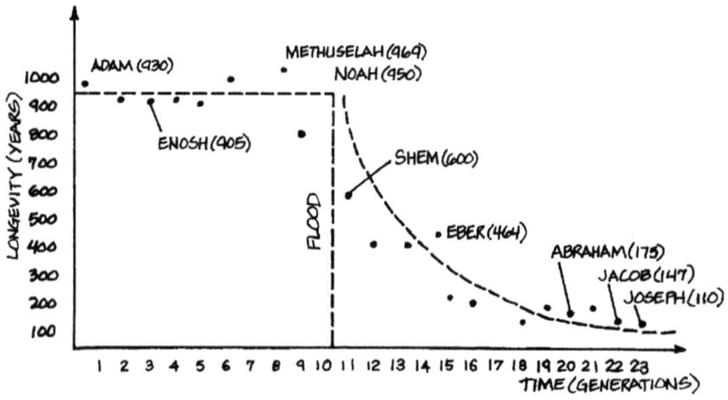

Ur
a wealthy, sophisticated pagan center in southern Mesopotamia

what others say

Samuel J. Schultz

To conclude the period of beginnings, the scope of developments is narrowed down to the Semites (Genesis 11:10–32)…. The climax is the introduction of Abram…who embodies the beginning of a chosen nation—the nation of Israel which occupies the center of interest throughout the rest of the Old Testament.[5]

Spotlight on Terah

God directs our attention to one particular family. Terah, a descendant of Shem, is the father of Abram, Nahor, and Haran. Abram's wife was Sarai, and Haran's son was Lot. We now have been introduced to characters who will play key roles in Genesis 12–24 as God works out his incredible plan of redemption.

The first scene is set in **Ur** (see Appendix B), a city that evidenced characteristics of an advanced, ungodly civilization.

what others say

Dr. Larry Richards

Ur was dominated by a giant three-stage ziggurat, reaching some 70 feet above the flat plain below. On it were shrines to Nunnar, the city's god. The city was enclosed by oval walls some 30 feet high, which protected not only the city but two harbors. Streets were carefully laid out. House walls faced the streets, and homes featured an inner courtyard onto which their rooms faced. Among the more spectacular finds from Ur's early period are beautifully worked gold jewelry and objects, gold-inlaid musical instruments, and colorful mosaics illustrating civil and military life. In addition, a number of clay tablets were recovered, including a Sumerian dictionary and a mathematical text recording cube roots. There were also business records, which show that the people of Ur were actively involved in international trade.[6]

something to ponder

God is sovereign. He works out his plans even while nations have ruled him out and are carrying on their own plans.

Chapter Wrap-Up

- The Table of Nations is a record of Noah's descendants through Shem, Ham, and Japheth. It was through them that the nations of the world began: Shem—Hebrews and Syrians; Ham—North Africa, the Far East, and Canaanites; Japheth—parts of Asia, Europe, and Spain. (Genesis 10)
- Nimrod, a descendant of Ham, was a mighty hunter and an aggressive empire-builder who rebelled against God in trying to build a tower to reach the heavens. This was in direct opposition to God's plan. (Genesis 10:8–12)
- God thwarted Nimrod's plans by causing the people to speak different languages, so they scattered and settled in various places. (Genesis 11:1–9)
- One of the descendants of Noah's son Shem was Terah, father of Abram, an important character in God's plan of redemption for all people. (Genesis 11:10–32)

Study Questions

1. God knew all about Nimrod but did not stop him. What does this tell us about God's attitude toward ungodly people—then and now?
2. How did Nimrod rebel against God? Are people today still rebelling against God? How?
3. How was the confusion of languages both a punishment and a protection from God?
4. What can we learn from Genesis 10–11 about God's plans?

Part Two
God and Abraham

Genesis 12 Abram

Chapter Highlights:
- **God Calls Abram**
- **Abram Moves to Canaan**
- **Abram Travels to Egypt**

Let's Get Started

God had created people for his own pleasure and for their blessing on earth and throughout eternity. But the first people chose to disobey him and brought sin into the world. When sin increased through each generation, God sent judgment through the Flood, saving only righteous Noah and his family. When sin increased and people turned from God, he reached out in **grace** to one man, Abram, who heard his call and responded in faith and obedience. God was not through with the human race. Reaching out to Abram was another new beginning. Abram's story vibrates with the truth that one person can make a difference when that person responds to God's call with trust and obedience. Through Abram, God founded a new nation that would receive his special blessing. Through that nation the **Savior** of the world would be born.

Three times in Scripture, Abram is called God's friend, a distinction not given any other character in the Bible. While it is true that Abram had faults and fell short of God's standards, he had faith, and over many years of testing, he continued to trust God.

go to

friend
2 Chronicles 20:7; Isaiah 41:8; James 2:23

grace
God's action to meet human need of deliverance from sin and its consequences

Savior
one who would deliver people from the consequences of their sin

God Calls Abram

In the four hundred years after the Flood, the descendants of Noah multiplied and spread out. In the fertile plains of Babylon (see Illustration #5), a civilization flourished in every way except in its acknowledgment of the true God. In the progressive city of Ur, God searched out one man and spoke to him.

the big picture

Genesis 12:1–3

God spoke to Abram, calling him to leave his country, his people, and his father's household. He was to go to an unknown land that God would show him. Then God gave Abram promises that would fill his life with amazing blessings that would extend through him to all peoples on earth.

The stream of daily life flowed on. The human race had chosen to go its own way and was living without regard for the God who had created them. Then God stepped in.

He interrupted the normal routine of Abram's life with a startling call. Abram was to leave his country, the large community of which he was a part, and his father's household. The call was to Abram from the God of heaven and earth.

God gave Abram promises that must have filled him with amazement and a deep sense of awe:

1. "I will make you a great nation" (Genesis 12:2 NKJV).
2. "I will bless you" (verse 2 NKJV).
3. "[I will] make your name great" (verse 2 NKJV).
4. "You shall be a blessing" (verse 2 NKJV).
5. "I will bless those who bless you, and I will curse him who curses you" (verse 3 NKJV).
6. "In you all the families of the earth shall be blessed" (verse 3 NKJV). These promises were not for Abram only but for the nation that would come from him and then ultimately for all peoples of the earth.

something to ponder

Abram was faced with a choice. He could ignore the voice and continue life in Ur. Or he could respond to that voice with trust and obedience. No matter which he chose, life could never be the same for him.

what others say

Gerrit Scott Dawson

The plan was always that the people who lived in such a particular relationship to God would lead the rest of the world back to harmony with the Creator.[1]

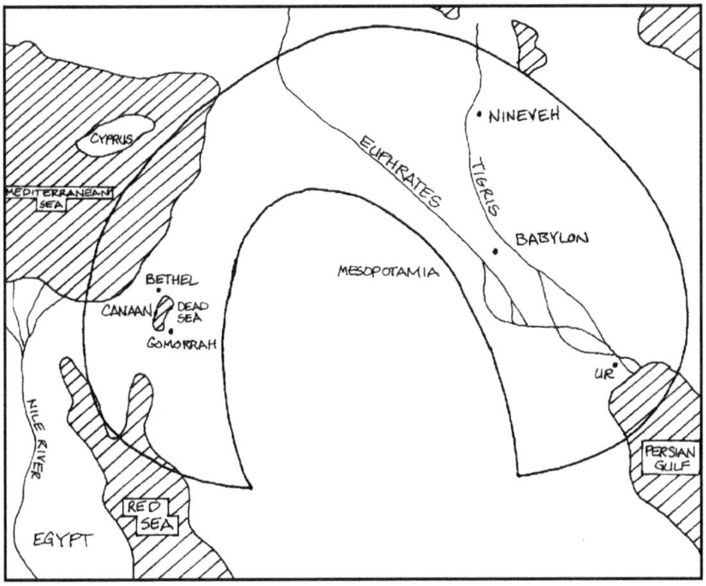

Illustration #5 The Fertile Crescent—The outlined area was called the Fertile Crescent. Broad river valleys supported agriculture and served as trade routes in Abraham's time.

go to

idol worshipers Joshua 24:2

Abram Moves to Canaan—Why Me?

the big picture

Genesis 12:4-9

Abram left, taking his wife, Sarai, and his nephew Lot with him, as well as all their possessions, arriving at Haran (see Appendix B), and from there they went on to Canaan (see Appendix A).

In Canaan the Lord appeared again and gave an additional promise of the land. Abram built altars to the Lord in this new land.

God called and Abram responded. Though he could see nothing that would encourage him to obey God, he trusted and stepped out into the unknown.

Looking at Abram, one would not judge him a likely candidate to receive God's great promises. Abram came from a family of idol worshipers. He was seventy-five years old when he left Haran (Genesis 12:4), hardly the typical age for making a major life change. As he pursued his journey, some of his relatives appeared to lose heart in the expedition and settled down before reaching the destination

God had chosen. And though God had promised to make a nation of Abram, Abram had no son. Sarai had been unable to bear children (Genesis 11:30).

go to

faith
Hebrews 11:8

It would seem that God's new beginning was off to a rough start—except for one all-important factor: Abram believed God. He had faith and was willing to obey even though he had no idea where God was directing him.

Sir Leonard Woolley, the archaeologist in charge of the excavation at Ur in the 1920s and 1930s, discovered that its inhabitants benefited from well-planned streets and houses with high standards of sanitation. The houses appear to have been constructed so they could remain cool in the hot summers, and some may have been two storied (see Illustration #6, this page). Abram left all that—for what? For what God had promised him.

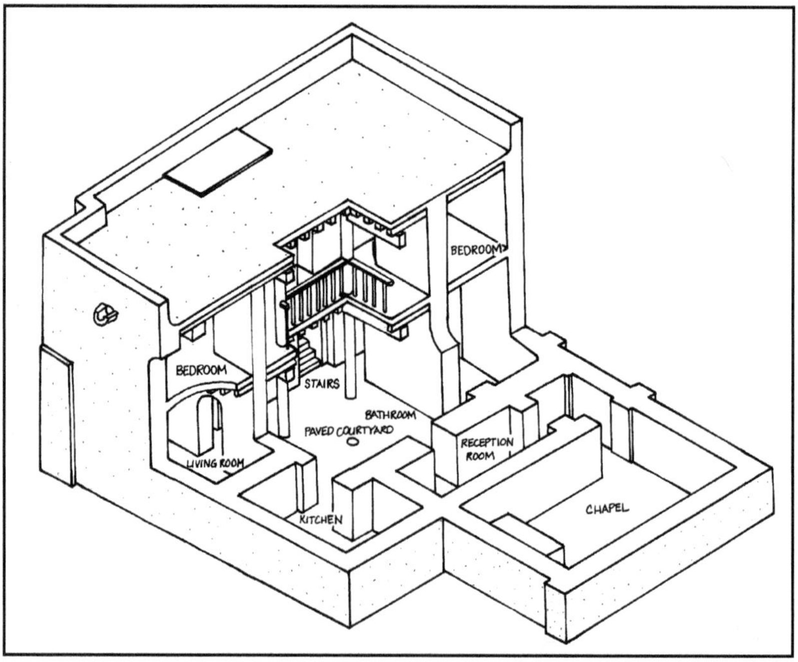

Illustration #6
Home in Ur—A home of a prosperous family in Ur offered the convenience of an inner courtyard with rooms around the side. A stairway gave access to second-story rooms.

what others say

J. Vernon McGee

The three great religions of the world go back to Abraham: Judaism, Islam, and Christianity. There are literally millions of people in Asia and Africa today who have heard of Abraham.[2]

It's You and Me, Lord

Pharaoh
ruler of Egypt

After Terah died in Haran, God spoke to Abram and gave him promises. Abram left with Sarai and Lot and traveled to the land of Canaan. Arriving at Shechem (see Appendix B), he received yet another promise from God: "To your descendants I will give this land" (Genesis 12:7 NKJV). Abram responded by building an altar to the Lord.

From Shechem, he moved to Bethel and pitched his tent between Bethel and Ai. There he built another altar to the Lord and called on the name of the Lord before moving on toward the Negev (see Appendix B for a map).

what others say

F. B. Meyer

As soon as Abraham had fully obeyed, this new promise [Genesis 12:7] broke upon his ear. And it is always this way. Disobey, and you tread a path unlit by a single star. Obey, living up to the claims of God, and successive promises beam out from heaven to light your steps, each one richer and fuller than the one before. Until this time, God had pledged himself only to show Abraham the land: now he bound himself to give it.[3]

Abram Travels to Egypt

the big picture

Genesis 12:10-20

A famine in Canaan caused Abram to go live in Egypt. En route, Abram decided to prepare for a problem that would surely arise. Sarai, at sixty-five, was in her prime—a beautiful woman. Her beauty would most certainly tempt Egyptian men. Believing they might kill Abram in order to have his wife, Abram told Sarai to say she was his sister.

When Abram and Sarai arrived in Egypt, **Pharaoh**'s officials were so struck by her beauty that she was taken into the palace as one of Pharaoh's wives, and Abram was treated as an honored guest. But God inflicted diseases on Pharaoh and his household. When Pharaoh discovered the deception, he returned Sarai to Abram and asked him to leave the country, taking with him all the wealth he had accumulated in Egypt.

A Killer Beauty

God had guided Abram to Canaan and had promised to give the land to his descendants, but the land had become so parched it did not produce vegetation needed for survival of people and animals. Because of the shortage of food, Abram decided on his own to proceed to Egypt, where there would be plenty of food. Instead of seeking God's direction, Abram made his own plans. He would not settle in Egypt, but would stay for a while (Genesis 12:10). His heart was not at peace as he moved across the desert toward Egypt. He looked at Sarai, who was beautiful, and knew the Egyptians would be attracted to her. He feared they would kill him in order to have Sarai. To solve the dilemma, Abram told her to tell the Egyptians that she was his sister. (She was, in fact, his half sister.) The plan seemed to work well. Sarai's beauty so appealed to the Egyptians that she was taken into Pharaoh's palace. Abram had crafted the deception "that it may be well" (Genesis 12:13 NKJV) with him, and as her "brother," he was treated so well that he was able to expand his wealth by accumulating sheep, cattle, donkeys, camels, and male and female servants. When we obey God, he assumes responsibility for the consequences of our obedience. When we disobey God, we assume the consequences of our actions.

what others say

James Montgomery Boice

> So far as earthly circumstances went, the decision of Abram was a wise one. There was a famine. Abram could have expected no food from the Canaanites; they were in the same fix too and, even if they had not been, he could hardly have expected them to assist a stranger. What else was he to do? Unfortunately, even though there were ample circumstances to justify his course of action, if that action evidenced a failure of belief in God, as it did, the unbelief was still unbelief and no one can please God who does not trust him (Hebrews 11:6).[4]

The Game Is Over

While Abram's plan seemed to be working flawlessly, God was also working out his own plan. He plagued Pharaoh and others in the palace with "great plagues" (Genesis 12:17 NKJV). Being superstitious, Pharaoh surmised what had happened and called Abram into account. When Abram confessed his deception, Pharaoh banished him from the palace and from the country.

Abram left with Sarai and all the wealth he had gained.

what others say

Bill Hybels

> We live in a society that minimizes the seriousness of lying. We've been conditioned to accept dishonesty with a sigh and a shrug of the shoulders. That's why it's so hard to break the behavioral pattern of lying.[5]

Among the Dead Sea Scrolls found in 1947 hidden in caves near the Dead Sea was a scroll which contained an interpretation of Genesis 12–15. It includes comments on Sarai's beauty, even describing her features.

God's Call Was Not Recalled

Pharaoh was through with Abram, but God was not. He did not let Abram's lapse of faith keep him from fulfilling his plan for Abram.

Returning to the Promised Land, Abram built an altar, showing his desire to be brought closer to God (Genesis 13:1–2).

Psalm 86:15–17
You, O Lord, are a God full of compassion, and gracious,
Longsuffering and abundant in mercy and truth.
Oh, turn to me, and have mercy on me!
Give Your strength to Your servant,
And save the son of Your maidservant.
Show me a sign for good,
That those who hate me may see it and be ashamed,
Because You, Lord, have helped me and comforted me. (NKJV)

When we are not listening closely to God, he sometimes uses difficult circumstances and even the rebuke of an ungodly person to put us back on the right path. We should resist the temptation to get angry when these things happen. As George MacDonald said, God is bringing us to perfection, and he'll stop at nothing to get us there.

something to ponder

Chapter Wrap-Up

- God spoke to Abram, a descendant of Noah's son, Shem, and from an idol-worshiping family in the land of Ur. God told him to leave his country, his people, and his father's household to go to a place that God would reveal to him. (Genesis 12:1)
- God promised Abram that he would make him into a great nation, bless him, make him a blessing, bless those who blessed him and curse those who cursed him, and bless everyone on earth through him. (Genesis 12:2–3)
- After a time in Haran, Abram headed for Canaan with his wife, Sarai, his nephew Lot, and their possessions. When they arrived in Shechem, God spoke to Abram again with an additional promise to give him the land. Abram responded by building an altar to the Lord. (Genesis 11:2–32; 12:4–5)
- Though Abram had no son, he believed God would keep his promises. Abram moved on to Bethel and built another altar before moving on toward the Negev. (Genesis 12:6–9)
- Because of a famine in Canaan, Abram went to live in Egypt without consulting God. Afraid that the Egyptians would want to kill him to take his beautiful wife, Abram had her pretend to be his sister. The Egyptian pharaoh took Sarai to his palace, but God protected her by inflicting Pharaoh and his household with diseases. (Genesis 12:10–19)
- Abram and Sarai left Egypt with much wealth gained during their stay there. (Genesis 12:20)

Study Questions

1. What was "unusual" about Abram's circumstances that could have kept him from believing God's promises?

2. What can we learn about obedience from Abram?

3. When Abram arrived in Canaan, God spoke to him again. What was Abram's response?

4. In Egypt, what caused Abram to rely on his own foolish schemes instead of on God?

5. How did God take care of Abram in spite of his foolishness? What does this reveal about God's character?

Genesis 13–14 Abram and Lot

Chapter Highlights:
- Abram and Lot Separate
- Abram Rescues Lot
- Abram and the King of Sodom

Let's Get Started

God engineered circumstances to bring Abram back to the Promised Land. Abram had gone to Egypt to escape a famine. Through deception, he escaped death and accumulated great wealth. Now we see what happens after Abram returns to the place where he had built an altar to the Lord God. For Abram it was an opportunity for a new beginning.

Jordan
a river that formed the eastern boundary of Canaan

As we turn now to the narrative in Genesis 13–14, we will see how Abram interacted with his nephew Lot over grazing space for their large herds. Though Abram had rights and certainly should have had the choicest part of the land, he did not try to work things out to his own advantage. Instead, he allowed Lot to make the choice.

When Herdsmen Collide

God can use even family disagreements and difficult interpersonal relationships to accomplish his purposes—purposes more far-reaching than to merely Abram's family. God was working out his plan for a nation and the whole world.

the big picture

Genesis 13:1–18

Abram had become very wealthy while he was in Egypt, amassing livestock and silver and gold. After he set up camp again in Bethel, a problem arose. His nephew Lot also had flocks and herds and servants. While Abram and Lot lived in close proximity, their combined livestock ran out of suitable grazing space. The herdsmen of Abram and Lot began to quarrel.

Abram went to Lot and said that they should part in order to avoid the quarreling. When he offered his nephew the choice of the land, Lot chose the well-watered plain of the **Jordan** and pitched his tents near Sodom, a city known for its wickedness. Later the Lord came to Abram and promised him the land, including the fertile plain that Lot had chosen.

The wealth Abram and Lot had gained while in Egypt did not bring peace and contentment. In time, their herdsmen began to quarrel because each group wanted the best grazing area for their employer in what was a small area of land. The disagreements escalated to striving and would become explosive if something was not done about it.

Abram took the initiative to bring peace. He confronted the problem and dealt with it. Approaching Lot, he pointed out that quarreling was not appropriate, because he and Lot were brothers. The time had come for the two to separate. Confrontation is uncomfortable, but when it is handled constructively, people assume responsibility for the choices they make.

what others say

Samuel J. Schultz

Frequent references indicate that Abraham was a man of considerable wealth and prestige. Far from being a wandering nomad in the Bedouin sense...it is likely that his wealth was represented by a large caravan when he migrated to Palestine. A force of 318 servants used subsequently to deliver Lot (Genesis 14:14) and a caravan of 10 camels (24:10) signify but a token of Abraham's material resources.... Palestinian chieftains recognized Abraham as a prince with whom they made alliances and concluded treaties (Genesis 14:15; 21:22; 23:6).[1]

A Lesson in Manners

In a gesture of unselfish generosity, Abram told Lot to choose what part of the land he would like for himself and his many possessions. Lot shrewdly noted that it would be greatly to his advantage to take the well-watered plain of the Jordan River. It was clearly the choice most favorable to him, so he asked for it, shamelessly violating the custom of deference to one's elders. Abram agreed to the division of land, and the two men parted company. Abram could have wondered, *Sure, I was unselfish in giving Lot the first choice—but how smart was that?*

Abram stayed in the land of Canaan, while Lot lived among the cities of the plain. Eventually he pitched his tents near Sodom. The area was beneficial for his livestock, but the neighbors were not suitable for Lot and his family: "The men of **Sodom** were exceedingly wicked and sinful against the LORD" (13:13 NKJV). There was more. By settling near Sodom, Lot had moved outside Canaan. He had chosen to leave the area God had promised to give Abram.

Sodom
one of five cities of the plain, in a fertile area at the southern end of the Dead Sea, which lay at the tip of the Jordan Valley

When God Speaks, Abe Listens

Abram's camp was suddenly peaceful. Quarreling between the herdsmen had stopped—but at what price? Now he was alone. He had allowed his nephew to rip him off from the very land God had promised to give him. While Abram had opportunity to reflect on his situation, God spoke to him.

A short while before, Abram and Lot had looked over the land available—north, south, east, and west. Now the Lord told him to repeat the scan—north, south, east, and west. God was promising to give to Abram and his offspring all that he could see in each direction. More than that, God promised Abram to multiply his offspring so that they would become uncountable multitudes. Then God challenged Abram to walk through the whole land in the sure knowledge that God was giving it to him.

Then Abram moved his tents near the shade of trees at Mamre at Hebron (see Appendix B). There he built an altar to the Lord. His relationship with his nephew Lot had changed. His relationship with God remained unchanged.

Two new aspects are highlighted in God's promise to Abram:

1. God had previously said Abram's descendants would inherit the land. Now He promised that Abram himself would have it.

2. God had previously said Abram would have descendants. Now he said Abram would have many, many of them; in fact, an uncountable multitude!

Gomorrah
one of five cities that lay in a fertile plain: Sodom, Gomorrah, Admah, Zeboiim, and Bela

Abram Rescues Lot—Trouble in Five Cities

the big picture

Genesis 14:1–17

Raiding armies from the north went to war against the kings of Sodom and its surrounding cities. After thirteen years of suppression, the peoples of the plain rebelled. A battle erupted, and the armies of Sodom and its allies were in trouble. As they fled from the enemy, some of the men fell into tar pits while others retreated into the hills. The victorious enemy captured goods and food from Sodom and **Gomorrah** (see Appendix B) and carried away captives. Lot was among the captives.

One captive escaped and reported the event to Abram. He immediately called out 318 of his men, led them out in pursuit, and bravely brought Lot and his possessions, as well as other captives, back home. Abram's band of faithful servants defeated the armies of four kings.

This passage reads like next week's newsmagazine. An army attacks, innocent citizens are taken captive, their goods seized. They are at the mercy of their captors. Will anyone come to their rescue? Wrong choices bring consequences. Lot experienced this. He also experienced God's grace expressed through Abram.

The prosperity Lot enjoyed in the area of Sodom was rudely interrupted when four kings from the east descended on them:

- Amraphel, king of Shinar (Babylon)
- Arioch, king of Ellasar
- Chedorlaomer, king of Elam
- Tidal, king of nations

These kings went to war against the kings in the valley where Lot lived (see Appendix B):

- Bera, king of Sodom
- Birsha, king of Gomorrah
- Shinab, king of Admah
- Shemeber, king of Zeboiim
- Zoar, king of Bela

For twelve years these five kings had been subject to Chedorlaomer, king of Elam. Finally, they rebelled against this suppression. They prepared for battle, but it was an ill-fated plan. As they fled before the four kings, some slipped into the tar pits in the valley while the rest escaped to the mountains. The four warrior kings swooped down to capture the people of Sodom and Gomorrah, carrying them and their possessions away.

Providence
God's foreseeing care and guidance

James Montgomery Boice points out, "Nothing is as common to the history of the human race as war. The earliest surviving monuments, known as steles, tell of wars. The earliest pictures show wars. In fact, the earliest of all historical records, a Sumerian bas-relief from Babylon (c. 3000 B.C.), shows soldiers fighting in close battle order, all with shields and helmets."[2]

General Abram's Rough Riders

One captured man escaped and ran to report the bad news to Abram. Suddenly Abram was thrust into the role of a general. No longer was he merely a wealthy gentleman cattle rancher. He immediately called 318 of his trained and trusted men and pursued his captured nephew, going as far as Dan (see Appendix B), some 140 miles away. With courage, strategy, and strength, he attacked at night and recovered all the loot, Lot, his possessions, and other captives. When Chedorlaomer's men took flight, Abram chased them north to Hobah, which was another one hundred miles north of Dan. God equips people of faith to do his will.

what others say

R. C. Sproul

Adam Smith referred to **Providence** as "the invisible hand of God." Because God is invisible to us, we often fail to recognize His active presence in human affairs. Because we cannot peer into the transcendent realm, many things appear to happen by chance or as mere contingencies.[3]

An Unexpected Encounter

the big picture

Genesis 14:18-24

When Abram returned from his victorious pursuit of the four kings, he was met by both the king of Sodom and Melchizedek, king of Salem (see Appendix B), a priest of the living God.

tithe
one-tenth of one's goods

> Melchizedek brought Abram bread and wine—and a blessing addressed to the God who had made him victorious. Abram, in turn, gave Melchizedek a **tithe** of all the goods he had recovered.
>
> The king of Sodom made Abram an offer: If Abram returned all the people who had been captured, he could retain all the loot he had recovered. Abram rejected the offer.

Abram had a stunning victory over the enemy kings. As he returned to his tent, a weary general thankful that his pursuit of the enemy had been so successful, he could not have guessed what God had in store for him.

Abram had an unexpected encounter with Melchizedek, king of Salem (later called Jerusalem, see Appendix B), who was also the priest of the Most High God. Abram may not have been acquainted with Melchizedek, but Melchizedek knew Abram.

Melchizedek greeted Abram with bread and wine and a blessing that revealed his knowledge of the living God. While accepting the blessing expressed by Melchizedek, Abram gave him a tenth of all the goods he had recovered from his rescue mission.

what others say

Jack W. Hayford

Uniquely occupying the offices of king and priest, [Melchizedek] worships God Most High (somewhat of a rarity in the area at that time). Prior to any legal requirement, Abram responds to [Melchizedek's] office, generosity, and blessing by giving him a tithe of all the spoils gathered in the recent war.[4]

The Bible Knowledge Commentary

Melchizedek's name (which means "king of righteousness") suggests a righteous ruler who was God's representative. (Some Bible students believe Melchizedek was a theophany, an appearance of the preincarnate Christ.)[5]

All I Want Is This Bagel

Abram was heralded as a hero. The king of Sodom tried to strike a deal with him. He suggested that since Abram had returned the captives, he was free to keep for himself all the goods he had recovered.

Here was a legitimate opportunity for Abram to be rewarded for his heroism. In fact, by rights the goods and the captives were his. But Abram rejected the offer. He told the king of Sodom that he had already promised the Lord that he would "take nothing, from a thread to a sandal strap" as a reward (Genesis 14:23 NKJV). Abram did not want the king of Sodom to take credit for adding to his great wealth. All Abram was willing to accept was the food his troops had already consumed in their hot pursuit of the enemy.

what others say

Bill T. Arnold

> The king of Sodom seems rude. He offers Abram nothing and speaks to him curtly: "Give me the people and keep the goods for yourself" (Genesis 14:21). As returning victor of the war, Abram was entitled to keep everything: people, animals, and captured property. Presumably, the king of Sodom feared he would do just that. So he proposed a compromise, without the usual common amenities that were associated with friendlier ancient Near Eastern conversations.[6]

When God prospers our efforts, we should give him all the credit and not covet rewards from the ungodly. We can be sure that God will honor the glory we give to him.

something to ponder

Chapter Wrap-Up

- While in Egypt, Abram and Lot became wealthy. When they came back to Bethel, there was not sufficient room for their livestock to graze. This caused conflict between their herdsmen. Abram suggested that they part, and he gave Lot first choice of where to move. Lot took advantage of Abram's generosity and chose the best grazing land near Sodom. (Genesis 13:1–13)

- God blessed Abram further by promising to give to him and his descendants all the land he could see in every direction. God also promised that Abram's descendants would be too many to count. (Genesis 13:14–17)

- Abram moved to Hebron and built an altar to the Lord. (Genesis 13:18)

- The peoples of the plain where Lot lived rebelled against the armies of the north after thirteen years of suppression and were defeated. Lot was among the captives taken. (Genesis 14:1–12)

- When Lot's capture was reported to Abram, he gathered an army of his men and set out in pursuit. He and his servants defeated the northern armies and brought Lot back home, with other captives and their possessions. (Genesis 14:13–16)

- Upon his triumphant return, Abram was met by the king of Sodom and by Melchizedek, king of Salem. Melchizedek gave Abram bread and wine and a blessing for his victory. Abram gave Melchizedek a tenth of the goods he had recovered. (Genesis 14:17–20)

- The king of Sodom told Abram that since he had returned the captives, he could keep the loot (which was rightfully his anyway). Abram refused, not wanting the king of Sodom to be able to take credit for any of his wealth. (Genesis 14:21–24)

Study Questions

1. What does Abram's treatment of Lot teach us about peacemaking?

2. How did Abram come out ahead in spite of Lot's selfishness with the land?

3. What does Abram's rescue of Lot teach us about forgiveness?

4. How did Abram show his thanks to God when Melchizedek met him?

5. What can we learn from Abram about giving God credit for his goodness to us?

Genesis 15 God's Covenant

Chapter Highlights:
- **The Center of Abram's Heart**
- **Abram's Question**
- **God's Confirmation**
- **Abram's Eye of Faith**

Let's Get Started

Abram had rescued his nephew Lot from a raiding army that had carried him away. He had refused a reward from the king of Sodom. Now he was alone back at his camp.

God had made wonderful promises to Abram, but it seemed to him that the one most important promise had not been fulfilled. All other promises hinged on God's promise to give him a son. How could God make a nation from Abram if he did not have a son? As the months went by, it seemed more and more unlikely that Sarai could ever give birth to a child.

However, in spite of the apparent impossibility of ever having a son, Abram believed God. We learn from Genesis 15 how God viewed his faith and confirmed the promise he had made when he first called Abram to his adventure in faith (Genesis 12).

At the Center of Abram's Heart

God's timing is perfect. He knew when Abram's heart was particularly sore, when his faith needed reassurance, and when he was ready for God to make himself known in yet another facet of his love and care for Abram.

the big picture

Genesis 15:1

After Abram's dramatic rescue of Lot, God spoke to Abram in a vision, saying, "Do not be afraid, Abram. I am your shield, your exceedingly great reward" (NKJV).

Abram is a hero, but he is also human. We see him perhaps feeling let down after the challenges he had overcome in his daring rescue of Lot. Perhaps he feared that the kings of the east might target him in retaliation for his attack on them. He had done right by refusing to accept the rewards offered by the king of Sodom, but in doing so, he had missed out on sizable wealth.

go to

shield
2 Samuel 22:31; Psalm 28:7; Proverbs 30:5

prophets
Numbers 12:6

God knew Abram's heart and spoke to him in a **vision**. He assured Abram in the two areas he felt need. God confirmed that he himself was Abram's protection or shield. He also confirmed that far more than any material reward, he himself was Abram's "exceedingly great reward" (Genesis 15:1 NKJV). No matter what was happening in Abram's life, God was at the center—the center of Abram's activity, his plans, his hopes.

what others say

Lloyd Ogilvie

> The Lord's constant word to us is "Fear Not!" There are 366 "Fear Not!" verses in the Bible—one for every day of the year and an extra one for Leap Year! Most of the admonitions are followed by a firm assurance of the Lord's presence or a stirring reminder of an aspect of His nature—like His faithfulness, goodness, lovingkindness, or intervening power in times of need.[1]

vision
a revelation from God received while in a dreamlike state

tabernacle
a portable shelter, as a tent, used for worship

missionary
a believer who traveled (often to other countries) to give God's message

From time to time God spoke to people, usually prophets, in a vision. Here are a few examples:

- Jacob, Abram's grandson (Genesis 46:2)
- Samuel, a boy serving the priest Eli in the **tabernacle** (1 Samuel 3:1–18)
- Ezekiel, a priest who prophesied while in exile in Babylon (Ezekiel 1:1)
- Daniel, a captive in Babylon who became God's prophet (Daniel 10:7)
- Zechariah, a priest serving in the temple (Luke 1:22)
- Ananias, a believer in the early church (Acts 9:10) and Saul, a new convert (Acts 9:12)
- Peter, a leader in the early church (Acts 10:9–23)
- Paul, a **missionary** and leader in the early church (Acts 18:9)

GOD AT WORK

Under the Stars—Abram's Question

the big picture

Genesis 15:2–6

Abram asked about the promised reward. What would God give him, since he was without a son? When Abram died, his heir would be his servant Eliezer. But God promised that Eliezer would not be the heir, since Abram was going to have a son. To confirm the promise, God took Abram out to look at the sky, for his offspring would number with the stars. Abram believed the Lord, and the Lord credited Abram's faith to him as righteousness.

God had promised to be Abram's reward, but what would that reward be? Abram raised a troubling question. What Abram longed for was a son, but no son had come since God had promised to make a nation of Abram's descendants. Abram yearned with all his heart to probe God's plan for him. He wondered why God had not kept his promise to give him a son.

According to custom, if Abram died without a son to be his heir, his servant Eliezer would receive the inheritance. It is probable that Eliezer was Abram's "chief of staff," or had been given the status of an adopted son and had been trusted to serve as a member of the family. Did God intend to fulfill his promise through Abram's servant?

God left no doubt in Abram's mind as he said, "This one shall not be your heir, but one who will come from your own body shall be your heir" (Genesis 15:4 NKJV). To make his promise even more clear, God took Abram outdoors where he could gaze at the night sky. He told Abram to look up. "Count the stars if you are able to number them" (Genesis 15:5 NKJV). Of course, Abram could not count all the stars that glittered overhead. God promised that Abram's descendants would become so multiplied that they could not be counted either. Abram's heart responded. He believed God. Abram "believed in the LORD, and He accounted it to him for righteousness" (Genesis 15:6 NKJV).

go to

God is righteous
Jeremiah 12:1

sin
wrongdoing that falls short of God's holy standard of perfection

righteousness
not sinlessness, but counted as sinless in God's eyes

key point

what others say

The Experiencing God Study Bible

God honored the boldness and confidence Abram showed in asking God hard questions.[2]

Elisabeth Elliot

When we are stalling over some difficult decision, or hesitating to make an affirmation, faith comes in to strengthen and encourage us, but faith's object is dim to our human eyes. In the face of obscurities Jesus is saying, "Trust Me." Grace then is given which confirms our will and helps us toward a faith which can rest with the unexplained.[3]

What, Me Righteous?

God is righteous. He is morally right in every way. Abram could not claim to be righteous, for like every person born into the human race, he had done wrong. God calls this wrongdoing **sin**. But Abram believed God, and God credited his faith as **righteousness**. Though what Abram believed is not clear in Genesis 15, his actions indicate he believed that God

- was his protector,
- was his reward,
- would give him a son, and
- would give him descendants that would become a great nation of many people.

We can learn a lot from Abram's response to God by looking at other passages in the Bible where Genesis 15:6 is explained.

Romans 4: Abraham (as he was later called) obeyed rules that God gave, but those rules came after God had credited Abram's faith as righteousness. Therefore, obeying God's laws does not earn credit for righteousness. Rather, even when faced with the fact that he and Sarah (as she was later called) were old, Abram "did not waver at the promise of God through unbelief, but was strengthened in faith, giving glory to God, and being fully convinced that what He had promised He was also able to perform. And therefore 'it was accounted to him for righteousness.' Now it was not written for his sake alone that it was imputed to him, but also for us. It shall be imputed to us who believe in Him who raised up Jesus our Lord from the dead" (verses 20–24 NKJV).

Galatians 3:6–9: "Just as Abraham 'believed God, and it was accounted to him for righteousness.' Therefore know that only those who are of faith are sons of Abraham. And the Scripture, foreseeing that God would justify the Gentiles by faith, preached the gospel to Abraham beforehand, saying, 'In you all the nations shall be blessed.' So then those who are of faith are blessed with believing Abraham" (NKJV). Abraham's faith encompassed more than we might think. Through these verses in Galatians, God tells us that when Abram believed God he was believing that God would provide **justification** not only for himself and for the nation that God had promised to come from him, but also for the **Gentiles**. This means that anyone who has faith as Abram did will be **blessed** as Abram was. Abram was declared righteous, not because he was perfect, but because he believed God.

justification
God's declaration of innocence—"just as if " I'd never sinned

Gentiles
non-Jewish peoples

blessed
God's favor communicated to a person or a people

something to ponder

what others say

James Montgomery Boice

Genesis 15:6 is one of the most important verses, if not the most important verse, in the entire Bible, for it tells for the first time how a sinful man or woman may become right with God. In ourselves we are not right with God. We are alienated from him by our sinful natures and by deliberate sinful choices. We are under God's wrath, and apart from him we are destined to perish miserably. If it is possible that we can become right with God once again—as this verse says we can—thereby passing from sin to holiness and from wrath to blessing, this is clearly great news, and the verse that tells us how this can happen is of supreme importance.[4]

God's Confirmation—A Solemn Encounter

the big picture

Genesis 15:7-21

God spoke to Abram, saying "I am the LORD, who brought you out of Ur of the Chaldeans, to give you this land to inherit it" (verse 7 NKJV). Again Abram raised a question. How could he know that he would gain possession of it? In a solemn ceremony, God revealed to Abram that in spite of mistreatment, his descendants would see his covenant promises fulfilled.

- God and Abram had opened their hearts.
- God had given an assurance (Genesis 15:1).
- Abram had raised a question (verses 2–3).
- God had answered (verse 4).
- God had confirmed his covenant by giving Abram a never-to-be-forgotten experience of looking to the starry heavens and learning that indeed his offspring would be just as uncountable (verse 5).
- Abram had responded by believing the Lord (verse 6). God had credited this to him as righteousness (verse 6).

It was fitting, then, that this solemn encounter between God and Abram be culminated in a further act of confirming the covenant God had made with Abram.

God told Abram to bring a heifer, a goat, a ram, a turtledove, and a young pigeon. Abram killed the animals, cut them in half, and arranged the halves on opposite sides. When vultures swooped down to eat the dead bodies, Abram drove them away.

At sunset Abram fell into a deep sleep. Through a thick and dreadful darkness God spoke to Abram saying that his descendants would be strangers in another country, enslaved and mistreated four hundred years. God promised that he would punish the nation that enslaved the people and would see that they would leave "with great possessions" (Genesis 15:14 NKJV).

In the darkness God revealed himself in the form of an image: a smoking firepot and a torch. Abram watched in the darkness as the two fiery objects moved between the pieces of the slain animals. This showed that God would judge the nations and fulfill the covenant promises he had made.

Then God gave specific geographic details regarding the land he was giving Abram's descendants—from the river of Egypt to the Euphrates.

God had answered Abram's question. In spite of pain and enslavement in another land, Abram's descendants would indeed have the land. He would not fail. He would keep his covenant with Abram.

what others say

Dr. Larry Richards

Usually covenants were confirmed by both parties. This implied that each accepted obligations related to carrying out the intentions the covenant expressed. How significant Abram's deep sleep becomes. God alone passed between the parts of the sacrificed beasts. Abram has no part in making the covenant, so nothing Abram does can cause it to be canceled. You and I contributed nothing to our salvation: Jesus did it all. All we must do, all we can do, is put our trust in God. He will keep His covenant promise to save us for Jesus' sake.[5]

Abram's Eye of Faith

What distinguished Abram was his eye of faith. He could see beyond the here-and-now to what lay ahead in life with God after his body died: "By faith Abraham obeyed when he was called to go out to the place which he would receive as an inheritance. And he went out, not knowing where he was going. By faith he dwelt in the land of promise as in a foreign country, dwelling in tents with Isaac and Jacob, the heirs with him of the same promise; for he waited for the city which has foundations, whose builder and maker is God" (Hebrews 11:8–10 NKJV).

what others say

A. W. Tozer

As Abraham staggered not at the promises of God through unbelief, but was strong in faith, giving glory to God, and was fully persuaded that what he had promised he was able to perform, so do we base our hope in God alone and hope against hope till the day breaks. We rest in what God is. I believe that this alone is true faith. Any faith that must be supported by the evidence of the senses is not real faith.[6]

Because Abram believed God, he could forgo the security and pleasures of this world, knowing that a far greater security and far more pleasures lie ahead.

something to ponder

Chapter Wrap-Up

- After Abram's rescue of Lot, God spoke to him again, in a vision, promising himself as Abram's protection and reward. (Genesis 15:1)

- Abram asked what God would give him, since he had no son. Would his servant be his heir? God promised that Abram would have a son. Then God told Abram to look at the stars in the sky. He explained to Abram that his offspring would be just as numerous. (Genesis 15:2–5)

- Abram believed God and that faith was credited to him as righteousness. Abram trusted that God would provide justification for him and the nation that would come from him. (Genesis 15:6)

- Abram asked how he could be sure of God's promises. God conducted a solemn ceremony with sacrificial animals to confirm his covenant with Abram. As Abram was in a deep sleep, God told him that his descendants would be slaves in another land for 400 years, but God would deliver them and punish their enemies. Then God moved between the animal pieces to show that he would fulfill his covenant promises. (Genesis 15:7–17)

- God gave geographic details of the land he was giving Abram's descendants: from the river of Egypt to the Euphrates. (Genesis 15:18–21)

Study Questions

1. What did God mean when he told Abram, "I am your shield, your exceedingly great reward" (Genesis 15:1 NKJV)?

2. In Bible times God often spoke to men, like Abram, through visions. How does God speak to us today?

3. To encourage Abram, God repeated his promises and even made them clearer. How does God encourage you in your walk of faith?

4. How did Abram's part in God's covenant with him compare to our part in God's covenant of salvation?

Genesis 16 Hagar and Ishmael

Chapter Highlights:
- Abram's Lack of Faith
- God's Intervention
- When God Heard Misery
- Something for Now and for the Future

Let's Get Started

We live in time, organizing our lives by years, months, days, hours, and minutes. We carry notebooks to remind us of appointments. We watch the news to hear how the weather and the traffic flow will impact our travel plans. We make reservations for vacations, enroll in advance for education, and set up schedules with deadlines for the next months or years.

In our efforts to be productive, we demand accountability of ourselves and our colleagues. We expect to meet our commitments, and we expect others to meet their commitments to us. That's why waiting is difficult. It's an affront to our pride, our sense that we need to be in control.

God had made a covenant with Abram, but it was a covenant with no specified time. Still, Abram had an expectation that he would see promises fulfilled in his lifetime. Months and years passed. Where was the action? In this chapter we will see what Abram did to make something happen. The results were imperfect, yet God in his mercy intervened.

Abram's Lack of Faith

the big picture

Genesis 16:1-6

Since Sarai had not borne a child, she suggested that Abram take her maidservant Hagar as a secondary wife. After Hagar became pregnant, she began to show contempt for Sarai. With Abram's consent, Sarai began to mistreat Hagar so badly that Hagar ran away.

Abram was seventy-five years old when God first promised to give him a son (Genesis 12:4, 7). He was now eighty-five years old and Sarai was seventy-five. Why had God not fulfilled his promise?

Abram had believed God, but now Sarai felt they could not wait any longer for God to keep the promises he had made. Sarai made a proposal that was well within the customs of that time. She suggested that Abram take Hagar, her Egyptian maidservant, as a secondary wife. She hoped that in this way she could "obtain children" through Hagar (Genesis 16:2 NKJV).

Gene Getz explains, "What Sarai had proposed was a very common practice. Archaeologists have discovered tablets containing marriage contracts that "specify that a barren wife must provide a woman for her husband for the purpose of procreation."'[1]

Building a Family Our Way

Without seeking God's direction, Abram followed Sarai's plan and Hagar became pregnant.

When she knew she would bear Abram's child, Hagar began to show contempt for Sarai. This, of course, irritated Sarai. Rather than assume her responsibility for the difficulty, "Sarai said to Abram, 'My wrong be upon you! I gave my maid into your embrace; and when she saw that she had conceived, I became despised in her eyes'" (Genesis 16:5 NKJV).

Abram didn't want to be involved in the problem, so he simply told Sarai to deal with Hagar in any way she wished. And Sarai wished to make life miserable for Hagar.

Before long, Hagar ran away from Sarai and Abram.

something to ponder

Hagar was an Egyptian maidservant, undoubtedly acquired as part of the wealth Abraham gained in his visit to Egypt, where he deceived Pharaoh and had to leave. While God forgives our wrongdoing, we have to live with the consequences of our lapses in faith and outright disobedience.

what others say

Henry M. Morris

However worthy and unselfish may have been the motives of Abram and Sarai, and perhaps even of Hagar, in carrying out this plan, it was bound to create problems. God's creative purpose included only monogamous marriage, and anything else was bound to generate problems. There are many instances

instances recorded of polygamous marriages in the Bible, which God allowed because of mitigating circumstances at the time...but none of a happy polygamous marriage.[2]

angel
a messenger from God

When God Heard Misery

the big picture

Genesis 16:7-16

While Hagar rested near a spring at the side of a road, an angel appeared and asked her,

"Hagar, Sarai's maid, where have you come from, and where are you going?" (verse 8 NKJV).

Hagar answered truthfully that she was running away from her mistress.

The angel told her to return to Sarai and submit to her. Then he promised that her descendants would become so numerous that "they shall not be counted for multitutde" (verse 10 NKJV). She would have a son, Ishmael, but he would live in hostility toward his brothers.

Sarai and Abram had stepped outside God's plan for them. Abram's faith, which had been vibrant and strong, faltered. Now Hagar, Sarai's maidservant, was pregnant and miserable. Sarai was hurt and angry. Abram was bewildered.

Hagar ran away, not because her life was in danger, but because she was miserable under Sarai's mistreatment. Actually, Sarai was within current custom in mistreating her slave, and Abram had given Sarai freedom to follow her inclinations. Hagar, though, decided she would not take the treatment she was given, so she headed into the barren wilderness.

While she rested near a spring beside a desert road, an **angel** spoke to her. He called her by name and identified her as Sarai's servant. "Where have you come from, and where are you going?" he asked (Genesis 16:8 NKJV).

Hagar told the truth. She admitted that she was running away from her mistress.

what others say

F. B. Meyer

We are all prone to act as Hagar did. If our lot is hard and our cross is heavy, we start off in a fit of impatience and wounded pride. We shirk the discipline; we evade the yoke; we make our own way out of the difficulty. Ah, we shall never get right with God this way! Never! We must retrace our steps and meekly bend our necks under the yoke. We must accept the lot that God has ordained for us, even though it may be the result of the cruelty and sin of others.[3]

Something for Now—Something for the Future

Surprisingly, the angel told her to go back and submit to her mistress. Then he gave her an amazing promise. He would increase her descendants so they eventually would be too many to count. He added that she would bear a son and she should call him Ishmael, "because the LORD has heard your affliction" (Genesis 16:11 NKJV). Nothing is beyond God's notice. He sees our distress.

He then gave a graphic description of Ishmael: "He shall be a wild man; his hand shall be against every man, and every man's hand against him. And he shall dwell in the presence of all his brethren" (verse 12 NKJV).

Hagar recognized that the God of Abram had communicated with her in her misery. She gave a name to God, "You-Are-the-God-Who-Sees" (verse 13 NKJV), knowing that she had seen the God who had seen her and would continue to see her.

In time, Hagar bore Abram a son, and Abram called him Ishmael. Abram was eighty-six years old when he became a father.

Nobody sins alone. What a person does has an effect on others—often far-reaching. In this case, Hagar's son Ishmael became the ancestor of the Arabs, who have been hostile to the descendants of Abram. Ishmael is the ancestor of Mohammed, the founder of Islam.

what others say

Kay Arthur

Where is God, you ask. Where is this sovereign God who promises that all things work together for good? Does he know what is going on? Does he see?

> Yes, He is El Roi, the God who sees. The omnipresent God is there, and His eyes are not shut. He isn't asleep, unaware of all the circumstances. He sees.[4]

While some may look at a pregnancy as an accident, a mistake, an error in judgment, or even a tragedy, God shows that he has intimate knowledge of that unborn child.

something to ponder

I Know Him Because He First Knew Me

David, who wrote Psalm 139, was filled with awe when he acknowledged that God saw all the details of his life—including his formation while he was yet unborn:

Psalm 139:13–18
You formed my inward parts;
You covered me in my mother's womb.
I will praise You, for I am fearfully and wonderfully made;
Marvelous are Your works,
And that my soul knows very well.
My frame was not hidden from You,
When I was made in secret,
And skillfully wrought in the lowest parts of the earth.
Your eyes saw my substance, being yet unformed.
And in Your book they all were written,
The days fashioned for me,
When as yet there were none of them.
How precious also are Your thoughts to me, O God!
How great is the sum of them!
If I should count them, they would be more in number than the sand;
When I awake, I am still with You. *(NKJV)*

what others say

J. I. Packer

> I am graven on the palms of his hands. I am never out of his mind. All my knowledge of him depends on his sustained initiative in knowing me. I know him, because he first knew me, and continues to know me. He knows me as a friend, one who loves me; and there is no moment when his eye is off me, or his attention distracted from me, and no moment, therefore, when his care falters.[5]

Chapter Wrap-Up

- Sarai, having no children, decided that Abram should have a child by her servant Hagar so that God's promise could be fulfilled. Abram agreed and Hagar became pregnant with his child. (Genesis 16:1–4)

- Hagar, once she was pregnant, began to feel contempt for Sarai, who could not get pregnant. Sarai became so irritated by her servant's attitude, she complained to Abram, who told her to take care of the problem herself. Sarai's solution was to mistreat Hagar. (Genesis 16:5–6)

- Tired of Sarai's mistreatment, Hagar ran away. God sent an angel to confront her and comfort her with the promise of a son and many descendants. Hagar said the name of the Lord was "You-Are-the-God-Who-Sees" (verse 13 NKJV), and she was encouraged. (Genesis 16:6–14)

- Hagar returned to Sarai as the angel had instructed her, and later gave birth to Abram's son Ishmael. (Genesis 16:15–16)

Study Questions

1. How did Sarai's plan for a child and Abram's agreement to it show their lack of faith?

2. How did Abram deal with the conflict between Sarai and Hagar? Was this wise? Why or why not?

3. What do God's dealings with Hagar teach us about him?

4. Why do you think God's treatment of Hagar gave her courage to return to Sarai?

5. What lessons could Sarai, Abram, and Hagar have learned from this experience?

Genesis 17 God's Covenant Confirmed

Chapter Highlights:
- Sarai: Mother of Nations
- God Includes Ishmael
- Abraham Commits Himself to God

Let's Get Started

Abram and Sarai had taken the matter of having a son into their own hands. As a result, Ishmael was born to Sarai's maidservant, Hagar. For thirteen years God was silent. Had Abram failed so badly that God had changed his mind?

In Genesis 17 we see God stepping into Abram's life again to confirm his covenant and to deepen Abram's faith in God's commitment to keep his promises. As if to impress on us the tremendous importance of the covenant, the word appears fourteen times in this chapter.

God gave Abram the rite of circumcision as a physical sign of the covenant between God and the covenant people. While it was a physical sign, it also was a symbol of a heart commitment to God.

The Mark of El Shaddai

If we ever wonder how close God wants to be to us and how close he longs for us to be to him, this chapter provides an awesome insight. The God of heaven and earth, Creator of the universe, appeared to Abram to reinforce his promises, even though Abram had stepped outside God's plan for giving him a son.

the big picture

Genesis 17:1–14

When Abram was ninety-nine years old, the Lord came to him to confirm his covenant that he would make a nation of Abram. He changed Abram's name to Abraham, to signify that he would become a "father of many nations" (verse 5 NKJV). He established his covenant as everlasting, to be the God of Abraham and of his descendants and to give them the land as an everlasting possession. As a sign of the covenant, God instituted circumcision to be an everlasting sign between Abraham's offspring and God.

go to

Almighty God
Genesis 28:3; 35:11; 43:14; 48:3

After thirteen years, God spoke to Abram, not to reprove him for his faithless fathering of Ishmael, but to strengthen Abram's trust in God's covenant.

God broke into the silence and came to Abram, saying, "I am Almighty God; walk before Me and be blameless. And I will make My covenant between Me and you, and will multiply you exceedingly" (Genesis 17:1–2 NKJV).

El Shaddai
the God who is sufficient

In identifying himself as **El Shaddai**, Almighty God, he reminded Abram that he had the power to fulfill every promise he had made. He confirmed his covenant to make a nation of Abram. Abram's response to God's appearance was to fall with his face to the ground, expressing his humility before God and his worship.

what others say

The Revell Bible Dictionary

In Scripture the word *El* is often combined with other nouns and adjectives to indicate the true God (El Shaddai, El Olam) in the same way that we capitalize God to distinguish the Lord from other gods.[1]

Why Put the "Ham" in Abraham?

God made five statements to Abram in making his covenant with him. They are found in Genesis 17:4–8:

- "You shall be a father of many nations" (verse 4 NKJV). To make this known by all, God changed Abram's name from Abram, which means "father," to Abraham, which means "father of nations."
- "I will make you exceedingly fruitful" (verse 6 NKJV).
- "I will make nations of you, and kings shall come from you" (verse 6 NKJV).
- "I will establish My covenant between Me and you and your descendants after you in their generations, for an everlasting covenant, to be God to you and your descendants after you" (verse 7 NKJV).
- "I give to you and your descendants after you the land in which you are a stranger, all the land of Canaan, as an everlasting possession; and I will be their God" (verse 8 NKJV).

what others say

Bill T. Arnold

Genesis portrays a loving God who seeks at every turn to reveal his true nature to humans in order to invite them into deeper relationship with him. In each case, his self-revelation presents Abram with an opportunity to draw closer to God. This time, God also reveals his deepest desire for Abram: "walk before me and be blameless" (Genesis 17:1). This expression is a call for Abram to live a life of unequivocal surrender to God's will. Perhaps you wonder what else Abram could surrender, having left everything to follow God's calling (Genesis 12). But the previous episode with Hagar is a subtle warning that Abram still has more to learn about dependence on God.[2]

Gerrit Scott Dawson

When Abram was 99 years old, the Lord appeared to him to reiterate the promises. It included a name change.... And from that moment on, the text uses the new name of Abraham—though the fulfillment of the promise was still more than a year away. He took the name of the promise into his present experience, and lived under its power and hope, even before the fulfillment came to pass.[3]

A Sign for All Generations

God had pledged to his part of the covenant. Now he gave Abraham a means by which he and his descendants would keep their part of the covenant. He gave a sign that would confirm the human side of the covenant. It was the rite of circumcision to Abraham and to all males who descend from him.

The physical aspect of the rite of circumcision would involve removing the flap of skin that covered the tip of the male's penis. The rite would be performed immediately on Abraham and in the future on all males born to Abraham and his descendants. For them it would be performed on the eighth day of a male's life. Circumcision was the physical mark of the covenant relationship with God for Abraham and his descendants. If anyone did not identify himself or his children with that physical sign, he would be cut off from God's covenant.

GOD AT WORK

Both the Old and the New Testaments of the Bible teach that the physical rite was only a formality that spoke of something far deeper.

circumcision of the heart
Deuteronomy 10:16; Romans 2:28–29; 4:9–12

There are several passages that refer to "circumcision of the heart," which means believing God and setting oneself apart for him.

Spotlight on Sarah

the big picture

Genesis 17:15–19

God changed Sarai's name to Sarah and specifically included her in his blessing. He would give Abraham a son by her and she would be the mother of nations.

Abraham laughed to think that a son could be born of a man of one hundred years with a wife ninety years old. If only God would bless Ishmael! But God confirmed that Sarah would bear a son whom Abraham should call Isaac. The covenant would be extended through Isaac, not Ishmael.

Most of God's communication had been with Abram. However, Sarai had not been overlooked. She was an essential part of God's plan from the beginning. God had promised to give Abraham a son through Sarai.

Ishmael, son of Abraham's union with Hagar, lived in the household. Abraham obviously loved the boy, but the very sight of the child must have stabbed Sarai's heart. God had promised Abraham a son, but she could not bear children.

God knew Sarai's pain and addressed it by bringing her into his promise to Abraham. Her name was changed to Sarah, and God would bless her and enable her to give birth to a son. With his blessing she would be the mother of nations, and kings would trace their ancestors back to her.

This incredible announcement caused Abraham to laugh. Abraham was one hundred years old and Sarah was ninety. They were past the child-bearing years.

Then Abraham's thoughts turned to Ishmael. "Abraham said to God, 'Oh, that Ishmael might live before You!' Then God said: 'No, Sarah your wife shall bear you a son, and you shall call his name Isaac; I will establish My covenant with him for an everlasting covenant, and with his descendants after him'" (Genesis 17:18–19 NKJV).

Sarah would indeed be blessed by God and would bear the son of God's promise.

In Bible times names had great significance. They communicated something about the individual that would identify not only qualities about that person's appearance, but more important inner qualities as well as the aspirations of their parents. When God gives a new name, he makes possible the fulfillment of that name.

something to ponder

What can we learn from names in Abraham's family?

It's All in the Name

Name	Meaning	Comment
Abram	"exalted father"	ironic name, since he had no son
Abraham	"father of a multitude"	a new name given by God
Sarai	"princess"	original name
Sarah	"princess"	a new name given by God (Genesis 17:15)
Ishmael	"God heard"	name given by God when he took note of Hagar's misery (Genesis 16:11)
Isaac	"laughter"	name given by God (Genesis 17:19)

what others say

Kathy Collard Miller

The life of this biblical matriarch (Sarai/Sarah) speaks to us today about believing and following God's directions. She had many winsome attributes and in the New Testament, she is described in a positive light. She also represents the truth that no woman is perfect. Women who are seeking to draw closer to God can learn from Sarai's strengths and weaknesses.[4]

go to

she is described
Hebrews 11:11

God Includes Ishmael—Bless Him Too!

the big picture

Genesis 17:20–22

God knew Abraham's love for Ishmael and gave a special blessing for him. He promised to make Ishmael the head of a great nation. But the covenant would be established with Isaac, the son who would be born to Sarah in the next year.

Though Ishmael was not to be the son God had promised to give Abraham, he was dearly loved by his father. Abraham's heart longed to see God extend his blessing to the boy. After all, every time he said the boy's name he could have remembered the meaning of Ishmael's name: God hears.

From one point of view, Ishmael should never have been born. But God did not ignore Ishmael, nor did God disappoint Abraham. In fact, God had a special blessing in store for Ishmael.

God told Abraham, "As for Ishmael, I have heard you. Behold, I have blessed him, and will make him fruitful, and will multiply him exceedingly. He shall beget twelve princes, and I will make him a great nation" (Genesis 17:20 NKJV).

James Montgomery Boice notes, "God had told Abraham that he would bless Ishmael, making him the father of twelve rulers. . . . Ishmael had 12 sons, according to Genesis 25:13–16, and these became the rulers of 12 peoples who settled in northern Arabia along the main caravan route between Egypt and Assyria."[5]

Abraham Commits Himself to God

the big picture

Genesis 17:23–27

On the very day God instituted the rite of circumcision, Abraham took Ishmael and all males in his household and all his servants and circumcised them.

God had given Abraham a solemn rite that would symbolize his part of the covenant. He had clearly outlined the implications for the rite of circumcision and had given it special meaning. Abraham responded "that very same day" (Genesis 17:23 NKJV).

He took first Ishmael, then all those born into his household, and then all his servants. All were circumcised that day. There could be no doubt in the mind of anyone in Abraham's large community that he had responded in faith to the covenant God had made with him.

apply it

We may speak about loving God, sing about it, and even use the word *love* in our prayers, but the proof that we love God is in our actions. Perhaps no Bible character models this for us better than Abraham. Abraham proved his commitment to God by his prompt obedience to God's Word.

Circumcision was not new. It was practiced by other people in the ancient world.

what others say

R. C. Sproul

> If we ignore his commandments absolutely and totally and completely, that would be the clearest proof that we don't love God. As Jesus himself said, "If you love me, keep my commandments." The keeping of the commandments is a manifestation of our love for God, and obedience is something that flows out of a heart that is inclined toward God and embraces God in love.[6]

go to

love
John 14:15

Chapter Wrap-Up

- Thirteen years after Ishmael was born, God spoke to Abram again to strengthen his trust in God's promises. God referred to himself as El Shaddai, "Almighty God," the one who had power to fulfill all that he had promised. He confirmed his promise to make a nation of Abram. Abram responded in humility by falling with his face to the ground. (Genesis 17:1–3)

- God gave Abram a new name, Abraham, which means "father of nations." (Genesis 17:4–8)

- God gave Abraham a sign to confirm the human side of his covenant: circumcision. This was a physical rite to be performed on all males to demonstrate the heart attitude of believing God and setting themselves apart for him. (Genesis 17:9–14)

- God changed Sarai's name to Sarah and promised to give Abraham a son through her. Abraham laughed at the idea of he and his ninety-year-old wife having a son, but God confirmed it, specifying that the son should be named Isaac. The covenant would be fulfilled through Isaac, not through Ishmael. (Genesis 17:15–19, 21–22)

- Ishmael was not to be the son of God's promise, but God promised to make him the head of a great nation. (Genesis 17:20)

- As soon as God had given Abraham the command for circumcision, Abraham was circumcised and so were Ishmael and all the males in his household, including his servants. (Genesis 17:23–27)

Study Questions

1. Why do you think God referred to himself as El Shaddai to Abram?
2. Why was Abram's simple name change so significant?
3. What does "circumcision of the heart" mean to you?
4. In what special ways did God let Sarai know that she was still an important part of his promise?
5. What can we learn from Abraham about obedience?

Genesis 18–19 Judgment on Sin

Chapter Highlights:
- Three Unexpected Guests
- Abraham Pleads for Sodom
- Gone Gomorrah

Let's Get Started

For anyone who thinks God may not have knowledge of the thoughts and activities of individuals, Genesis 18–19 will present a very different picture. Here we see God accepting hospitality, being aware of heart desires, seeing gross sin, stepping in to judge it, and sparing a few in response to earnest prayers.

One day Abraham was surprised to receive three visitors and to hear some unexpected news. Before the end of the visit, he learned that Sarah would have a son in a year. This was the first time the promise of a son was linked to a specific time. He also learned that the Lord was aware of the gross sins of the people of Sodom and that he was ready to judge the city.

Abraham pleaded that the righteous would be spared. The Lord promised that if ten righteous people were found in the city, he would not destroy it. However, the city was destroyed. Only Lot was saved with his wife and daughters.

Three Unexpected Guests

the big picture

Genesis 18:1–15

When Abraham noticed three men standing near his tent, he welcomed them and offered refreshments. While they ate the meal Abraham served them, the Lord spoke: "I will certainly return to you according to the time of life, and behold, Sarah your wife shall have a son" (verse 10 NKJV).

Sarah laughed, but when questioned about it, she denied having laughed. The visitor, however, knew she was doubting that the Lord could give her the promised son.

The day was hot and Abraham was sitting at the doorway of his tent when he saw three men standing nearby. In a time when travel

go to

entertaining angels
Hebrews 13:2

was by foot or riding on an animal, drop-in guests were not frequent. It was customary to welcome any visitors and provide for their needs. Abraham welcomed them, offering them water to wash their feet and a seat under the shade of a tree.

Hurriedly, he alerted Sarah to the need to honor the visitors with a fine meal. While Sarah began to prepare flour for baking bread, Abraham looked for the choicest calf to be killed. As soon as the food was prepared, he served freshly baked bread, curds, milk, and veal. He stood nearby while the visitors ate, demonstrating his desire to provide the best hospitality to his guests.

We may wonder if Abraham was extending just the usual level of hospitality to strangers or if he understood immediately who the visitors were.

something to ponder

Many Bible experts believe that one of the guests was Jesus Christ in human form (Genesis 18:1) and the other two were angels. The appearances of Jesus in human form in Old Testament times are called "theophanies."

V. Gilbert Beers explains, "Hospitality to guests was one of the most important social functions of the ancient East. A guest was highly honored even if he was a stranger passing by."[1]

Abraham extended himself in entertaining his guests—almost as if they were angels, which indeed they were. We too should extend gracious hospitality, for we too may unknowingly be entertaining angels.

what others say

Billy Graham

Some places in the Old Testament tell us that the second person of the Trinity appeared and was called either "the LORD" or "the angel of the LORD." Nowhere is it clearer than in Genesis 18 where three men appear before Abraham. Their leader is clearly identified with the Lord, whereas the other two are merely angels. There are no grounds for questioning the very early and traditional Christian interpretation that in these cases there is a preincarnation manifestation of the second person of the Trinity, whether he is called 'the LORD' or 'the Angel of the LORD.'

We must remember, then, that in some cases in the Old Testament God himself appeared in human form as an angel.[2]

A Cynic Caught

The guests inquired where Sarah was. Abraham responded that she was in the tent, as would be the custom of that time.

Then the Lord told Abraham that he would come back to him in about a year and that Sarah would have a son.

We don't know how Abraham responded because the narrative shifts to Sarah, who was standing in the doorway listening in on the conversation. Well aware that she was beyond the child-bearing years, she laughed to herself as a question came to her mind. "After I have grown old, shall I have pleasure, my lord being old also?" (Genesis 18:12 NKJV). Unlike Abraham, who had laughed with joy at God's announcement of a son (Genesis 17:17), Sarah laughed with unbelief.

Sarah's response was no secret. The Lord asked Abraham why she had laughed and raised that doubt-filled question. Then he asked, "Is anything too hard for the LORD?" (Genesis 18:14 NKJV). He confirmed that he would indeed return next year and Sarah would have a son.

Sarah was afraid, knowing that the visitor had accurately discerned her silent laugh and her thoughts of unbelief. She added to her problem by telling a lie as she denied having laughed.

The Lord answered simply, this time directing his words to her instead of Abraham: "No, but you did laugh!" (Genesis 18:15 NKJV).

Abraham Pleads for Sodom

the big picture

Genesis 18:16-38

The Lord asked of the other two guests, "Shall I hide from Abraham what I am about to do?" (see verse 17). In supplying the answer, he reviewed the promises God had made to Abraham. Then he spoke of the iniquity of Sodom and Gomorrah. Abraham pleaded for the Judge of all the earth to spare the city for the sake of the righteous who lived there—even if there were only ten righteous people in the city.

The three guests prepared to leave Abraham. As a good host, he walked along with them for a while. The Lord asked, "Shall I hide from Abraham what I am about to do?" (see Genesis 18:17). He reviewed the qualities in Abraham that were important:

- Abraham would surely become a great and mighty nation.
- All nations on earth would be blessed in him.
- God had chosen him, so that he would direct his children and his household to keep their part of the covenant God had made with him—to keep the way of the Lord by doing what is right and just. As Abram did this, the Lord would bring about the covenant promises.

Then God added one more revelation: he intended to do a little private investigating.

Abraham Intercedes

The iniquity of Sodom and Gomorrah was so great that its outcry had reached God. He said he would go to the cities to confirm that the actions of the people were as bad as the outcry had indicated.

The two angels proceeded to Sodom, leaving Abraham standing before the Lord. Abraham approached the Lord to plead for Lot and his family. He asked three questions, made a declaration, and then asked a final question:

Questions:

- "Would You also destroy the righteous with the wicked?" (Genesis 18:23 NKJV).
- "Suppose there were fifty righteous within the city?" (Genesis 18:24 NKJV).
- "Would You also destroy the place and not spare it for the fifty righteous that were in it?" (Genesis 18:24 NKJV).

Declaration:

- "Far be it from You to do such a thing as this, to slay the righteous with the wicked, so that the righteous should be as the wicked; far be it from You!" (Genesis 18:25 NKJV).

Final question:

- "Shall not the Judge of all the earth do right?" (Genesis 18:25 NKJV).

The Lord answered that if he found fifty righteous people in the city of Sodom, he would spare the city for their sake.

Then Abraham pleaded for the city to be saved if the Lord found forty-five righteous there. Then forty . . . thirty . . . twenty . . . ten. And the Lord promised that he would not destroy the city if he found ten righteous people there.

Abraham stopped pleading. He could not bring himself to ask the Lord to spare the city if he found only one righteous person in Sodom.

what others say

Jack Hayford

At least three important principles emerge from God's conversation with Abraham in [Genesis] 18.

1. We learn that wicked Sodom could have been spared for the sake of only ten righteous people. From this we learn that it is not the presence of evil that brings God's mercy and longsuffering to an end; rather, it is the absence of good!
2. Although God sometimes inspires us to pray by showing us things to come (verse 17), our intercession must be in line with God's character and covenant with men. Like Abraham, we may appeal to God to preserve His name, honor, and perfect justice before the world (verse 25).
3. Although we often measure influence by numbers, man's arithmetic cannot be used to estimate the impact of the righteous. God saves by many or by few.[3]

Here Today, Gone Gomorrah

the big picture

Genesis 19:1–29

When the two angels arrived at Sodom, Lot invited them to spend the night at his home. That night men of Sodom surrounded Lot's house demanding to meet the two angels for homosexual rape. Lot offered his daughters to them, but the men would not stop their demands. Finally, the angels caused

go to

Sodom
Isaiah 3:9;
Jude 7

the men of Sodom to become blind so that they could not find the door into Lot's family and guests.

The angels told Lot to take his family and leave the city, because the Lord would destroy it. When dawn arrived, the angels dragged the family out of the city. While running for their lives, Lot's family was forbidden to look back. Lot's wife disobeyed and was turned into a pillar of salt.

God sent judgment. Raining brimstone and fire charred the cities so that there was no life left. From a distance, Abraham stood looking toward Sodom and saw the dense smoke rising to the sky.

The two angels who visited Sodom observed evidence of the wickedness that had risen up to God as an outcry. Up until the moment of destruction, the men of Sodom "were exceedingly wicked and sinful against the LORD" (Genesis 13:13 NKJV).

He Climbed the Ladder of Success (But It Was Leaning on the Wrong Wall)

Lot had chosen the fertile fields around Sodom for his financial advantage (Genesis 13:10–11). This required moving his family to Sodom and associating closely with its people. In time, he became a respected leader in the community, even becoming a judge who sat "in the gate of Sodom" (Genesis 19:1 NKJV), giving his opinion on legal transactions. It seems that Lot said the right words, but his lifestyle proved that he was compromising with the wrong people.

Trouble in Sodom

God's angels came to confirm that the sins of Sodom and Gomorrah were as great as had been indicated by the outcry that had reached God. He knew with absolute certainty, of course, but he was demonstrating his justice.

The on-site visit of the angels served only to confirm the evil in Sodom. The demands of the male citizens gave evidence of the wickedness that God knew was rampant.

When the men of Sodom demanded that Lot release his guests to them for sexual abuse, Lot showed the degree to which he had bought into the thinking of his neighbors. He went outside to talk with them, closing the door behind him. While refusing to surrender his guests to their evil designs, he offered instead his two unmarried daughters for their evil designs. This compromise did not satisfy the men. They continued their rude demands, adding derision to Lot as an alien who was now daring to act as their judge. They began to threaten Lot himself. Lot lost credibility with his neighbors because he had compromised his spiritual values.

Suddenly, the angels opened the door, reached out, and pulled Lot back into the house, closing the door behind him. Then they caused the men to be blind so that they could not even locate the door to break it down.

go to

merciful
Deuteronomy 4:31

No Laughing Matter

There was no turning back. God's judgment was imminent. The angels told Lot to round up his family members: his wife, daughters, and sons-in-law who were pledged to marry his daughters. Lot went to warn his sons-in-law of the impending judgment. But they didn't hasten to join Lot in the family exodus; to his sons-in-law, Lot "seemed to be joking" (Genesis 19:14 NKJV).

Long before this night, Lot had lost his credibility with the two men who were pledged to become members of his family. As a result, the two men perished with the other citizens of Sodom.

Running for Our Lives

Just at dawn the two angels urged Lot to hurry out of the city, taking with him his wife and two daughters. They were in danger of being "consumed in the punishment of the city" (Genesis 19:15 NKJV). "While he lingered, the [angels] took hold of his hand, his wife's hand, and the hands of his two daughters, the LORD being merciful to him, and they brought him out and set him outside the city" (verse 16 NKJV).

Once out of the city, the angels issued warnings: "Escape for your life! Do not look behind you nor stay anywhere in the plain. Escape to the mountains, lest you be destroyed" (Genesis 19:17 NKJV).

Instead of complying with the warning, however, Lot tried to negotiate, asking instead to flee only as far as Zoar (see Appendix B).

The angels gave their permission, and left Lot. By the time the family reached Zoar, the sun had risen. Then suddenly the Lord rained down brimstone and fire on Sodom and Gomorrah. It was a terrible destruction with burning flames and thick smoke ascending to the sky. Lot's wife could not resist the urge to look back on it, which was exactly what the angels had said they must not do. When she looked back, she became a pillar of salt.

what others say

Charles Caldwell Ryrie

Deposits of sulfur (brimstone) and asphalt (see Genesis 14:10) have been found in this area. Possibly an earthquake occurred and lightning ignited the gases that were released, causing a rain of fire and smoke.[4]

Lloyd Ogilvie

If you had to choose one word to describe the nature of God, what words would you choose? *All-powerful? All-knowing? Forgiving? Gracious?*

My word would be *merciful.* Whatever other words I might use are all part of this magnificent quality of mercy. I'm not alone in my choice. In the Old Testament the word is used nearly 200 times to describe the nature of God. The Hebrew word *chesedh* means both identification and empathy, involvement and intense feeling. . . . The mercy of God, from my experience and the biblical witness, is his favor, forgiveness, forbearance, and fortuitous intervention.[5]

Charles R. Swindoll

Why was [Lot's wife] "behind him"? Who knows for sure? I'd suggest she was still attached to that lifestyle. She willfully refused to cut off her emotional ties. All this business of running away and not looking back was awfully extreme, terribly unrealistic. . . . The bottom line of Mrs. Lot's philosophy could have been etched on her salt-block tombstone: THERE IS NO NEED TO TAKE GOD SERIOUSLY.[6]

something to ponder

Jesus is coming again. We do not know when this will be, but we know it will happen. Jesus warned that in the days of Noah, people were carrying on life as usual when the Flood came (Genesis 6–7). Then he added:

"Likewise as it was also in the days of Lot: They ate, they drank, they bought, they sold, they planted, they built; but on the day that

Lot went out of Sodom it rained fire and brimstone from heaven and destroyed them all.

"Even so will it be in the day when the Son of Man is revealed. In that day, he who is on the housetop, and his goods are in the house, let him not come down to take them away. And likewise the one who is in the field, let him not turn back. Remember Lot's wife. Whoever seeks to save his life will lose it, and whoever loses his life will preserve it. I tell you, in that night there will be two men in one bed: the one will be taken and the other will be left. Two women will be grinding together: the one will be taken and the other left. Two men will be in the field: the one will be taken and the other left" (Luke 17:28–36 NKJV).

go to

tormented
2 Peter 2:6–9

Desperate Daughters in the Dark

the big picture

Genesis 19:30–38

Lot and his two daughters settled in a cave some distance from the ruins of Sodom. There the young women succeeded in getting their father drunk so they could become pregnant by him.

Years before, Lot had left Ur (see Appendix B) with his uncle Abram. The potential of being under the covenant blessing had been his, and he had prospered. But he chose to leave all that when he decided to move to the lush area of the Jordan Valley.

He was not completely happy in Sodom. We know he was tormented by the filthy lives of lawless men. Though he kept living among them, his righteous soul was tormented.

He ran for his life from Sodom to the little town of Zoar, but was afraid to stay there. At the end of his life story, we see him living in a mountain cave with his daughters, lying senseless. The daughters, thinking they were the sole survivors of their people, seduced Lot so that their family could continue. The descendants of their sons, Moab and Ben-Ammi, became the Moabites and the Ammonites, people who became enemies of the descendants of Abraham.

Lot's biography is a series of steps downward, all tragic:

- He left Ur and Haran (see Appendix B) with his uncle Abram to travel to an unknown destination. (Genesis 12:1–5)

- When given an opportunity to choose the grazing area for his herds, he selfishly chose the fertile valley near Sodom. (Genesis 13:1–11)
- He pitched his tent on the outskirts of Sodom. (Genesis 13:12–13)
- He fit into the new community so well that he became a leader, even a judge who sat at the gate to give judgment on issues. (Genesis 19:1)
- Because he fit so well in the community, the men of Sodom did not hesitate to demand that he release his two guests for their homosexual purposes. (Genesis 19:4–5)
- Not wanting to give his guests to the townsmen's disgusting designs, he offered them instead his virgin daughters. (Genesis 19:6–8)
- He tried to get his sons–in-law to escape the destruction of Sodom with his wife and daughters. They thought he was only joking. (Genesis 19:12–14)
- Angels dragged him out of Sodom and told him to run to the mountains for safety. (Genesis 19:16–17)
- Lot negotiated with the angels, seeking approval to stay closer to Sodom. (Genesis 19:18–22)
- Lot was afraid, so he hid in a cave with his daughters. (Genesis 19:30)
- Lot's daughters got him drunk and used him to impregnate themselves. (Genesis 19:31–36)
- The sons born of the daughters become the Moabites and the Ammonites, enemies of Abraham's descendants. (Genesis 19:37–38)

Where did Lot lose his dignity and faith? Not in big earthshaking decisions but in making numerous small choices that left God out of his life.

Chapter Wrap-Up

- Abraham had three special visitors—angels and, possibly, the Lord himself. He welcomed them and fed them. One visitor told him that Sarah would have a son within the year. Sarah, hearing this, laughed in disbelief. When the visitor accused her of laughing, she denied it. (Genesis 18:1–15)
- The Lord reviewed his promises to Abraham, then told Abraham he was going to destroy Sodom and Gomorrah because of the people's wickedness. Abraham asked him not to destroy the city if fifty righteous people could be found there. The Lord agreed not to. Then Abraham changed the number to forty-five and the Lord again agreed. Abraham continued changing the number until God agreed to spare the cities if ten righteous people could be found there. (Genesis 18:16–33)
- The two angels who had visited Abraham went to Sodom. Lot invited them to spend the night at his home. Later, men of Sodom surrounded the house and demanded that Lot bring out his guests so they could have sex with them. Unable to disperse the crowd, Lot offered them his daughters instead. When this didn't appease them, Lot's life became endangered. The two angelic visitors brought him inside and struck the crowd with blindness. (Genesis 19:1–11)
- The angels told Lot to gather his family members to leave the city, which was going to be destroyed. Lot tried to get his daughters' fiancés to come, but they laughed at him and didn't believe him. (Genesis 19:12–14)
- The angels led Lot, his wife, and their two daughters out of the city, then told them to run to the mountains for safety. Lot begged to go only as far as Zoar and was allowed to do so. Then God destroyed Sodom and Gomorrah. Though Lot's family had been warned not to look back, his wife did. She was turned into a pillar of salt. (Genesis 19:15–26)
- Lot and his daughters hid in a cave. There the daughters got him drunk so they could become pregnant by him to continue their family line. (Genesis 19:30–38)

Study Questions

1. Abraham laughed when God told him that he and Sarah would have a son (Genesis 17:17). Sarah also laughed when she heard the special visitor say she would have a son within a year. What was the difference in their laughter?

2. Why do you think Abraham kept asking God to spare the city of Sodom for fewer and fewer righteous people?

3. What indications were there that Lot had been greatly influenced for wrong by living in Sodom?

4. What does this story teach us about God's mercy?

5. What can we learn about Jesus' second coming from Lot's story?

Genesis 20 Abraham and Abimelech

Chapter Highlights:
- Abraham's Deception Exposed
- On the Move
- A Mutual Agreement
- God's Protection

Let's Get Started

While we may show our heroes in only a positive light, God tells the truth about their weaknesses and lapses.

Abraham knew God to be the Judge of all the earth who does only what is right (Genesis 18:25). Yet we see Abraham in a lapse of faith again, lying about Sarah in order to save his life. Abraham left Mamre and stayed at Gerar (see Appendix B), a Philistine city. Abimelech, king of Gerar, took Sarah into his household, believing that she was Abraham's unmarried sister.

We then see God's mercy as he intervenes and protects all parties. Abraham was afraid that the godless king would kill him in order to take Sarah, but the king showed respect for God and sent Abraham away.

afraid
Proverbs 29:25

Abraham's Deception Exposed

Fear can turn a brave person into a coward. Abraham discovered this when he moved to Gerar. Fearing for his life, he told a lie and immediately put Sarah in jeopardy!

the big picture

Genesis 20:1-13

When Abraham arrived in Gerar he introduced Sarah as his sister. Abimelech, king of Gerar, felt free to add her to his harem, thinking she was unmarried. God revealed to Abimelech in a dream that he was in great danger because he had unknowingly taken a married woman.

Abimelech advised all his officials of the alarming situation and then confronted Abraham with his deception. Abraham made excuses for himself, saying that he feared for his life and that Sarah was in fact his half sister.

Sodom and Gomorrah had been destroyed. Abraham had not heard from Lot and did not know he had been saved. Perhaps the view from Abraham's tent was a painful reminder of his lost nephew, so he decided to move from Mamre, where he had lived for twenty years. Or, as some suggest, there may have been another famine impending in that part of the land.

He came to Gerar, a Philistine city ruled by a powerful king, Abimelech. His name means "my father is king" and was an inherited title rather than his personal name. On arriving, Abraham and Sarah introduced themselves as brother and sister, a practice they had agreed to follow (Genesis 20:13).

Abraham was afraid that if the king knew Sarah was his wife, he would kill Abraham in order to marry Sarah. Even though Sarah was almost ninety years old, the king took her into his household. Abraham's fear of the king led to his lapse of faith.

what others say

Derek Kidner

The episode is chiefly one of suspense: on the brink of Isaac's birth-story here is the very Promise put in jeopardy, traded away for personal safety. If it is ever to be fulfilled, it will owe very little to man. Morally as well as physically, it will clearly have to be achieved by the grace of God.[1]

Elisabeth Elliot

Hundreds of times in Scripture we are told not to be afraid. How can we help it? If someone we love is in danger, if awful possibilities constantly present themselves, what are we to do? The psalmist gives the answer: "When I am afraid, I will trust in you" (Psalm 56:3). He brings the two conflicting powers, emotion and will, into a single verse. He's a realist. He does not deny the feeling, but he doesn't let that govern his life either, or drain the energy God gives for his work. He feels one thing, he does another. He applies the antidote. I think the best way to do that is simply to offer up to the Lord each fear as it arises, and pray for grace to go on peacefully doing the work he has given us to do.[2]

Trouble in the Royal Household

One night Abimelech had a dream in which God spoke to him: "Indeed you are a dead man because of the woman you have taken, for she is a man's wife" (Genesis 20:3 NKJV).

Abimelech was stunned at the news and very frightened. Thankful that he had not gone near Sarah, he asked God, "Will You slay a righteous nation also? Did he not say to me, 'She is my sister'? And she, even she herself said, 'He is my brother.' In the integrity of my heart and innocence of my hands I have done this" (20:4–5 NKJV).

go to

Egypt
Genesis 12:10–20

God replied, "Yes, I know that you did this in the integrity of your heart. For I also withheld you from sinning against Me; therefore I did not let you touch her. Now therefore, restore the man's wife; for he is a prophet, and he will pray for you and you shall live. But if you do not restore her, know that you shall surely die, you and all who are yours" (20:6–7 NKJV).

That Same Lie, Take Two

Wisely, Abimelech took his dream very seriously. Rising early, he called in all his officials. When he related to them all that had occurred, they "were very much afraid" (Genesis 20:8 NKJV).

Abimelech summoned Abraham to a meeting in which he confronted him with his wrongdoing. "What have you done to us?" he asked accusingly. "How have I offended you, that you have brought on me and on my kingdom a great sin? You have done deeds to me that ought not to be done." He then went beyond accusing and demanded an answer: "What did you have in view, that you have done this thing?" (See 20:9–10 NKJV.)

Abraham gave two excuses in his deception. First, he feared for his life because he viewed the people of Gerar as not fearing God. Second, he said that Sarah was really his half sister, so he had not told a complete lie. Abraham did not trust God to take care of him if he told the truth.

something to ponder

Abraham had been scolded for this sin once before when he was in Egypt. Even a person who has a long-standing trust in God can fall into the same sin for which he has previously repented.

go to

pride
Proverbs 16:18

what others say

F. B. Meyer

In a certain sense, no doubt, Sarah was his sister. She was the daughter of his father, though not the daughter of his mother. But she was much more his wife than his sister, and to withhold that fact was to withhold the one fact that was essential to the maintenance of his honor and the protection of her virtue. We are not bound to tell the whole truth to gratify an idle curiosity, but we are bound not to withhold the one item that another should know before completing a bargain if the knowledge of it would materially alter the result. A lie consists in the motive quite as much as in the actual words. We may unwittingly say that which is actually false, meaning above all things to speak the truth, and, though a lie in kind, there is no lie in fact. On the other hand, like Abraham, we may utter true words, meaning them to convey a false impression, and in the sight of heaven, we are guilty of a deliberate and shameful falsehood.[3]

A Mutual Agreement

the big picture

Genesis 20:14–18

Abimelech was desperate to be relieved of his guilt and God's judgment on him. He returned Sarah to Abraham, gave him gifts, and invited him to live wherever he liked in Philistine country. Abraham prayed for all in Abimelech's household to be healed.

Abimelech wanted to make things right with Abraham and his God.

- He gave sheep, cattle, and slaves to Abraham.
- He returned Sarah.
- He offered Abraham permission to live wherever he wished in the land.
- He told Sarah that he was giving her "brother" one thousand pieces of silver (Genesis 20:16 NKJV).

For his part, Abraham prayed to God, and the Lord healed Abimelech and all his household. To protect Sarah, God had "closed up all the wombs of the house of Abimelech" (Genesis 20:18 NKJV).

Who was the better man? Abraham, the father of our faith, or a Philistine king? We have an amazing revelation of character in Genesis 20. Abraham had been chosen by God to be the conduit of blessing to the whole world. He had been privileged to have conversations with God and had received promises from God that no one else had received. He felt that in going to the Philistine city of Gerar he would be mingling with people who had no fear of God. That was his excuse for lying about Sarah. He certainly stumbled in his walk of faith and caused God's judgment to come on Abimelech.

something to ponder

Still, God called Abraham his **prophet**, and he answered Abraham's prayer for judgment to be lifted, thus saving Abimelech's life and removing the barrenness of all of Abimelech's household.

go to

wisdom
James 1:5

Abimelech

Abimelech, on the other hand, recognized that God was speaking to him through his dream (Genesis 20:3–7). He also understood that to take another man's wife would be wrong and would make him guilty before God. He, the **pagan** king, confronted Abraham with his lie and then took steps to be relieved of his guilt. In offering Abraham a generous compensation, Abimelech acknowledged his wrongdoing, though in his reference to Sarah's brother he seemed to be insisting upon his innocence.

prophet
one who declares a message on behalf of God

pagan
one who does not believe in the true God

God's Protection

Through his lack of faith, Abraham was prepared to jeopardize God's covenant promises to him. God was not caught off guard. He protected Sarah by keeping Abimelech from her and by informing the king through a dream of the lies that both Abraham and Sarah had told.

Abraham stumbled when he relied on his own problem-solving skills while he should have trusted the Lord for protection. God promises to give wisdom to all who ask him for it.

something to ponder

Chapter Wrap-Up

- Abraham and Sarah moved to Gerar. They told King Abimelech that Sarah was Abraham's sister, so the king felt free to take her into his household for himself. However, God spoke to the king in a dream and warned him that he must return Abraham's wife to him or he was a dead man. God had shown mercy on the king by not allowing him to touch Sarah. (Genesis 20:1–7)
- The king confronted Abraham with his deceit. Abraham's excuses were fear for his life in an ungodly land and that technically Sarah was his half sister. (Genesis 20:8–13)
- Abimelech returned Abraham's wife to him and also gave him gifts. He invited Abraham to live wherever he wanted in the country. (Genesis 20:14–16)
- Abraham prayed and God healed the women in the king's household whose wombs he had closed up. (Genesis 20:17–18)

Study Questions

1. What were Abraham's excuses for not telling Abimelech that Sarah was his wife?
2. What does God's dealing with Abimelech teach us about God's righteousness? About God's mercy?
3. Why do you think Abraham, who had demonstrated his faith in God in so many ways for so many years, had lapses in his faith, such as this one?
4. What can we learn from this story about our daily interaction with people who do not know God?

Genesis 21 Reordering Life

Chapter Highlights:
- The Birth of Laughter
- Hagar and Ishmael Are Sent Away
- Agreement with Abimelech

Let's Get Started

Life on planet Earth has its ups and downs, its pleasures and its frustrations. This is illustrated clearly in Genesis 21.

Sarah giving birth to Isaac was a tremendous high. God had kept his promise. As Abraham held little Isaac in his arms, he must have laughed with joy. His years of waiting were over. It would seem that joy would pervade the lives of Abraham and Sarah forever.

Then a cloud settled over the household when during a great feast celebrating Isaac's weaning, Sarah watched Ishmael mock her son. Furious, she insisted that Abraham banish Hagar and Ishmael. This, of course, caused great grief to Abraham because of his love for Ishmael.

Family problems needed to be set aside when a difficulty arose with Abraham's Philistine neighbors. Having observed Abraham's prosperity and strength, Abimelech arrived to ask for a treaty. Abraham settled a controversy over water rights, and life with the neighbors went on peacefully.

The Birth of Laughter—Centennial Son

Weeks, months, years of trusting, hoping, wondering were about to end. It was God's time to fulfill the promise he had made to Abraham years before. Laughter was soon to bubble up in the hearts of Abraham and Sarah.

the big picture

Genesis 21:1–7

God was gracious in keeping his promise to Sarah. She became pregnant at the time God had said, and she gave birth to the son he had promised her. Following God's instruction (Genesis 17:19), Abraham named the baby Isaac, which means "laughter." Again following God's instruction (17:9–14), Abraham circumcised Isaac when he was eight days old.

go to

Hannah
1 Samuel 2:21

Elizabeth
Luke 1:13, 24

GOD AT WORK

> Joyfully, Sarah announced that in her old age God had brought her laughter.

God was very much involved in the birth of Isaac. He was gracious to Sarah, enabling her to become pregnant, as he had promised long before. He scheduled Isaac's birth precisely at the time he had predicted. A year before, when God had told Sarah that she would have a son, she had laughed silently with unbelief. After years of waiting, hoping, and longing, it seemed impossible that she could ever have the son God had promised (Genesis 18:9–15). Now she laughed aloud with purest joy. She said, "God has made me laugh, and all who hear will laugh with me . . . Who would have said to Abraham that Sarah would nurse children? For I have borne him a son in his old age" (21:6–7 NKJV).

The word translated "visited" (Genesis 21:1 NKJV) has also been translated "gracious." God was gracious in enabling Sarah to become pregnant. The same word is used in connection with Hannah becoming pregnant with Samuel and, many years later, Elizabeth becoming pregnant with John the Baptist.

what others say

Dallas Willard

Abraham fell on the ground laughing when told by God that he, a one-hundred-year-old man, would have a child by ninety-year-old Sarah (Genesis 17:17). Later Sarah herself laughed at the same "joke" (Genesis 18:12–15). God specified to Abraham that the child of promise would be named "Laughter." Isaac means "Laughter." "Your wife shall bear you a son, and you shall call his name Laughter, and I will establish my covenant with him" (Genesis 17:19). Was this a penalty imposed upon them because they laughed? Hardly. Rather, it was a perpetual reminder that God breaks through. What joy they had when little Laughter came into their home and as he grew to become a young man![1]

Hagar and Ishmael Are Sent Away

It seemed the laughter that had filled Abraham's household would go on forever. Isaac had brought so much joy to them all. But one day the laughter was choked in Sarah's throat. She lost her joy and immediately took steps to remove the source of her unhappiness.

expel
to drive away

weaned
gradually stopping dependence on the mother's milk

persecuting
directing hostility toward another

the big picture

Genesis 21:8–21

Isaac grew, and when he was weaned, Abraham hosted a feast to celebrate. Sarah observed Ishmael mocking Isaac, so she insisted to Abraham that he **expel** Hagar and Ishmael from the household.

Abraham was greatly distressed, but God told him to comply with Sarah's demand. God would keep his promise to make Ishmael into a nation.

Abraham sent Hagar and Ishmael away, giving them food and water for their journey. Before long, as they were in the desert, they ran out of water needed for their survival. God heard the boy's cries and sent an angel to rescue Hagar in her desperate need and to assure her that he would make Ishmael into a great nation. God opened Hagar's eyes and she saw a well of water which provided for their need.

A Feast That Turned Sour

Abraham and Sarah celebrated with a feast when Isaac was **weaned**. Family members, servants, and neighbors were probably in attendance. The happy event was marred, however, when Sarah observed Ishmael mocking Isaac. In the New Testament, Paul refers to Ishmael **persecuting** Isaac (Galatians 4:28–31).

In ancient times, a child was not weaned until he was two or three years old. When this important stage was reached in the child's development, the father would host a celebration.

During the process of weaning, a child would cry for his mother's milk and express distaste for the substitute nourishment. The psalm-writer referred to this when he wrote about the way he had "calmed and quieted" his soul before the Lord, like a "weaned child with his mother" (Psalm 131:2 NKJV).

what others say

Gene Getz

Ishmael was probably in his mid-teens. As an alert teenager, he saw clearly what was happening. Ever since he was old enough to understand, he had been told by his parents that he was the promised seed. But for the last three years, he had been getting another message. He discovered his parents had made a serious mistake. Naturally, he would feel deceived and victimized.

> Anger welled up within Ishmael as Isaac became the center of attention. The great feast and the glad speeches in Isaac's honor were the last straws for Ishmael. His growing feelings of bitterness erupted with ridicule and mockery (Genesis 21:9). We can only conjecture what he did and how he did it, but one thing is certain—Ishmael pushed Sarah too far, and she reacted with intense anger.[2]

A Journey That Ended with a Promise

Sarah was extremely upset to see Ishmael, now a teenager, teasing Isaac. She now saw his very presence in the camp as a threat to Isaac. There could be no mistaking her decisiveness as she demanded that Abraham "cast out this bondwoman and her son" (Genesis 21:10 NKJV). She wanted to be sure that Ishmael did not receive any portion of the inheritance that was rightfully Isaac's.

Abraham was in anguish because he loved his son Ishmael. How could he send him away? But God spoke to him, telling him not to be distressed but to listen to what Sarah was saying. The promises of God were to come through Isaac, not through Ishmael. However, since Ishmael was Abraham's son, God would make a nation of him also.

Early the next morning, Abraham sent Hagar and Ishmael away, giving them food and water for the journey. However, the water was soon consumed as they walked in the desert.

When they could no longer go on, Hagar put Ishmael under the shade of a bush. She seated herself at a little distance, unable to bring herself to watch her son die. They both wept. Hagar cried in total despair. Ishmael cried out to God, and he heard the boy.

God sent his angel to speak with Hagar. "What ails you, Hagar? Fear not, for God has heard the voice of the lad where he is. Arise, lift up the lad and hold him with your hand, for I will make him a great nation" (Genesis 21:17–18 NKJV).

The angel's instructions must have seemed like mockery to Hagar. It would be cruel to expect the boy to move in his condition. Cruel—until God opened Hagar's eyes. A well of water was close by. She hurried to fill the waterskin and give Ishmael a lifesaving drink.

God was with Ishmael as he matured. He lived in the desert, became an archer, and married a woman from Egypt.

what others say

Stephen Fortosis

In a sense, Ishmael was a symbol of Abraham and Sarah's lack of faith. God knew that they should have faithfully waited for the promised son. However, when Ishmael was conceived, God did not angrily reject him and toss him aside. Instead, God loved the boy and agreed to bless him. When our frail faith results in costly mistakes, God can turn our penitent regret into blessing for his own purposes.[3]

go to

wrath
Psalm 76:10

Same Dad, Different Destinies

Ishmael	Isaac
Birth arranged by Sarah	Birth promised by God
Conceived by Hagar	Conceived by Sarah
Son of a slave	Born free
Abraham named him after his birth	God named him before he was conceived
Circumcised as a boy when God instituted the rite	Circumcised when eight days old, as God had directed

It was God's purpose that Ishmael be removed from Abraham's household. Nothing should be allowed to distract Abraham from raising Isaac as the child of God's covenant promise. God used the ridicule of Ishmael and Sarah's anger to accomplish his purpose. He comforted Abraham's aching heart with special promises for Ishmael's future. This was an act of mercy, since Ishmael's birth had been Abraham's attempt to help God provide the son he had promised. God can use even the wrath of imperfect humans to accomplish his purposes.

something to ponder

Agreement with Abimelech—Payback Time

Abimelech had been aware of God's blessing on Abraham. To protect himself from any aggression on Abraham's part, Abimelech arrived one day with his army chief of staff to negotiate a treaty with Abraham.

the big picture

Genesis 21:22-34

Abimelech approached Abraham to ask for a treaty. He wanted assurance that Abraham would show kindness to him and his descendants, much as he had shown kindness to Abraham. After they agreed, Abraham raised a complaint. Abimelech's servants had taken over one of Abraham's wells, but Abimelech denied any knowledge of it. To seal the treaty, Abraham gave sheep and cattle to Abimelech. After Abimelech returned home, "Abraham planted a tamarisk tree in Beersheba, and there called on the name of the LORD, the Everlasting God" (verse 33 NKJV).

It had been about three years since Abimelech had offered Abraham permission to live wherever he wished in Philistine territory (Genesis 20:15). Abraham was living about twenty-five miles from Gerar. Already a wealthy man, Abraham continued to prosper. The possibility of disputes arising over the land was great. It was time for the two men to make an agreement.

Abimelech arrived with Phichol, the commander of his forces, and asked for a treaty. He said, "God is with you in all that you do. Now therefore, swear to me by God that you will not deal falsely with me, with my offspring, or with my posterity; but that according to the kindness that I have done to you, you will do to me and to the land in which you have dwelt" (21:22–23 NKJV).

Abraham willingly gave his word.

Then There's the Matter of the Well

Abraham raised a complaint to Abimelech. One of Abraham's wells had been seized by Abimelech's servants. Abraham had agreed to the treaty, so he would not take aggressive action to get his well back, but he was free to voice his complaint.

Abimelech excused himself, saying that he did not know who had taken the well and that he had not been advised of the wrong until that day.

Surprisingly, the Bible account does not say how the issue was resolved. Instead, we learn that Abraham brought a gift of sheep and cattle to Abimelech and the treaty was formally made.

Abraham set aside seven ewe lambs. When Abimelech asked the meaning of this action, Abraham explained that they were a gift that sealed the fact that Abraham was the legitimate owner of the well.

what others say

Derek Kidner

The Hebrew verb suggests that Abraham had to make his complaint several times; perhaps Abimelech was adept at evasive tactics. The glimpse of a running rivalry over the wells makes the reopening of the whole matter with Isaac in chapter 26 highly predictable.[4]

Victor P. Hamilton

No sacrificial activity is involved, nor is there any covenant meal. The parties swear to the pact simply in words. In accepting the lamb Abimelech releases rights over the well and concedes ownership to the patriarch. In other words, Abimelech is challenged to accept the reliability of Abraham's word, I dug this well, and to side with him in any future altercation. Of course, in an incident not too far removed from this one, Abraham's earlier word to Abimelech had been anything but reliable. If Abraham can cheat on the truth about Sarah, can he do the same with the truth about a well?[5]

Chapter Wrap-Up

- God kept his promise and Sarah gave birth to a son who was named Isaac. Sarah laughed, this time with joy. Following God's command, Abraham circumcised Isaac when he was eight days old. (Genesis 21:1–4)

- When Isaac was weaned at age two or three, Abraham gave a celebration feast. During the celebration Sarah saw Ishmael, a teenager, mocking her son. She angrily insisted that Abraham get rid of Hagar and Ishmael immediately. (Genesis 21:8–10)

- God told Abraham to do what Sarah said, and with great sorrow, he gave them food and water and sent Hagar and Ishmael away. (Genesis 21:12–14)

- Running out of water in the desert, Hagar was sure her son would die, but she cried out to God, and God sent an angel to speak to Hagar. The angel assured the anguished mother that God had heard her. Not only would Ishmael not die, he would become a great nation. God provided water for them, and Ishmael grew up to be an archer living in the desert, married to an Egyptian woman. (Genesis 21:15–21)

- King Abimelech asked Abraham to make a treaty with him. Abraham agreed, but complained that the king's servants had taken over one of Abraham's wells. Abimelech denied knowing anything about the well. The treaty was made and Abraham sealed the treaty, giving the king sheep and cattle. Abraham challenged Abimelech to accept his word that the well was his. (Genesis 21:22–32)
- Abraham settled down in Beersheba (see Appendix B) and, living peacefully, worshiped God. (Genesis 21:33–34)

Study Questions

1. How did Isaac's birth once again show that God is El Shaddai, Almighty God?
2. In Genesis 21, how did God use human emotions to further his plan?
3. What do you think might have happened if Ishmael and Isaac had grown up together?
4. How did God help Ishmael, even though he was not the son God had promised Abraham?

Genesis 22–23 A Heartrending Test

Chapter Highlights:
- God Gives Abraham a Test
- Abraham Responds
- Family Affairs
- A Cave for Sarah

Let's Get Started

It all began in Ur of the Chaldeans when Abraham was seventy-five years old. God spoke to him, calling him to leave his country, his people, and even his household to go to a land that God would yet show him. God also promised to make Abraham into a great nation, a nation through which all peoples of the world would be blessed. Abraham started out in faith, trusting God to keep his word. That was just the beginning.

Through the years Abraham's relationship with God had involved one call to faith after another. For twenty-five years, Abraham waited for God to give him a son through whom God would bring other covenant blessings. When Sarah was ninety years old and Abraham was one hundred, God sent that son.

In Genesis 22, Abraham comes to the ultimate test—would he give up his son? If God told him to, would Abraham offer Isaac as a sacrifice?

The text then turns to Abraham's relatives: who they were and whether they fit in with God's covenant with Abraham.

Finally, Genesis 23 turns to the poignant account of the death of Sarah, and Abraham's desire to give her a burial place in the land that God had promised to him.

A Painful Assignment

GENESIS 22:1–2 ***Now it came to pass after these things that God tested Abraham, and said to him, "Abraham!" And he said, "Here I am." Then He said, "Take now your son, your only son Isaac, whom you love, and go to the land of Moriah, and offer him there as a burnt offering on one of the mountains of which I shall tell you."*** *(NKJV)*

go to

image
Genesis 1:27

offerings
Leviticus 5:17–19

Savior
Genesis 3:15

blood
Genesis 9:5–6

children
Leviticus 20:1–5; Jeremiah 32:35

burnt offering
a sacrifice in which an animal is consumed by fire

Molech
a pagan deity associated with sacrificing children

God had told Abraham to send Ishmael away, and Abraham had obeyed (Genesis 21:8–21). Now God was telling him to sacrifice Isaac, the son of promise. He was to take Isaac to Mount Moriah (future site of Jerusalem, see Appendix B) and sacrifice him as a **burnt offering**.

Sacrificing children as an offering to pagan gods was practiced in that time, but never by a godly person. The command must have been abhorrent to Abraham, first as it would be to any loving parent and then because God's covenant promises were bound in Isaac and his offspring.

How God values humans:

- God created life, making man and woman in his image. He loved the people he made and desired to have a close friendship with them.
- When sin became a barrier that separated people from their holy Creator, he provided offerings and the promise of the Savior to make a way for friendship to be restored.
- After the Flood, God said he would demand an accounting of anyone who shed the blood of a person, since people were made in God's image.
- Later, God expressly stated in strongest terms that he would set his face against a person who sacrificed his children to **Molech**. God was testing Abraham.

what others say

The Bible Knowledge Commentary

It is one thing to claim to trust God's word when waiting for something; it is quite another thing to trust and obey His word after it is received. This was a test of how much Abraham would obey God's word. Would he cling to the boy now that he had him, or would he still obey and return him to the Lord? In other words how far would Abraham go in obedience? Did he really believe that God would still keep his word and raise the seed of promise?[1]

Abraham Responds

We cannot imagine the anguish in Abraham's heart as he thought about the painful duty that lay ahead. We do know, though, how he acted. He took action early the following morning to obey God.

the big picture

Genesis 22:3-11

Early the next morning Abraham took Isaac and two servants, along with wood for the burnt offering, and set out on a three-day journey to the place God had specified. On the third day, Abraham left the servants with the donkey while he and Isaac went further up to worship. "Abraham took the wood of the burnt offering and laid it on Isaac his son; and he took the fire in his hand, and a knife" (verse 6 NKJV). When Isaac asked about the lamb they would need for the sacrifice, Abraham replied that God would provide it.

When they reached the place God had specified, Abraham built an altar, arranged the wood on it, and then bound Isaac and laid him on the altar. He took the knife and prepared to kill Isaac, but an angel called out to him.

A Painful Journey

God had given clear directions, but he did not force Abraham's obedience. Abraham chose his response.

He did not delay. Early the next morning he made his preparations for the fifty-mile journey to Mount Moriah. He saddled his donkey and cut wood for the offering. Taking Isaac and two servants, he started out.

key point

What explanation did he offer? What did they talk about as they headed north? We do not know. But we do know that Abraham did not falter in his faith. God had promised, "In Isaac your seed shall be called" (Genesis 21:12 NKJV). He knew God would be true to his word. God is true to himself. He is always consistent with his character.

When the party arrived at Mount Moriah, Abraham told his servants, "Stay here with the donkey; the lad and I will go yonder and worship, and we will come back to you" (22:5 NKJV). There was no doubt in Abraham's mind—Isaac would be returning with him.

temple
2 Chronicles 3:1

Golgotha
Mark 15:22–24

Abraham placed the wood for the burnt offering on Isaac, while he carried the fire and the knife. As father and son started to walk a distance from the servants, Isaac took note of what they were carrying and asked his father, "Where is the lamb for a burnt offering?" Abraham replied, "My son, God will provide for Himself the lamb for a burnt offering" (22:7–8 NKJV).

They approached the place God had specified. Abraham "built an altar there and placed the wood in order; and he bound Isaac his son and laid him on the altar...And Abraham stretched out his hand and took the knife to slay his son.

"But the angel of the LORD called to him from heaven and said, 'Abraham, Abraham!' So he said, 'Here I am'" (22:9–11 NKJV).

Faith in Action

Abraham did not know what God would do, but he knew God would keep his promise that the covenant blessings would come through Isaac. He expressed his faith by telling the servants that he and Isaac were going apart to worship and would come back to them. He expressed his faith when he told Isaac that "God will provide for Himself the lamb" (Genesis 22:8 NKJV). He also believed that if he did in fact sacrifice Isaac, God would raise him from the dead (Hebrews 11:17–19).

what others say

F. B. Meyer

What a significant expression is that word *worship*! It reflects the mood of the patriarch's mind. He was preoccupied with that Being, at whose command he had gone forth on this sorrowful errand. He looked upon his God, at the moment when he was asking so great a gift, as only deserving adoration and worship. The loftiest sentiment that can fill the heart of man swayed his whole nature, and it seemed to him as if his costliest and dearest treasure was not too great to give to that great and glorious God who was the one object of his life.[2]

God directed Abraham to go to Mount Moriah. The temple was later built on that mountain. Jesus was crucified outside the walls of Jerusalem at Golgotha, a rock formation that resembled a skull. This was in the general area where Abraham built the altar on which he was prepared to sacrifice his son.

Abe Earns an A

Abraham passed his test. We read the report in the New Testament:

"By faith Abraham, when he was tested, offered up Isaac, and he who had received the promises offered up his only begotten son, of whom it was said, 'In Isaac your seed shall be called,' concluding that God was able to raise him up, even from the dead, from which he also received him in a figurative sense" (Hebrews 11:17–19 NKJV).

something to ponder

God assures us that he will never tempt us, but he does test us. His tests are intended to be learning experiences through which we can grow stronger: "Blessed is the man who endures temptation; for when he has been approved, he will receive the crown of life which the Lord has promised to those who love Him. Let no one say when he is tempted, 'I am tempted by God'; for God cannot be tempted by evil, nor does He Himself tempt anyone. But each one is tempted when he is drawn away by his own desires and enticed" (James 1:12–14 NKJV).

Ramming the Lesson Home

God never intended that Abraham would actually sacrifice Isaac. He let Abraham make the preparation, and then he intervened. Abraham had passed the test.

the big picture

Genesis 22:12-19

The angel spoke from heaven telling him not to harm Isaac. Abraham had demonstrated his fear of God by being willing to sacrifice his son. Abraham saw a ram caught by its horns. He took it and sacrificed it as a burnt offering.

The angel spoke again to Abraham confirming God's promises to be fulfilled through Isaac so that all nations of the earth would receive the blessing.

Abraham had taken the test and passed. God stepped in at just the right moment.

When Abraham took the knife to sacrifice his son, the angel of the Lord stopped him, calling Abraham by name.

Abraham responded, "Here I am" (Genesis 22:11 NKJV), indicating that he was alert and attentive both to hear the next directive and to do whatever was asked of him.

The reply that came from the angel must have washed over Abraham's heart like balm from heaven. "Do not lay your hand on the lad," the angel said, "or do anything to him; for now I know that you fear God, since you have not withheld your son, your only son, from Me" (22:12 NKJV).

"Abraham lifted his eyes and looked, and there behind him was a ram caught in a thicket by its horns. So Abraham went and took the ram, and offered it up for a burnt offering instead of his son" (22:13 NKJV).

"Abraham called the name of the place, 'The-LORD-Will-Provide'" (22:14 NKJV). Again the angel spoke from heaven: "By Myself I have sworn, says the LORD, because you have done this thing, and have not withheld your son, your only son—blessing I will bless you, and multiplying I will multiply your descendants as the stars of the heaven and as the sand which is on the seashore; and your descendants shall possess the gate of their enemies. In your seed all the nations of the earth shall be blessed, because you have obeyed My voice" (22:16–18 NKJV).

Then Abraham and Isaac returned with the servants to Beersheba.

what others say

Warren Wiersbe

Our faith is not really tested until God asks us to bear what seems unbearable, do what seems unreasonable, and expect what seems impossible.[3]

Charles Caldwell Ryrie

God assures Abraham again that his covenant with him would be fulfilled. About 3,000 stars can be counted with the naked eye, but the comparison of Abraham's seed to dust and sand increases the number almost immeasurably.[4]

Family Affairs—News from a Far Country

It had been sixty years since Abraham had seen his family members who lived in Mesopotamia. Abraham and Sarah must have received news of the family as an indication of God's pleasure in his willingness to sacrifice Isaac.

the big picture

Genesis 22:20-24

Abraham received news of his brother Nahor and his wife Milcah. They had eight sons. Nahor also fathered four sons with his concubine.

Abraham must have been concerned about one part of God's promised blessing. Isaac was the key to producing offspring that would develop into a multitude. In order to do this, he needed a wife, but the women in Canaan (see Appendix B) were pagans and were not suitable to be part of God's covenant.

Abraham had not heard from his family since he left Haran many years before (see Appendix B). Now receiving news of his brother's expanded family must have given Abraham hope. Nahor had twelve sons and daughters. Surely somewhere in the extended family was a God-fearing woman who would be a suitable wife for Isaac. Within the list of family members were two names: Bethuel, Abraham's nephew, and Rebekah, his grandniece. Rebekah would later become Isaac's wife (see Illustration #7).

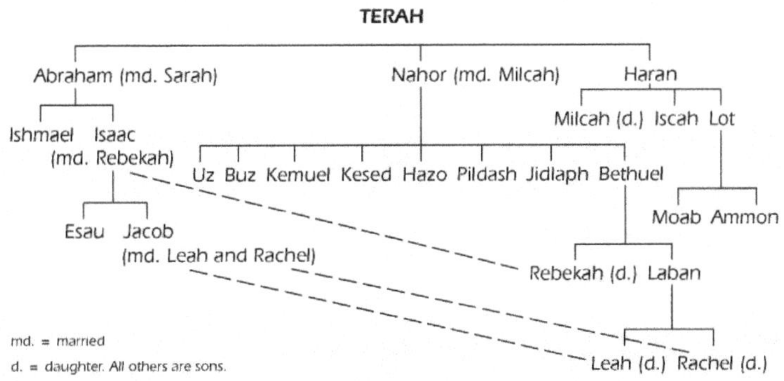

Illustration #7
Terah's Family—This chart shows Terah's family and how a number of his sons' offspring became a part of Abraham's family.

A Cave for Sarah

One indication of the closeness of the family unit is the level of grief when a loved one dies. When Sarah died, Abraham grieved. So did their son Isaac.

the big picture

Genesis 23

Sarah died when she was 127 years old. Abraham mourned for her and wept.

Abraham needed a place to bury her, but he had no burial ground. He approached the men of Heth and asked to purchase a piece of land. The men invited him to choose from the choicest of their tombs, and they would give it to him. Abraham had a particular cave in mind, but insisted on paying the fair price for it. The transaction was witnessed, and the field was deeded to Abraham as his property to be used as a burial site.

Buying What God Had Already Given

Abraham mourned the death of Sarah. They had been married more than sixty years and had gone through the tests of faith together. It was appropriate that he yield to his grief and express it with tears.

This is the first mention of Abraham weeping. There was no mention of tears when he went through other painful experiences that could have caused crying, for example:

- when he left Ur
- when he left Haran
- when Lot chose the better land for himself
- when he heard that Lot had been captured
- when he witnessed the destruction of Sodom
- when Sarah had insisted that Ishmael be sent away
- when God tested him by telling him to sacrifice Isaac

Abraham Buys a Burial Site

Abraham, having found a suitable cave for burying Sarah, initiated a somewhat delicate process of purchasing it. First he went to the Hittites and asked them to sell him property for a burial site. The Hittites responded respectfully, "Hear us, my lord: You are a mighty prince among us; bury your dead in the choicest of our burial places. None of us will withhold from you his burial place, that you may bury your dead" (Genesis 23:6 NKJV).

Abraham wisely countered the offer. If they would intercede with Ephron on his behalf for the cave of Machpelah, which Ephron owned, Abraham would pay the full price for it.

When Ephron heard of Abraham's request, he too offered to give the field with the cave to Abraham. Again Abraham respectfully insisted on paying the fair price for the field. Now Ephron stated the value of the field as four hundred shekels of silver, but again told Abraham he was welcome to accept it as a gift. Abraham still insisted on making it a business deal. He paid the four hundred shekels of silver, making the field his permanent possession by formal agreement witnessed by others.

The cave of Machpelah was the only property Abraham had purchased in the land God had promised him. In the time of Abraham, it was customary to bury remains in a tomb and to add the remains of other family members over a period of time. The cave Abraham purchased in order to bury Sarah later received Abraham's remains. Other family members were added. According to Jewish tradition, the tomb was in Hebron. King Herod built a wall around it, a wall which still stands two thousand years later.

How would Sarah be remembered?

- As a woman who risked everything to accompany her husband on a journey to an unknown destination?
- As a woman who joined her husband in believing promises that God made—believing even though they waited year after year for those promises to be fulfilled?
- As a woman who lied, claiming on two separate occasions that she was Abraham's sister instead of acknowledging she was his wife?
- As a woman who proposed that her husband use her maidservant to produce the son who would be heir to God's promises?
- As a woman who laughed silently when God promised that she would indeed have a son, even though she would be ninety years old when he was born?
- As a woman who laughed aloud with pure joy and delight when God fulfilled his promise, and she gave birth to a baby boy?
- As a woman who banished the maidservant and Abraham's son,

Ishmael, because she could not tolerate the thought that Ishmael might take part of the inheritance she wanted for her son-of-promise, Isaac?

In the New Testament the apostle Peter defines why we should remember Sarah, and his words are directed to women:

"Do not let your adornment be merely outward—arranging the hair, wearing gold, or putting on fine apparel—rather let it be the hidden person of the heart, with the incorruptible beauty of a gentle and quiet spirit, which is very precious in the sight of God. For in this manner, in former times, the holy women who trusted in God also adorned themselves, being submissive to their own husbands, as Sarah obeyed Abraham, calling him lord, whose daughters you are if you do good and are not afraid with any terror" (1 Peter 3:3–6 NKJV).

God values inner beauty of the heart more than outer beauty of adornment.

Chapter Wrap-Up

- God told Abraham to sacrifice his only son Isaac as a burnt offering on Mount Moriah. Abraham immediately set out with Isaac, two servants, and the items needed for the offering. (Genesis 22:1–3)
- Abraham and Isaac left the servants for the last part of the trip, but Abraham said he and Isaac would both return. When Isaac questioned where the lamb was that would be used for the offering, Abraham assured him that God would provide the lamb. (Genesis 22:4–8)
- After Abraham built an altar and got it ready for an offering, he tied up Isaac and laid him on the altar. As he raised the knife to kill his son, the angel of the Lord stopped him. (Genesis 22:9–12)
- God provided a ram, which Abraham sacrificed in place of his son. The angel confirmed God's promises to bless all nations through Isaac. Then Abraham and Isaac returned home. (Genesis 22:13–19)

- Abraham received news of his brother Nahor and Nahor's children. Within the list of family names was the name of Isaac's future wife. (Genesis 22:20–24)

- Sarah died at the age of 127, and Abraham wept. He inquired of the men of Heth about land to buy for her burial. They offered to give him a tomb, but Abraham refused. Instead, he bought the cave of Machpelah from Ephron, and Abraham buried Sarah there. This was the only property Abraham bought in the land God promised to give him. (Genesis 23)

Study Questions

1. Why do you think God chose to test Abraham's faith through his son Isaac?

2. What was so unusual about God instructing Abraham to sacrifice his son?

3. What evidences of faith in God did Abraham give as he was preparing to sacrifice his son?

4. What is the purpose of God testing people?

5. What was significant about Abraham burying Sarah in Canaan, rather than taking her back to their homeland?

Part Three
God and Isaac

BE SMART. BE INSPIRED.

Genesis 24 Isaac and Rebekah

Chapter Highlights:
- Abraham Seeks a Wife for Isaac
- A Trusted Servant Prays
- God Answers
- Time Out for Praise
- Here Comes the Bride

Let's Get Started

Abraham had a concern. Isaac needed a wife, but not one from the godless women in Canaan. He called his chief servant and commissioned him to go to his relatives and select a wife for Isaac. It was important to Abraham that the bride come to the land God had promised to give him and his descendants.

After a 450-mile journey, the servant arrived at the town where Abraham's relatives lived. He stopped at the well outside town and prayed that God would use a sign to guide him to God's chosen woman for Isaac. Rebekah came to the well and fulfilled the sign and even more. She invited the servant to stay, and he wound up dining with her brother, Laban.

When the servant told Laban of his mission, Laban gave Rebekah the choice to stay or go, and she consented to go with the servant to be Isaac's bride. Rebekah made the long journey to Canaan to meet her husband, and God brought joy to their hearts.

Abraham Seeks a Wife for Isaac

A loving parent cares deeply about the person who marries his child. But in Abraham's case, the issue was crucial. God's promised blessing to him and his descendants would be accomplished through the children born to Isaac and his wife. As an important part of God's promise, the woman needed to be a follower of the true God.

the big picture

Genesis 24:1–9

"Well advanced in age" (verse 1 NKJV), Abraham decided that he needed to take action in securing a wife for Isaac. He called in his chief servant and asked him to swear by the God of heaven and earth that he would not find a wife from the women in Canaan but would travel to the place where Abraham's family lived and to find a wife there.

Remember . . . No Pagan Brides!

Abraham was 140 years old. Isaac was forty. It was time for reflection. If God's promise of offspring was to be fulfilled, it was necessary for Isaac to have a wife.

Many years before, God had promised to bless Abraham. As he looked around, it was obvious that God had kept his promise:

"The LORD had blessed Abraham in all things" (Genesis 24:1 NKJV).

Abraham called in his chief servant, a man identified in Genesis 15:2 as Eliezer of Damascus. As chief servant, he would have been Abraham's heir if Abraham had died without a son. We cannot know for certain if Eliezer was still alive or if another man had been given this significant role in Abraham's household. Whoever the chief servant was, it is obvious that Abraham trusted him implicitly to understand the significance of God's covenant and to follow through to ensure that God's promises would not be thwarted.

Abraham asked the chief servant to swear by the Lord, the God of heaven and the God of earth, that he would not look for a wife for Isaac from among the women in Canaan. They were pagans and did not acknowledge Abraham's God. It was imperative that Isaac's wife would know God and would bear a son who would carry out God's covenant promise to Abraham. She needed to acknowledge the true God of heaven and earth.

The only place to find such a wife was in the community where Abraham's family lived. They at least had an understanding of Abraham's God and, hopefully, acknowledged him.

Still, this was another venture of faith for Abraham. There were no guarantees that the servant would find a wife that would fulfill Abraham's expectations.

what others say

Derek Kidner

To the very end, God's will for Isaac continued to make demands on Abraham's faith. With old age and wealth to anchor him to the past or present, he now looked on steadfastly to the next stage of the promise and acted with decision.[1]

What If . . . ?

Abraham's servant raised a logical question. In the event he went and found the prospective bride, what if she refused to move to the arid part of Canaan where Abraham lived. To Isaac, it was the Promised Land, but to her . . . ?

For Abraham, there was no discussion on this point. If the woman refused to come, the servant would be released from his oath. It was imperative that Isaac's future bride understand God's covenant and its tie to the land. Isaac, the son of promise, must not be removed from Canaan, the land of promise.

A Trusted Servant Prays

The servant had raised his questions and received his master's answers. Now was the time for action. He set out on his mission, committing its details to the Lord in prayer.

the big picture

Genesis 24:10-14

Abraham's servant followed his master's directions and trusted God for guidance. Arriving at the town of Nahor, he waited by the well and prayed that God would use a sign to identify the young woman who should become Isaac's wife.

I Can't Do It Alone!

Abraham's servant had been given a challenging assignment. He was to travel from Canaan to Aram Naharaim in northwest Mesopotamia (see Appendix B), a distance of about 450 miles that would take at least a month. His objective was to find a God-fearing

go to

put out a fleece
Judges 6:36–40

prayed
talked with God audibly or silently

sign
an indication of God's presence or purpose

woman from among Abraham's relatives who would be willing to return with him to marry a man she had never seen.

The servant traveled with ten camels, loaded with gifts to present to the young woman and her family as the bride-price. When he arrived at the town of Nahor, where Abraham's brother's family had settled, he stopped by the well outside the town. At evening the women would come out to draw water from the well. As he waited, the servant **prayed** that God would give him success and would show kindness to his master, Abraham. God usually guides through the Scripture and the counsel of godly people. Lacking these resources, the servant asked God to show him by a sign which woman should become Isaac's wife. This was the **sign**: when the women came, the servant would ask them for a drink of water from the well. If the woman would comply and then offer to water the camels as well, she would be the woman of choice for Isaac's bride.

what others say

Leith Anderson

Well, then, does prayer change things—or doesn't it? Before we try to answer this important question, think about what prayer is. Prayer is communion with God. Prayer is communication within relationship. From a biblical standpoint, change isn't what prayer is all about. It is more about love and relationship with God.[2]

Warren Wiersbe

The servant did what Gideon would do years later, "put out a fleece." This is not the best way for God's people to determine the will of God, because the conditions we lay down for God to meet might not be in his will. We are walking by sight and not by faith, and we may end up tempting God. However, God accommodated himself to the needs of the servant (and Gideon) and guided them as they requested.[3]

Jack W. Hayford

Many archaeologists have claimed that camels were not being domesticated at this time and for several centuries to come, in spite of a continuing record of camels through the early books of the Old Testament. However, camel bones have been dug from houses near Haran, and a record of expenditure for camel feed has been found in southern Turkey, both excavations dating from the patriarchal age.[4]

God Answers

God honored the simple faith of Abraham's servant. He had asked for guidance and a specific sign to indicate the woman of God's choice for Isaac. God answered with unmistakable clarity.

beka
half a shekel, .25 ounce

shekels
units of weight, about .4 ounce

the big picture

Genesis 24:15-53

Rebekah appeared and fulfilled the sign and took the servant to her father's house. There he discovered that he had arrived at the house of his master's relatives. The servant explained the purpose of his visit and how God had answered his prayer. After Rebekah's brother Laban and father Bethuel consented to the arrangement, the servant brought out gifts of jewelry and clothing for Rebekah and gifts for her brother and her mother.

Courting Becky by Proxy

Even before the servant had finished praying, Rebekah arrived with her jar to be filled from the well. She was very beautiful and was unmarried. As soon as she had filled her jar, the servant approached her and asked for a little water to drink. She immediately complied and then volunteered, "I will draw water for your camels also, until they have finished drinking" (Genesis 24:19 NKJV).

The servant must have watched with breathless anticipation. Was she the answer to his prayer? He had some time to observe her as she filled her jar and poured water into the trough for the thirsty camels. It is known that camels have three stomachs and can carry a three-day supply of water. To go to the well and draw water for ten camels would require hard work and persistence. When the camels had finished drinking, the servant presented her with a gold nose ring weighing a **beka** and two gold bracelets weighing ten **shekels**.

He then inquired about her family and asked if there was room in her father's house for him to spend the night.

She replied that she was the daughter of Bethuel, the son of Nahor, Abraham's brother. Then she confirmed there was room for him in her father's house and kindly offered to supply straw and food for the camels.

hairs
Matthew 10:29–31

what others say

F. B. Meyer

It is our privilege to talk with God about everything in life. The minutest things are not too small for him who numbers the hairs of our heads.[5]

Elisabeth Elliot

Prayer sets spiritual forces in motion, although the effect is often invisible, perhaps for a long time.[6]

James Montgomery Boice

A camel drinks more than twenty gallons of water, especially after a long day's journey in hot lands. Here were ten camels. Would her pitcher hold a gallon? If so, she must have made two hundred trips from the spring to the watering trough. It would have taken several hours.[7]

Time Out for Praise

The servant was overwhelmed. "Then the man bowed down his head and worshiped the LORD. And he said, 'Blessed be the LORD God of my master Abraham, who has not forsaken His mercy and His truth toward my master. As for me, being on the way, the LORD led me to the house of my master's brethren'" (Genesis 24:26–27 NKJV).

The servant was on a mission for his master Abraham and was being guided by Abraham's God. Assuming he expressed his worship aloud, he was careful not to reveal the purpose of his visit and the part Rebekah might have in it.

what others say

Richard J. Foster

Try to recall a time and place that is your "grateful center": a place that was restful, comforting, free of anxiety, and good to be in. It may be a memory from your childhood or something that is more recent. When you have found your "grateful center," try to call it to mind in all its detail. Go there in your memory; see the light and shadow, hear the sounds, touch it and smell it. Stay there for as long as you wish and gradually allow yourself to express your thankfulness to God in simple words.[8]

The servant clearly understood that he was on a mission for both Abraham and Abraham's God.

Meet the Family

Rebekah hurried home and told her mother's household what had occurred. Her brother Laban heard the story and saw the jewelry (see Illustration #8) and hastened to meet the man at the spring and to welcome him to the family home.

They unloaded the camels and gave them straw and fodder. They provided water for the servant and his men to wash their feet. When they began to serve a meal, the servant said that he would not eat until he had told them the purpose of his visit.

Have I Got a Story for You!

The family listened as the servant told how God had blessed Abraham so abundantly that he was wealthy in sheep and cattle, silver and gold, servants, camels, and donkeys. In their old age, God had enabled Sarah to bear a son who would inherit all that Abraham owned.

The servant then gave the real intent of the journey. He was to find a wife for Abraham's son. And if the woman would not come? The servant quoted Abraham: "The LORD, before whom I walk, will send His angel with you and prosper your way; and you shall take a wife for my son from my family and from my father's house" (Genesis 24:40 NKJV).

As the servant gave the account of his prayer, how he met Rebekah, and the obvious way God had answered his prayer, Rebekah's father and brother agreed that the Lord was directing, and they gave their permission for Rebekah to become Isaac's wife.

Illustration #8
Gold Jewelry—The pieces of gold jewelry that Abraham's servant gave to Rebekah may have looked like this.

Presenting the Gifts

Overjoyed, the servant presented gifts appropriate for a dowry, sealing a marriage arrangement and demonstrating that Abraham was indeed wealthy. He gave gold and silver jewelry and articles of clothing to Rebekah. He also gave costly gifts to Laban and to Rebekah's mother. Then the servant was ready to eat the meal that had been prepared for him and his men.

The servant had prayed about every aspect of his important mission. He had also planned wisely how he would meet the right woman, how to present his mission, and when to seal it with appropriate gifts. Sincere prayer, wise planning, and timely action go together in accomplishing God's plan.

Here Comes the Bride

Waiting is a theme that runs throughout Genesis. In the weeks while the trusted servant was on his mission to secure a bride for Isaac, the prospective groom waited, eager to see how God would honor Abraham's faith in this crucial matter.

the big picture

Genesis 24:54–67

After a night's rest, the servant prepared to leave for the return journey to Canaan. Laban and Rebekah's mother asked for a ten-day delay, but Rebekah agreed to leave immediately. The family gave her their blessing and sent her on her way with her maids. On Rebekah's arrival in Canaan, she and Isaac were married, and Isaac was comforted after his mother's death.

Time for Decision

The next morning when the servant made preparation to leave, Laban and Rebekah's mother asked for a ten-day delay in the departure in order to prepare for the parting. The servant pled for leaving immediately, so they turned the decision over to Rebekah. Would she go with the servant immediately? She answered simply, "I will go" (Genesis 24:58 NKJV).

go to

meditating
Psalm 48:9

veil
a cloth that covered a woman's face for modesty, worn especially at her wedding

The family sent her with their blessing, and she and her maids mounted the camels and began the long journey to the land God had promised Abraham and Isaac.

> what others say
>
> **Warren Wiersbe**
>
> Her parents and friends could have given Rebekah many arguments for waiting or even for saying no. "You have never seen the man!" "Maybe the servant is a fraud!" "It's nearly 500 miles to where Isaac lives. That's a long trip!" "You may never see your family again!" But she was determined to make the long, difficult journey and become the wife of a man she knew only by hearsay.[9]

Meet the Bride

One evening Isaac was meditating in the field. When he looked up and saw the camels approaching, he went to meet the party. After the servant identified Isaac to Rebekah, she took her **veil** and covered herself.

The servant told Isaac all that God had done, so Isaac took Rebekah as his bride. He loved her, and in loving Rebekah he at last found comfort after his mother's death.

Chapter Wrap-Up

- Abraham, not wanting Isaac to marry an ungodly Canaanite woman, sent his servant back to his homeland to find a bride for his son from among Abraham's relatives. (Genesis 24:1–9)
- The servant committed himself to finding the bride God had for Isaac. He traveled to the town of Nahor, where Abraham's brother lived, stopping by the well outside town. Women would be coming to draw water, and the servant prayed that God would show him the right woman for Isaac by this sign: he would ask for a drink and the woman would give him water and also volunteer to provide water for his camels. (Genesis 24:10–14)

- A beautiful woman named Rebekah fulfilled the servant's requirement and revealed that she was a relative of Abraham. (Genesis 24:15–25)
- The servant praised God and went to Rebekah's home for the night. He explained his mission to her family, and they agreed that Rebekah could marry Isaac. (Genesis 24:26–51)
- The servant gave expensive gifts to Rebekah and to her family. Then after a meal and a night's rest, he prepared to leave and take Rebekah with him. Her mother and brother wanted them to wait for ten days, but Rebekah agreed to leave immediately. (Genesis 24:52–60)
- When they arrived back at Abraham's home, Isaac saw them coming and went to meet them. Isaac loved Rebekah, and she became his wife. (Genesis 24:61–66)

Study Questions

1. Why was Abraham so determined not to let Isaac marry a woman from Canaan, where they lived?

2. What can we learn about the importance of prayer from this story?

3. What does Rebekah's willingness to water the camels tell us about her character?

4. What does Rebekah's experience teach us about the value of kindness and helpfulness?

5. How did God reveal his will to Abraham's servant? How does he reveal his will to us today?

Genesis 25–26 God's Covenant Is Passed On

Chapter Highlights:
- **Abraham Dies**
- **Hostility Among All the Brothers**
- **Two Nations**
- **Jacob Purchases the Birthright**

Let's Get Started

God's covenant had been with Abraham for almost a century. He lived thirty-seven years after Sarah died. Then it was time for Abraham to die and for Isaac to carry on God's plan. From now on, the Bible account shifts to Isaac and his heir who will receive the promised blessings.

Abraham's sons, Isaac and Ishmael, shared in the burial ceremonies for their father. It is the last account we have that these two had contact with each other. The Scripture gives an account of Ishmael's descendants and finally his death.

The story returns to Isaac and the covenant blessings. Isaac prayed for a son and God gave him twin boys, Jacob and Esau. The twins, who grew up to have very different personalities and values, provide us with important character-building lessons.

In a time of famine, Isaac follows his father's example in seeking relief by going to Egypt. God stops him en route, and Isaac stays in Gerar (see Appendix B), where Abimelech is king. Like his father had done, Isaac claims that his wife is his sister. His deception is discovered, and Isaac is asked to leave Gerar, though he is welcome to stay in the area. God confirmed his covenant with Isaac, and Isaac built an altar to the Lord.

Abraham Dies

Abraham had a long life, and in much of it he enjoyed communication with God. Though the Bible does not record God speaking to him after he had tested Abraham with the sacrifice of Isaac, Abraham's faith remained steady to the end of his life.

the big picture

Genesis 25:1–11

After Sarah's death, Abraham married Keturah and fathered six sons. Knowing he would soon die, he gave gifts to these sons and sent them away. Everything else he owned was left to Isaac.

go to

concubine
1 Chronicles 1:32

Ishmael
Genesis 21:8–14

grave
Genesis 25:17; 35:29; 49:29, 33

concubine
a secondary wife with a few rights

> When Abraham had lived 175 years, he died. Two of his sons, Isaac and Ishmael, buried him in the cave Abraham had purchased when Sarah died 37 years earlier.

Even in his old age Abraham fathered six sons by Keturah, his **concubine**. Keturah, as a secondary wife, had certain rights but not those Sarah, the primary wife, had. None of these sons would be allowed to interfere with the covenant promises that were reserved for Isaac alone. Abraham gave them gifts and sent them away, as he had sent Ishmael away many years before. These sons moved "to the country of the east" (Genesis 25:6 NKJV), where they multiplied and grew to become tribes, thus fulfilling God's promise to Abraham that he would be "a father of many nations" (Genesis 17:4 NKJV).

what others say

Ray Ortlund

> The good memories of his first marriage gave [Abraham] the courage to do it again. Some people are content to remain widowed the rest of their lives, and that's okay, but Abraham was not one of those. And for all we know, this marriage to Keturah was a good one and blessed of God.[1]

Back at Sarah's Cave

key point

When Abraham had lived 175 years, he died and "was gathered to his people" (Genesis 25:8 NKJV). This is the first indication we have in Genesis that there is life beyond the grave. Ishmael joined Isaac in burying their father in the cave he had purchased to bury Sarah.

what others say

Warren Wiersbe

> The phrase "gathered to his people" (25:8) does not mean "buried with the family"; for Sarah's body was the only one in the family tomb. This is the first occurrence of this phrase in the Bible; and it means to go to the realm of the dead, referring to the destiny of the spirit, not the body (James 2:26). The Old Testament word for the realm of the dead is *sheol*; the New Testament equivalent is *hades*. It is the temporary "home" of the spirits of the dead awaiting the resurrection (Revelation 20:11–15).[2]

The Other Half of the Family

the big picture

Genesis 25:12-18

Here we read an account of Ishmael's family, who settled in the south near the border of Egypt. Ishmael lived 137 years and then died. His descendants were continually hostile with other members of their family.

go to

promised
Genesis 17:20

Ishmael and Isaac were half brothers, both loved by their father Abraham. But God's chosen line of blessing was to come through Isaac. God had told Abraham to listen to Sarah's demand that Hagar and Ishmael be exiled from the camp (Genesis 21:8–21).

But God had other promises for Ishmael. He had promised that he would increase his descendants so that they would "not be counted for multitude" (Genesis 16:10 NKJV). Ishmael had twelve sons who became tribal rulers. God also said that Ishmael would "be a wild man; his hand shall be against every man, and every man's hand against him"; and he would "dwell in the presence of all his brethren" (16:12 NKJV).

In this passage we see God's predictions being fulfilled. Ishmael's descendants became tribes who settled in the Arabian peninsula (see Appendix B) and they did indeed live "in the presence of all his brethren" (25:18 NKJV).

prophecy

what others say

Henry M. Morris

Ishmael at that time was 90 years old. His own 12 sons were grown and they had become prolific and powerful enough to have settled towns and strongholds of their own, and to be called princes, as God had promised.[3]

Two Nations, One Womb

Again the theme of waiting comes to Isaac's life. When he married Rebekah, he longed to have a son to whom he could pass on the blessing that had come to him through Abraham. He waited twenty years for God to provide that son.

go to

covenant
Genesis 12:2–3, 7

the big picture

Genesis 25:19–26

Isaac was forty years old when he married Rebekah, his cousin from Nahor's family in Paddan Aram. When Rebekah was barren, Isaac prayed for her. God answered his prayers, and she became pregnant with twins. Rebekah turned to God in prayer when there was conflict in her womb, and God revealed to her the future of the twin sons that would be born. Two nations were in her womb, two peoples who would not live in harmony, one younger being stronger than the other, and the older son serving the younger.

At their birth, the first son, who was red and hairy, was called Esau. The second son, who was born grasping his twin's heel, was named Jacob.

Isaac was a wealthy man. He had inherited everything Abraham had owned. He was also under the covenant that God had made with Abraham. However, the promises God had made required Isaac to have a son. How else would God make a great nation of Abraham's descendants, giving the land to his seed and blessing all families of the earth?

GOD AT WORK

Isaac had married Rebekah when he was forty years old. Now he was approaching sixty and he still had no son. Rebekah was barren. Isaac prayed, and God answered. Rebekah became pregnant. God, who knows every detail of our lives, knows the heart cry of a couple who long for a child.

what others say

Elisabeth Elliot

Waiting on God is an act of faith—the greatest thing ever required of us humans. Not faith in the outcome we are dictating to God, but faith in his character, faith in himself. It is resting in the perfect confidence that he will guide in the right way, at the right time. He will supply our need. He will fulfill his word. He will give us the very best if we trust him.[4]

Why This Struggle?

Rebekah conceived twins. How her heart must have rejoiced. However, when she felt the babies moving in her womb, she sensed that something unusual, even disturbing, was happening. Instead of the normal movement, the babies were actually struggling with each other. Wondering what the significance of this was, Rebekah went to the Lord. His answer showed that he has intimate knowledge of the unborn.

go to

heel
Hosea 12:3

God told her that the founders of two nations were within her womb. The struggle she felt would endure in the two nations throughout history. Further, though custom would dictate that the firstborn would be the favored one, this would not be true of her twin sons. The firstborn would serve the second born.

what others say

Dr. Larry Richards

The older will serve the younger: Romans 9 emphasizes the importance of God's statement to Rebekah before her twin sons were born. God's choice of Jacob, the younger, to inherit his covenant promise was made before the boys were born. This showed that the choice did not depend on what either did. God is free to choose as he wills. The fact that Esau proved to be uninterested in spiritual things shows how wise God's choices are.[5]

"Hairy" and "Heel-Catcher"

The twins were born. The first "came out red. He was like a hairy garment all over" (Genesis 25:25 NKJV). His parents named him Esau, which meant "hairy." The second twin was born actually grasping Esau's heel. His parents named him Jacob, which meant "one who grasps the heel (figuratively, he deceives)" or "a supplanter" (Genesis 25:25–26).

The twins, who had appeared so unlike at birth, grew up to be very different from each other. Esau became an outdoorsman, skilled at hunting. Jacob, on the other hand, was a quiet person, content to stay by the tents, probably tending his father's flocks and herds. The Hebrew word for quiet, *tam*, means "perfect" or possibly "mature" (see Job 1:8).

Isaac favored Esau, because Esau brought home the wild game that he enjoyed eating. Rebekah favored Jacob. The Bible account shows the pain that follows when a parent shows favoritism.

birthright
special inheritance rights given a first-born son

what others say

Cynthia Ulrich Tobias

If you are a parent with more than one child, you've already discovered that even children growing up in very similar circumstances and environments can have dramatically dissimilar approaches to life. You begin to realize that people are fundamentally different. The individual bents that cause each person to be unique, often bring an overwhelming challenge to parents. It is not enough to simply decide how children should be reared and then apply the same techniques to each child. Parents need to get to know their children, and no two will be the same![6]

Gene Getz

Esau's "whole body was like a hairy garment" (25:25). Even today, children are sometimes born with an excessive amount of hair on their bodies, a condition known as 'hypertrichosis.'"[7]

A Business Deal That Wasn't Win-Win

the big picture

Genesis 25:29–34

One day when Jacob was cooking red stew, Esau came from the open fields feeling famished. He implored Jacob to give him a serving of the stew. Jacob offered the food on the condition that Esau first sell him his birthright. Esau complied, ate the food, and left. In that transaction he showed that he despised the birthright.

In his role as the stay-at-home son, Jacob was cooking a thick soup of lentils when Esau came from the fields. Lentils, which were probably grown as crops, turn a rich chocolate-red color when boiled.

The colorful food cooking in the pot and its tempting aroma reminded Esau that he was very hungry. In fact, he felt so famished that he could not bear to wait to eat until he had prepared something for himself. He begged Jacob to give him some of it right away.

Jacob seized the opportunity to make a proposal. Yes, he would give a serving of lentils to Esau, but Esau must give his **birthright** in exchange for the meal.

The fact that Esau agreed to the proposal so quickly indicates how little he prized the birthright. Jacob, on the other hand, must have been amazed that Esau placed so little value in it.

Esau reasoned that if he were to die of hunger, the birthright would be of no use to him, so he agreed to the proposal. Jacob, wisely, insisted that Esau swear formally to the sale of the birthright.

profane
unholy, not set apart for God

The business deal was consummated. Esau ate the lentils and Jacob got the birthright. In making this deal, both men lost out. Esau betrayed himself as a **profane** person who did not care about spiritual values. Jacob, on the other hand, made a deal for something that God had promised he would have anyway.

What's a Birthright Worth?

In patriarchal times, the custom was for the firstborn son to inherit a double portion of the estate. On occasion, this valuable inheritance was traded for something of lesser value that could be obtained for immediate use.

key point

In Isaac's case, however, he would be passing to the son receiving the birthright the covenant promise that God had first made to Abraham. This part of the birthright was worth far more than the material aspects of the inheritance. Esau lived for the here-and-now and had no regard for the spiritual part of the birthright. Isaac clearly favored Esau, while Rebekah favored Jacob. Isaac had known from before the birth of his sons that Jacob had been chosen by God to receive the special covenant blessings that had first been given to Abraham.

what others say

Henry M. Morris

> The eldest son customarily received a double portion in the division of the inheritance (Deuteronomy 21:17) and the right to lead the household (Genesis 27:29). The eldest son, of course, also had sober responsibilities. If he was to rule over the household, then he had to provide for the household, both materially and spiritually. In fact, in this particular family, the spiritual responsibilities were paramount (Genesis 18:19). In particular, there was the responsibility of building and officiating at the altar (Genesis 22:9; 26:25; 35:1, etc.) as well as the transmission of God's Word and his promises.[8]

something to ponder

Jacob didn't have to bargain to get the birthright. God had already promised that it would be his. How often do we manipulate others to get what we want instead of committing our desire to the Lord and letting him work things out in his time and in his way?

That Same Lie, Take Three

It is not hard to trust God when all is going well in life, but when trouble comes, we are tempted to rely on our own resources. In a time of crop failure and famine, Isaac followed his father's faulty example and decided to go to Egypt to find food.

the big picture

Genesis 26

When a famine came to Canaan, Isaac decided to relocate. He moved his family, servants, flocks, and herds to Gerar, where Abimelech, king of the Philistines, lived. There the Lord appeared to Isaac and told him not to proceed further to Egypt, as planned, but to stay where he was. God would be with him and bless him. Then God confirmed that the promises he had made to Abraham were continued to Isaac.

When the men of Gerar made inquiries about Rebekah, Isaac said she was his sister. Abimelech confronted Isaac with his deception and issued a death warrant for anyone who would molest Isaac or Rebekah. Isaac settled in, planted crops, and reaped a hundredfold. The Philistine neighbors became so envious that they stopped up the wells Abraham had dug. At Abimelech's request, Isaac moved to the Valley of Gerar, where he reopened wells Abraham had dug. Quarrels broke out with Philistine herdsmen over the wells. Isaac refused to fight, but moved away and dug another well. Finally, Abimelech came to Isaac to make a treaty.

Famine—and a Secure Promise

Famine came to Canaan and there was a shortage of food and water for Isaac's family and for his extensive flocks and herds. Isaac decided it was necessary to relocate to a more favorable area. When he reached Gerar, where Abimelech, king of the Philistines, ruled, the Lord appeared to Isaac and told him not to go down to Egypt, but to stay in the land that he would indicate.

The Lord confirmed his covenant with Isaac: "Do not go down to Egypt; live in the land of which I shall tell you. Dwell in this land, and I will be with you and bless you; for to you and your descendants I give all these lands, and I will perform the oath which I swore to Abraham your father. And I will make your descendants multiply as the stars of heaven; I will give to your descendants all these lands; and in your seed all the nations of the earth shall be blessed; because

Abraham obeyed My voice and kept My charge, My commandments, My statutes, and My laws" (Genesis 26:2–5 NKJV).

what others say

Warren Wiersbe

We can never successfully run away from trials, because God sees to it that his children learn the lessons of faith regardless of where they go. We can never grow in faith by running from difficulty.[9]

Killer Beauty: The Next Generation

Isaac's conduct in Gerar was a sad replay of his father's deception on two occasions (Genesis 12:10–20; 20:1–13). When the men of Gerar asked Isaac about Rebekah, he answered that she was his sister. He did this because he was afraid that if they knew she was his wife, they would kill him in order to be free to take her.

One day Abimelech saw Isaac caressing Rebekah and discerned that she was his wife, not his sister. Alarmed by what had come to light, Abimelech called Isaac in to give an account of his lie. He asked accusingly, "What is this you have done to us? One of the people might soon have lain with your wife, and you would have brought guilt on us" (Genesis 26:10 NKJV).

This pagan king gave orders to all in Gerar, "He who touches this man or his wife shall surely be put to death" (26:11 NKJV).

What if Isaac's marriage to Rebekah had been violated? What would have happened to the promises to Abraham? God intervened and used a pagan king to protect his covenant. Isaac faltered in his faith, but God was faithful.

something to ponder

Like Father, Like Son

The Bible account of Isaac's conduct when a famine came to Canaan is strikingly similar to Abraham's conduct on two occasions (Genesis 12:10–20 and 20:1–13). Some Bible experts have surmised that the writer was confused, but while there are similarities, there are also differences in the three accounts.

Since there is a ninety-year gap between the account of Abraham in chapter 20 and the account of Isaac in chapter 26, it is quite unlikely that Abimelech is the same man. Abimelech was a title, similar to president or king.

hundredfold
one hundred times as great

Abraham and Isaac: What They Did During Famines

	Abraham 1st time	Abraham 2nd time	Isaac
Famine in Canaan	Genesis 12:10		Genesis 26:1
Plans to go to Egypt	Genesis 12:10		Genesis 26:2 (implied)
God confirms his covenant			Genesis 26:3–6
Stays in Gerar		Genesis 20:1	Genesis 26:6
Motivated by fear for his life	Genesis 12:12–13	Genesis 20:2, 11	Genesis 26:7
Calls his wife his "sister"	Genesis 12:12–13	Genesis 20:2, 11	Genesis 26:7
Wife's beauty	Genesis 12:11, 14		Genesis 24:16
Deception is exposed by God	Genesis 12:17–18	Genesis 20:3–7	
Abimelech's alarm at possible adultery		Genesis 20:4–7	Genesis 26:10
Receives a rebuke	Genesis 12:18	Genesis 20:9–10	Genesis 26:10
Asked to leave	Genesis 12:19–20	Genesis 20:15	Genesis 26:16
Treaty requested by Abimelech		Genesis 21:22–32	Genesis 26:26–31

Bumper Crops and Stopped-Up Wells

Isaac stayed in the land, planted crops, and, even in a time of famine, was blessed with bumper crops that yielded a **hundredfold**. As his wealth increased, so did the envy of the Philistines around him. One way they could sabotage his abounding prosperity was to dry up his water supply. They did this by filling his wells with earth. These were wells that Abraham's servants had dug many years before.

Abimelech decided it was in the best interest of all for Isaac to move away. He complied by settling in the Valley of Gerar, where Abraham had dug wells. These had been stopped up by the Philistines, but Isaac restored them and assigned them the same names Abraham had given them. No matter how the Philistines opposed Isaac, God worked out his plan to give Abraham's descendants the land.

No Peace in the Valley

Before long, the herdsmen of Gerar fought with Isaac's men, claiming that the water was theirs. Isaac named the well Esek, which means "dispute." Soon after he had fresh water from a second well, another quarrel erupted. This well he named Sitnah, which means "opposition." Isaac refused to fight for what was rightfully his. Eventually the Philistines left him alone. The third well was called Rehoboth, which means "room."

go to

altars
Genesis 12:7–8; 21:33

Time for Worship

After a time Isaac moved to Beersheba. There God appeared to him and confirmed again the covenant he had given to Abraham. Abraham had built altars at Beersheba. Now Isaac built an altar there and called on the name of the Lord.

> what others say
>
> **Derek Kidner**
>
> The altars built by the patriarchs were a response, rather than an initiative: for the most part they gratefully record God's coming and speaking to his servants (see Genesis 12:7; 13:17–18; 35:7).[10]

Abimelech Renews a Treaty

Abimelech arrived with his personal adviser and the commander of his forces. Surprised, Isaac asked why he had come, since Abimelech had been hostile and had sent him away from Gerar. The delegation replied that it was obvious that God was with Isaac, so they felt the need of a sworn treaty that Isaac would not do them harm.

Isaac prepared a feast for them. Early the next morning the parties swore an oath, thus renewing the treaty Abraham had made with Abimelech almost a century before. Isaac was a peacemaker and eventually was able to live at peace with his neighbors.

something to ponder

We can learn from Isaac's dealing with Abimelech. He approached the potential controversy with candor as he questioned the sincerity of his guest. He showed restraint in not even replying to the statement that the Philistines had always treated him well. Then he dignified the treaty by preparing a feast for his guests.

Marriage Griefs

Hittites
group of migrants in Canaan originally from an empire that included Syria

When Esau was forty years old, he brought grief to Isaac and Rebekah by marrying two Hittite women, Judith and Basemath. These women were from an ungodly background and would have no understanding of God's covenant with Abraham and Isaac or of the special privileges available to them to know the true and living God.

what others say

Donald Joy

> Esau's vulnerability was that he wanted it all. Now! Maybe that is the real definition of worldly minded—to regard this present world as "all there is," and to take a tragically terminal view of reality. If we are willing to settle for a tangible, transient, sensuous experience as the ultimate reality, we will likely get it, one way or another.[11]

Chapter Wrap-Up

- Abraham married again and had six more sons, then died at age 175. His sons Isaac and Ishmael buried him in the cave where he had buried Sarah. (Genesis 25:1–11)
- Ishmael had twelve sons who became tribal rulers near Egypt and, as God had predicted, they lived in hostility toward other family members. Ishmael died at age 137. (Genesis 25:12–18)
- Isaac and Rebekah had been married for twenty years and still had no children. Isaac prayed and God gave them twin sons, Esau and Jacob. (Genesis 25:19–26)
- While still in the womb, the babies struggled with each other. God told Rebekah the babies would be the founders of two nations that would struggle with one another throughout history. God also told her that the younger of the two would be the favored one, not the older one according to custom. (Genesis 25:22–23)
- When the twins were born, Esau, the older, was red and hairy. Jacob, the younger, was born grasping Esau's heel. Esau grew up to be an outdoorsman who hunted. Jacob was quiet and enjoyed staying close to home. Isaac favored Esau, while Rebekah favored Jacob. (Genesis 25:24–28)
- One day Esau came home feeling very hungry. Jacob was cooking stew and Esau asked for some. Jacob offered to trade stew for Esau's birthright, and Esau agreed. Jacob, by scheming, got the birthright God had promised him anyway. (Genesis 25:29–34)
- When a famine came to Canaan, Isaac decided to move. He went to Gerar, where the Lord appeared to him and told him to stay there rather than going on to Egypt. God confirmed that the promises he had made to Abraham continued with Isaac. (Genesis 26:1–5)
- Isaac, like his father before him, told everyone that Rebekah was his sister, not his wife. When Abimelech discovered the truth, he confronted Isaac, and Isaac said he had lied because he was afraid someone would kill him and take his wife. Abimelech let it be known that anyone who harmed Isaac or Rebekah would be killed. (Genesis 26:6–11)

- Isaac settled down in Gerar and had fantastic crops. His neighbors were envious and stopped up his wells (which Abraham had dug years before). (Genesis 26:12–15)
- At Abimelech's request, Isaac moved farther away. When Isaac opened up wells that Abraham had dug there, conflict broke out over them with Philistine herdsmen. Isaac would not fight. Eventually the Philistines left him alone. (Genesis 26:16–22)
- Isaac moved to Beersheba (see Appendix B), where God appeared to him and confirmed his promises. Isaac "built an altar there and called on the name of the LORD" (verse 25 NKJV). (Genesis 26:23–25)
- Abimelech came with two other men to make a treaty with Isaac. Isaac fed them well and the next morning they renewed the treaty Abraham had made with Abimelech many years before. (Genesis 26:26–33)
- When Esau was forty, he married two women from an ungodly Hittite background. This saddened his parents. (Genesis 26:34–35)

Study Questions

1. How does Genesis 25 show that God is interested in details?

2. What does Esau's experience teach us about the importance of right priorities?

3. Since God had already promised that Jacob would get the birthright, why do you think Jacob felt he had to scheme to get it?

4. Abraham and Isaac both had weaknesses in the same area. What can we learn from this about the importance of a father's example to his children?

5. What does Isaac's experience teach us about peacemaking?

Part Four
God and Jacob

Genesis 27–28 God's Blessing for Jacob

Chapter Highlights:
- Jacob Gets the Blessing
- Isaac's Remaining Duty
- Jacob Leaves Home
- Isaac's Blessing
- Jacob Dreams

Let's Get Started

God does not camouflage human weakness nor the high cost of taking matters into one's own hands and not looking to him for direction. In Genesis 27 and 28, we get the inside story of Isaac's family life. It isn't a pleasant picture, but in the end we see God reaching out with grace and mercy.

Jacob had made a deal to get the birthright from his twin brother, Esau (Genesis 25:27–34). From Jacob's perspective, it was imperative to have Isaac's blessing that would ensure the covenant blessing being passed on to him and his descendants. Rebekah masterminded the scheme to seize the blessing, which Isaac fully intended to give to Esau. The scheme worked flawlessly—until Esau found that he had been cheated.

The result was tragic for each member of the family. Isaac was heartbroken, Esau was furious, Rebekah had to send her favored son away, and Jacob became a fugitive and would never see his mother again.

what others say

James Montgomery Boice

There is probably no more pathetic episode in Genesis than Jacob's deception of Isaac to gain his father's blessing. Yet strangely, it is handled in radically different ways by Bible commentators. Some praise Jacob and the equally deceptive Rebekah for their concern to see the will of God done—since God had promised the supremacy to Jacob (Genesis 25:23). Others condemn them. In some works, Esau is regarded as a worldly but nevertheless genuine believer. In others, he is considered an utter pagan. Most writers sympathize with at least one of the people in the narrative.[1]

go to

younger
Genesis 25:21–23

Jacob Gets the Blessing

Jacob had won the birthright by taking advantage of his brother's weakness. Now he moved in to seize the blessing which his father intended to give Esau. Rebekah was keenly aware of Isaac's decision and quickly took steps to get what she wanted for Jacob.

the big picture

Genesis 27

Isaac had become old, more than 100 years old, and was nearly blind. Knowing death was coming, he asked Esau to hunt some game and prepare a special meal for him as a prelude to a solemn event. He was ready to give Esau his blessing.

Rebekah overheard and immediately involved Jacob in a plan to prevent this from happening. They must secure the blessing for Jacob before Esau returned. Their plan was executed with speed and bold deception. Soon after Isaac blessed Jacob, thinking it was Esau, the deception was discovered.

Isaac could not retract the blessing he had given Jacob, but he did bestow a lesser blessing on Esau. Rebekah discovered that Esau planned to kill Jacob as soon as he could after his father's death. She sent Jacob away to stay with her brother Laban in Haran (see Appendix B), giving Isaac the excuse that Jacob was seeking a wife there.

Isaac's One Remaining Duty

Jacob had purchased the birthright from Esau. Now he participated in taking one more step to ensure his place in receiving the covenant blessings.

Isaac was old and virtually blind. Knowing death could come at any time, he summoned his favorite son, Esau, and asked him to hunt game and prepare his favorite savory dish. He promised that following the special meal, he would give Esau his blessing. He did this, even though he had known since before the birth of his twin boys that God had said Jacob, the younger, would receive the covenant blessing. Isaac had favored Esau for all his life.

This occasion was significant, for Esau understood that bestowing the blessing was virtually legalizing Isaac's will. A double portion of his possessions would go to Esau, and the blessing of the covenant God had made with Abraham would be carried through Esau's descendants. Isaac fully intended Esau to receive this blessing.

what others say

Gene Getz

[Isaac] probably knew that Esau had already sold his birthright to his younger son. Perhaps he was so angry at Jacob's tricky plot against his favorite son that he determined to carry his frustration to the ultimate level of self-deception and try to blatantly ignore God's predetermined plan.[2]

go to

choice
Genesis 25:21–23

Rebekah Springs into Action

Rebekah was eavesdropping on Isaac's conversation with Esau. She knew there was no time to be lost. As soon as Esau left to hunt the game for Isaac's meal, she recruited Jacob to cooperate with her in a daring scheme to deceive Isaac and secure the blessing for Jacob.

Tension was high. Rebekah spoke with highest confidence that she could make the scheme work. If Jacob would bring her goat meat, she would cook a dish that would duplicate the texture and flavor of what Esau would prepare—at least enough to deceive Isaac. Jacob raised an objection. He feared that he could not fool his father. What if Isaac touched his smooth skin? Though almost completely blind, he would know he wasn't touching Esau's hairy skin.

Rebekah had a solution. She prepared the food. Then she dressed Jacob in Esau's clothes and covered his hands and neck with goatskins to resemble Esau's hairy skin.

what others say

Henry M. Morris

Rebekah, indeed, had always been a woman of quick decision and action, as is evident from the time she first made her <u>choice</u> to follow Abraham's servant and marry Isaac. Probably, also, she and Jacob had often discussed the whole problem, and perhaps she had foreseen this development and already decided what she must do if the time should ever come.[3]

The Great Deception

Jacob approached his father, carrying the tasty food and bread Rebekah had prepared. "I am Esau your firstborn," he said. "Please arise, sit and eat of my game, that your soul may bless me" (Genesis 27:19 NKJV).

Isaac asked his son, "How is it that you have found it so quickly, my son?" (27:20 NKJV).

"Because the LORD your God brought it to me," he replied (27:20 NKJV).

As Jacob had anticipated, Isaac asked him to come near, so he could touch him. Clearly, Isaac was suspicious. He recognized the voice as Jacob's, but the hairy hands he identified as Esau's.

Again Jacob asserted that he was Esau. Now satisfied, Isaac ate the meal. Then he called Jacob to come and kiss him. Immediately he picked up the scent of Esau's clothes and was ready to bestow the blessing on Jacob. The covenant blessings God had given Abraham had been passed on to Isaac and now were passed on to Jacob. The birthright was ensured!

The Deception Unveiled

Jacob left Isaac's tent only moments before Esau entered with the meal he had prepared. Immediately the great deception was exposed. Isaac "trembled exceedingly" (Genesis 27:33 NKJV). Esau "cried with an exceedingly great and bitter cry" (verse 34 NKJV). Blaming Jacob, Esau said, "He has supplanted me these two times. He took away my birthright, and now look, he has taken away my blessing!" (verse 36 NKJV).

He then asked if his father had reserved any blessing for him. Isaac answered, "I have made him your master, and all his brethren I have given to him as servants" (27:37 NKJV).

For Esau, he said, "By your sword you shall live, and you shall serve your brother; and it shall come to pass, when you become restless, that you shall break his yoke from your neck" (27:40 NKJV).

what others say

James Montgomery Boice

God does not call upon us to sympathize with Esau but to learn from him, warning that although God is exceedingly gracious and is forever tempering justice with mercy, there are nevertheless choices in life that cannot be undone and consequences of sin that are thereafter unavoidable.[4]

From our point of view, Isaac had failed. Yet we read in the New Testament that Isaac exercised faith in the blessings he gave to each son: "By faith Isaac blessed Jacob and Esau concerning things to come" (Hebrews 11:20 NKJV). God uses imperfect people to accomplish his purposes.

something to ponder

Emergency Measures: Plan B

Esau was very angry and determined that after his father died and the days of mourning had ended, he would kill Jacob.

Rebekah learned of the plan and again took action. She persuaded Jacob to leave home and flee to her brother Laban in Haran. She promised that as soon as Esau's desire for revenge cooled, she would send word for him to return home.

To Isaac, she used an excuse that she knew would strongly appeal to Isaac's desires. She explained Jacob's departure by saying that she could not bear to have Jacob find a wife from among the ungodly Hittite women.

what others say

Derek Kidner

Rebekah's quick grasp of situations and characters shows itself again, first in her recognition that she must lose Jacob to save him, and then in her persuasive handling of both son and father.[5]

Jacob Leaves Home

Jacob's grandfather Abraham had set out on a lonely journey, now Jacob makes his way through the wilderness alone. There the similarity ends. Abraham traveled with the assurance that God was with him and was guiding him. Jacob had no such assurance as he started out.

the big picture

Genesis 28:1–9

Isaac called for Jacob and told him not to marry a woman from the local area, but to go to find a wife from among the relatives in Haran. Isaac blessed Jacob, reinforcing the covenant promises, then sent him on his way.

Isaac's Blessing

Canaanites
people in Canaan who followed a religion focused primarily on fertility

We have one dysfunctional family here. Isaac had favored Esau and was devastated that Jacob had cheated Esau from the blessing. Rebekah had favored Jacob and now feared for his life because of Esau's wrath.

Once Isaac heard that Jacob was leaving to find a wife from among Abraham's relatives living in Haran, he called Jacob to him to give him a blessing. He understood that anyone inheriting the blessings God had given to Abraham must not intermarry with **Canaanites**. The line must be kept spiritually pure. So Isaac reminded Jacob of the covenant blessings and sent him on his way. When Esau learned what had transpired and that Isaac had sent Jacob to find a God-fearing wife in Haran, he tried to buy his father's favor by also marrying a woman from Abraham's family—Ishmael's daughter, who was Esau's cousin. He now had a third wife.

what others say

The Bible Knowledge Commentary

All participants were at fault. Isaac knew of God's oracle to Rebekah (Genesis 25:32) that the elder would serve the younger; yet he set out to thwart it by blessing Esau! Esau, agreeing to the plan, broke the oath he had made with Jacob (25:33). Rebekah and Jacob, with a just cause, each tried to achieve God's blessing by deception, without faith or love. Theirs would be the victory, but they would reap hatred and separation, for Rebekah never saw Jacob again! So the conflict between Jacob and Esau was greatly deepened by Jacob's pursuit—he wanted what belonged to the firstborn, the blessing. Yet the story is not just about Jacob. He alone did not destroy the family: parental preference did.[6]

Esau's Tears

Esau discovered that for him there was no turning back. We are warned: "Pursue peace with all people, and holiness, without which no one will see the Lord: looking carefully . . . lest there be any fornicator or profane person like Esau, who for one morsel of food sold his birthright. For you know that afterward, when he wanted to inherit the blessing, he was rejected, for he found no place for repentance, though he sought it diligently with tears" (Hebrews 12:14–17 NKJV).

what others say

Donald Joy

There seems to be an irreversible fatalism in the Hebrews text suggesting that Esau was at a point of no return. The ultimate tragedy of life is that if I lost sight of my goals, I may never find the way home![7]

. . . And That's How Jacob Invented the Escalator

the big picture

Genesis 28:10–22

Jacob started on his journey and stopped at Bethel for the night. As he slept, he had a dream of a stairway from earth to heaven. Angels were ascending and descending it. Above it stood the Lord, who restated the covenant promises to Jacob, adding that he would be with him, watch over him, and bring him back to the land he had promised to give Abraham. When Jacob awoke in the morning, he set up a stone pillar and poured oil on it, calling the place Bethel. By this action he expressed his worship and further promised to give a tithe of all God's material blessings back to God.

After all Jacob and Rebekah had done to ensure that he receive the blessing, Jacob had to run for his life.

Now Jacob was on his way, escaping for his life from his revenge-filled brother. Before him lay a 450-mile journey to find his relatives in Haran. As he walked along, he must have reflected on recent events in his life. Did he have regrets? Was he feeling lonesome? Did he wonder when he would ever return home?

He stopped for the night, finding a stone to put under his head as a pillow and lay down for sleep. God gave him a dream. He saw a stairway that reached from earth to heaven. Angels of God were moving up and down the stairway.

Above it, the Lord stood. He spoke to Jacob, giving his covenant promises in even more detail than he had given to Abraham and Isaac.

GOD AT WORK

When Jacob awoke, he recognized that the Lord had spoken to him—he was in the very house of God. He took the stone he had

tithe
one-tenth of one's possessions

used as a pillow and set it up as a pillar. Pouring oil on it, he called the place Bethel, which means "the house of God."

Jacob made a vow to God that if God would be with him and care for him until he returned to Bethel, he would honor the Lord as his God and would give him a **tithe** of all his material blessings.

something to ponder

Esau was waiting to give Jacob what he deserved—death for his conniving, deceitful conduct. God gave Jacob what he didn't deserve—a vision that connected Jacob with God and a promise that he would bring Jacob back to the Promised Land. How thankful we can be that God gives us what we don't deserve—his love and forgiveness. He promises to give us a new beginning.

what others say

Jerry Bridges

God said nothing in the dream about Jacob's deceitful character or actions. God did not reprimand him or threaten to punish him. Instead he gave Jacob five astounding promises related to possession of the land of Israel, a multitude of descendants, being a blessing to everyone on earth, and enjoying God's protective guidance and his continual presence.

What was Jacob's reaction to such a wealth of promised blessings? Did he wake up rejoicing and praising God as we might have expected? . . . Instead of exaltation, Jacob was afraid. . . . The reason for Jacob's fear was the realization that he had somehow been in the very presence of God. It was not the consciousness of his sin but the consciousness of his creaturehood in the presence of deity that created his sense of awe.[8]

Chapter Wrap-Up

- Isaac was old and nearly blind. He knew he would die soon, so he told Esau to go hunting, cook the meat, and bring it to him to eat. Then he would give Esau his blessing. This was in direct opposition to God's plan. (Genesis 27:1–4)

- Rebekah, overhearing Isaac's directions, involved Jacob in an alternate plan to get the blessing for him. She told Jacob to bring her some goat meat, which she cooked to resemble wild game. She dressed Jacob in Esau's clothes and covered his arms with goatskin so Isaac would think he was Esau. When Jacob, pretending to be Esau, took the food to his father, Isaac would give him the blessing. (Genesis 27:5–17)

- Rebekah's plan worked. Though Isaac was suspicious at first, he gave the blessing to Jacob and the birthright was ensured. (Genesis 27:18–29)

- Shortly after Jacob left Isaac's tent, Esau came with his wild game meal, and the deception was exposed. Isaac was upset, but he was able to give Esau a lesser blessing. (Genesis 27:30–40)

- Esau angrily vowed to kill Jacob. Rebekah advised Jacob to leave home and go live with her brother until Esau cooled down. She told Isaac that Jacob was going to Haran to find a wife. (Genesis 27:41–46)

- Isaac blessed Jacob and reinforced the covenant promises, then sent him away. (Genesis 28:1–5)

- Jacob left, stopping at Bethel for the night. As he slept, God gave him a dream of angels going up and down a stairway from earth to heaven. The Lord stood at the top of the stairway. He spoke to Jacob, giving his covenant promises in more detail than he had given Abraham or Isaac. (Genesis 28:6–15)

- When Jacob woke up and realized that God had spoken to him, he set up a stone as a pillar and poured oil on it for a memorial. He called that place Bethel, "the house of God." (Genesis 28:16–19)

- Jacob vowed that if God would be with him and care for him until he returned to Bethel, he would honor the Lord as his God and give him a tenth of all his possessions. (Genesis 28:20–22)

Study Questions

1. How was each person in Isaac's family at fault in Genesis 27?
2. What happens when we deliberately go against God's will, as Isaac was prepared to do?
3. What does this account teach us about the way God carries out his plans?
4. How did God show mercy to Jacob instead of giving him what he deserved?
5. Do you think Jacob regretted what he had done? How did he respond to God speaking to him?

Genesis 29–31 Jacob in Paddan Aram

Chapter Highlights:
- **Jacob and Uncle Laban**
- **Jacob Marries**
- **Jacob's Wealth Increases**
- **Jacob Runs from Laban**
- **Laban Pursues Jacob**

Let's Get Started

Jacob made the long, lonely trek to meet his mother's relatives. When he arrived in Paddan Aram, he was welcomed by family members and invited to stay. In time, he worked out an agreement with his uncle Laban. Jacob would work for Laban seven years in return for marrying his younger daughter Rachel. After the seven years, the wedding day arrived, but Laban cheated Jacob by instead giving him Leah, Rachel's older sister. In order to have Rachel, Jacob agreed to work another seven years, and then more years to build up his flocks and herds. During his time with Laban, Jacob experienced firsthand the ugliness of deception.

After staying twenty years, Jacob was directed by the Lord to return home. So he fled from his cheating Uncle Laban while Laban was away from home for a few days. But Laban chased him until the two men made a reluctant truce.

Throughout the years in Paddan Aram, Jacob must have been lonely at times and must have thought about his parents and the covenant blessings that were first given to his grandfather Abraham, then to his father, Isaac, and now to him. During all that time God faithfully kept his promise to bless Jacob, and now Jacob was returning to the Promised Land.

Jacob and Uncle Laban

We can only imagine the thoughts that filled Jacob's mind as he trudged across the wilderness to find his relatives. Somewhere in the five hundred miles, he must have wondered if he could find his uncle and what kind of welcome he would receive.

the big picture

Genesis 29:1-14

Jacob arrived in Paddan Aram and stopped at a well, which was a regular meeting place for shepherds. He inquired about his uncle Laban and learned that Laban's daughter Rachel was a shepherdess. When she arrived with her flock, he identified himself. Laban arrived at the well and took Jacob to his home.

Is She the One?

Jacob made the 450-mile journey alone. He must have been anxious to link up with his relatives and find a place to settle down. Arriving at Haran, he stopped at a well that served as an information center for the shepherds of the area. The custom was to wait until the flocks had been led to the well, then remove the heavy stone that covered it. After the sheep had been watered, the shepherds would replace the stone and leave with their flocks.

Jacob greeted the waiting shepherds and asked if they knew Laban. He learned that Laban's daughter Rachel, a shepherdess, was even then approaching with her father's flock of sheep. Jacob suggested that the men water their sheep immediately. He may have wanted the men to leave before Rachel arrived so he could meet her alone. The men, however, did not cooperate, saying that they always waited until all the shepherds had come before removing the stone that covered the well.

As soon as Rachel arrived, Jacob took the initiative to remove the stone and to water her sheep. Then he identified himself as her cousin.

Rachel ran home and gave the news to her father. Laban immediately hurried to meet Jacob and welcome him into his home, saying, "Surely you are my bone and my flesh" (Genesis 29:14 NKJV).

what others say

Gene Getz

I think Jacob had a strong sense that this woman could be the wife God had chosen for him. He must have heard his own mother, Rebekah, share many times how she had come to the well near Haran—years ago now—and met Abraham's chief servant, Eliezer. He was there to find a wife for Jacob's father, Isaac, and his mother, Rebekah, of course, was the woman who appeared at the well.[1]

Laban welcomed Jacob with the words, "You are my bone and my flesh" (29:14 NKJV). This statement has been found in ancient adoption ceremonies. Bible experts suggest that Laban may have adopted Jacob as his son.

Jacob Marries

Jacob stayed with his uncle Laban and was prepared when Laban opened a discussion of paying Jacob for his work. Jacob did not ask for money. He had something very different in mind.

the big picture

Genesis 29:15-35

After Jacob had lived with Laban for a month, Laban offered to pay Jacob for his work. Jacob, who was in love with beautiful Rachel, said he would work for Laban seven years to have her as his wife. Laban agreed.

At the end of that time, Laban hosted a wedding feast. However, that night he substituted Leah, Rachel's older sister, for the bride. When Jacob discovered that he had been tricked, he agreed to work another seven years to have Rachel. He could have her after the week of wedding festivities were completed, and he would work for her the next seven years. Thus, within a week Jacob had acquired two wives and two servant girls.

Will Work for Food (and a Wife)

After living as a guest, enjoying the hospitality of his uncle, Jacob was being put to work as a member of the family. In actuality, however, he ended up being treated as a servant—a big step down from the lifestyle he had enjoyed in his father's tents. However, Jacob was not put off by his uncle's proposal. Sometimes love requires a "step down."

Laban had two daughters. Leah, the older, had delicate eyes, whereas Rachel, the younger, was strikingly beautiful in face and form. The meaning of Leah's "delicate" eyes is unclear (Genesis 29:17 NKJV). They may have been visually weak, or possibly they lacked the sparkle that was so valued in her culture. On the other hand, some Bible scholars interpret the Hebrew word to indicate that her eyes were beautiful, enabling her to appear younger than she was.

When Rachel arrived at the well with her father's flock, Jacob immediately noted her beauty. By now he knew he wanted her for his wife. When Laban offered to pay Jacob for the work he would be doing, Jacob was ready to make a deal with him.

According to custom, a groom would pay the father of his bride an agreed-upon amount. This was only fair because the father was losing a productive member of his family. Though Isaac was wealthy and Jacob would inherit that wealth upon his death, Jacob had no money or livestock to offer. Instead, he offered to work for Laban seven years to have Rachel for his bride. Laban agreed, reasoning that he would rather have his daughter marry Jacob than anyone else. It would be to his advantage to have the services of Jacob for seven years. This was a long time to wait, but to Jacob it seemed but a few days, so great was his love for her. There is no indication that Jacob asked the Lord for guidance in the arrangements he made with Laban.

At the end of seven years, Jacob needed to remind Laban of their agreement. Jacob had fulfilled his part of the bargain. Now he wanted his bride. Laban then invited everyone in the community to come to the wedding feast.

what others say

Gene Getz

Jacob kept careful and accurate records during this seven-year period. Can you imagine a tree with 2,555 notches (365 x 7)? We're not sure, of course, how Jacob calculated the time, but he did.[2]

Elisabeth Elliot

The love by which one person puts his very self at the service of another, for that other's sake, is the bond that unites them. For in so willing the good of his beloved, the lover makes that good his own as well. And in their sharing of that good, the two are one without ceasing to be two. Self-giving love, to God and to others, is the only way to fulfillment and joy.[3]

"Did Laban Think We Wouldn't Notice?"

That night Laban delivered the bride in the dark—but it was Leah, not Rachel. Morning light revealed that Laban had cheated Jacob. Jacob wasted no time in angrily confronting Laban with the trickery. Laban excused himself, saying that it was not customary to marry off a younger daughter before the firstborn daughter. He placated Jacob by saying that after the **bridal week** was over, he could have Rachel as his second wife—if he would agree to work another seven years for her.

bridal week
wedding festivities that lasted seven days

Thus, in one week Jacob acquired Leah and her maid Zilpah and Rachel and her maid Bilhah. However, all was not at peace. Jacob loved Rachel more than he loved Leah, and this brought conflict and anguish that escalated through the family.

God was aware of Leah's secondary place in Jacob's heart and enabled her to bear six sons, while Rachel was barren.

something to ponder

How it hurts to be cheated! Laban's deception in giving Leah to Jacob on his wedding night must have been a painful reminder to Jacob of the way he had deceived Isaac. Jacob was deceived in much the same way as he had deceived his father. Jacob learned from first-hand experience the pain of being cheated.

- Jacob was determined to get Isaac's blessing; Laban was determined to have his firstborn daughter married before Rachel.
- Jacob had taken advantage of Isaac's blindness; Laban had taken advantage of darkness.
- Jacob had worn Esau's clothes; Leah may have worn Rachel's clothes.

Jacob's Family and Wealth Increase

Though Jacob was in a "school of hard knocks" with Laban, he was not abandoned by God. Laban could not help but see that God was blessing his son-in-law and causing him to prosper and grow in wealth.

the big picture

Genesis 30

The next few years involved rivalry between Leah and Rachel in an unhappy contest of childbearing. After Jacob had fulfilled his fourteen years of work, he asked Laban to release him so he could return home with his wives and eleven sons. Laban and Jacob made an agreement regarding the livestock and flocks that had flourished greatly under Jacob's care. Laban agreed to give Jacob part of the flock as payment for his years of work. He tried to trick Jacob so that he would not get his fair share, but God overruled, and Jacob's flocks multiplied.

mandrake
a large-leafed plant that bears violet flowers and yellow fruit. The fruit is thought to have aphrodisiac properties.

Sons and More Sons

Jacob was married to two sisters and, at their insistence, had accepted their maids as secondary wives. Though Jacob loved Rachel, she was unable to bear children. She was desperately unhappy. Leah was also unhappy because even though God had blessed her and given her sons, she yearned for Jacob's love. In competing with Leah's fertility, Rachel persuaded Jacob to take her maid as a secondary wife. Leah followed by insisting he take her maid as well. In their culture, children born to a maid were considered to be children of the mistress.

Behind the Scenes

One day while the men were harvesting wheat, Leah's oldest son Reuben found **mandrake** plants which he brought to his mother. Rachel wanted them for herself, and arranged with Leah that if Rachel took the mandrakes, Leah could sleep with Jacob that night. This incident gives insight into the inner workings of Jacob's family (see Illustration #9).

Illustration #9
Jacob's Family

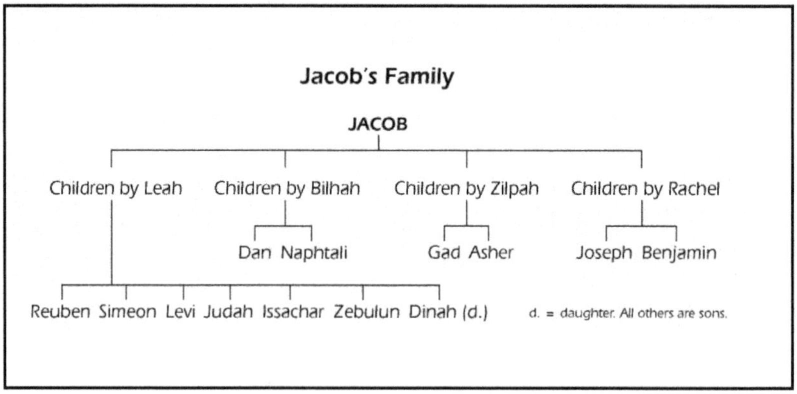

what others say

Dr. Larry Richards

Despite their flaws, God used each of these individuals to create a family that would become the channel of his blessing to the world. And, despite the dissatisfaction each felt, each truly was blessed. How we need to accept ourselves and our limitations. How we need to rejoice in what we have, rather than make ourselves and others miserable in pursuit of what we do not have.[4]

Of Speckled Goats and Black Sheep

After the birth of Joseph, Jacob asked Laban to release him so that he could return home, taking his wives and children with him. He made it clear that he had fulfilled his commitment of work for Laban. However, Laban asked Jacob to stay, observing that the Lord had prospered him because of Jacob.

The two men made an agreement. Jacob would stay and work, but he would be paid by developing his own flock of sheep and goats. Jacob would take "all the speckled and spotted sheep, and all the brown ones among the lambs, and the spotted and speckled among the goats; and these shall be my wages" (Genesis 30:32 NKJV). By this arrangement, if Jacob took any of Laban's sheep it would be easily observed. Laban agreed, for it seemed that Jacob would get only a small part of the animals. He separated these animals from the rest of the flocks, putting a three-day journey between the two flocks.

The Trickster Is Tricked

Laban thought he had the advantage over Jacob, since only a small number of the total flock was speckled and spotted. But Jacob was not to be outdone. He made efforts to increase his flock by having Laban's monochrome flock produce spotted and speckled offspring. He arranged peeled tree branches in the watering troughs, where they would be viewed when the animals came to drink. An accepted but unfounded notion was that something distinctive viewed during conception and pregnancy would leave its mark on the embryo. Jacob hoped that the dark tree branches, with their light stripes where bark was peeled away, would produce spotted and speckled animals. His strategy worked only because of God's intervention. Jacob "became exceedingly prosperous, and had large flocks, female and male servants, and camels and donkeys" (Genesis 30:43 NKJV).

Loaded Comments: Remarks Made When Naming Jacob's Sons

Name	Significance of Name	Reference in Genesis
	Leah's Sons	
Reuben	"The LORD has surely looked on my affliction."	29:32 (NKJV)
Simeon	"The LORD has heard that I am unloved."	29:33 (NKJV)
Levi	"This time my husband will become attached to me."	29:34 (NKJV)
Judah	"Now I will praise the LORD."	29:35 (NKJV)
Issachar	"God has given me my wages."	30:18 (NKJV)
Zebulun	"God has endowed me with a good endowment."	30:20 (NKJV)
	Rachel's Sons by Bilhah (Rachel's Maid)	
Dan	"God has judged my case."	30:6 (NKJV)
Naphtali	"With great wrestlings I have wrestled with my sister, and indeed I have prevailed."	30:8 (NKJV)
	Leah's Sons by Zilpah (Leah's Maid)	
Gad	"A troop comes!"	30:11 (NKJV)
Asher	"I am happy, for the daughters will call me blessed."	30:13 (NKJV)
	Rachel's Sons	
Joseph	"God has taken away my reproach."	30:23 (NKJV)
Benjamin	Son of My Sorrow, or Son of the Right Hand	35:18

Jacob Runs from Laban

Jacob's relationship with Laban had deteriorated because Laban and his sons became jealous of Jacob's prosperity. When Laban's hostility grew, God told Jacob it was time to return to Canaan, the Promised Land.

the big picture

Genesis 31:1–21

Jacob heard complaints from Laban's sons that he had gained his wealth by taking what belonged to Laban. He also observed Laban's growing hostility. The Lord spoke to Jacob, telling him to go back home. Jacob talked with Rachel and Leah, giving his perspective of how he had become so wealthy and telling them of God's message that they should leave. Rachel and Leah supported Jacob and told him to do whatever God had said he should do. Jacob took everything that belonged to him and left Haran without telling Laban that he was leaving.

You Can't Fire Me—I Quit!

Jacob had become very wealthy because God had blessed him. Laban's sons did not see it that way. They grumbled that Jacob had taken from Laban. At the same time, Jacob could see that Laban's attitude toward him had changed and was becoming hostile. The Lord spoke to Jacob in his dilemma: "Return to the land of your fathers and to your family, and I will be with you" (Genesis 31:3 NKJV). God had promised to bless and prosper Jacob. He fulfilled his promise. He also used circumstances to discipline Jacob and strengthen his character.

key point

Family Conference

Jacob called Rachel and Leah to come from the fields to discuss the situation. He explained that though Laban's attitude toward him had changed, the God of his father Isaac had been with him. He reviewed his honorable conduct toward Laban, though Laban had cheated him by changing his wages ten times. The tremendous increase in his flocks was because of God's intervention in the agreement between Laban and Jacob. He went on to say that the God who had met him at Bethel so many years before was calling him to return to the land he had come from.

Rachel and Leah supported Jacob, saying that they had no hope of inheritance from Laban. They felt Laban had reduced them to the status of **foreign women**. The wealth God had given Jacob was theirs and their children's.

So Jacob loaded up the camels and left, driving the animals in front of him. He was able to leave secretly while Laban was away shearing his sheep. Without Jacob's knowledge, Rachel stole her father's **household gods** and carried them away with her.

go to

ten times
Genesis 31:6–7

what others say

Stephen Fortosis

Laban tried every trick in the book to defraud Jacob. Ten times he renegotiated Jacob's "salary," giving him less each time. Jacob was cheated so flagrantly and so often that surely being cheated became hateful in his eyes.[5]

foreign women
women with no rights

household gods
small idol figurines supposed to bring prosperity

Laban Pursues Jacob

Jacob slipped away while Laban was away. When Laban discovered what had occurred, he was very angry and set out in a fury to catch up with Jacob.

the big picture

Genesis 31:22-55

Three days later, Laban heard about Jacob's departure and set out in pursuit. God spoke to Laban in a dream warning him to be careful of what he said to Jacob. He caught up with Jacob and asked why he had left so secretly. He would have given them a farewell party. He professed to understand why Jacob longed to return to his homeland, but he asked why they had stolen his household gods.

Jacob defended his actions, but the two men were not reconciled. Instead, they agreed to make a covenant and build a stone marker as a witness that they would not go into the other's territory to inflict harm.

You Can Keep My Daughters If You Return My Gods

Jacob had been gone three days before Laban got word of his departure. Laban took off in hot pursuit, but it took a week before he caught up with the party in the hill country of Gilead (see Appendix B). He confronted Jacob, asking, "Why did you flee away secretly, and steal away from me, and not tell me?" (Genesis 31:27 NKJV). He claimed that he would have hosted a farewell party and sent them off with goodwill. But with Jacob's deception, he had the right to do him harm, except that God had spoken to him and warned him to be careful what he said to Jacob. The burning issue, though, was the stolen gods. Jacob was unaware that Rachel had hidden the gods in her camel's saddles. Laban made a thorough search of the camp, but did not discover them because Rachel was sitting on the saddle and declined to stand up.

what others say

Samuel J. Schultz

The teraphim . . . may have had more legal than religious significance for Laban. According to Nuzu law, a son-in-law who possessed the household idols might claim the family inheritance in court. Thus Rachel was trying to obtain some advantage for her husband by stealing the idols.[6]

Finally a Truce

Obviously the men could not be reconciled, so they built a stone marker and set a boundary that they would respect. Jacob took an oath in the name of God and offered a sacrifice there. He served a meal that evening. The next morning, Laban kissed his daughters and grandchildren and returned home to Haran.

God used Laban to discipline Jacob so that when he returned home and eventually met Esau again, he was a changed man. God allows difficulties in our lives to shape us and to cause us to turn to him in humble dependence.

something to ponder

what others say

Victor P. Hamilton

Laban appears anxious to end this meeting with Jacob, and so rises early in the morning. He gives a kiss and a farewell blessing to his grandsons and daughters, but not to Jacob. Laban appears to ignore him. This last encounter between Jacob and Laban contrasts vividly with their first meeting, when Laban ran to meet him, and embraced him, and kissed him (29:13).[7]

Chapter Wrap-Up

- Jacob arrived in Haran and stopped at a well where some shepherds were waiting. He asked them about his uncle and they pointed out to him that the woman coming to the well with a flock of sheep was Laban's daughter Rachel. Jacob watered Rachel's sheep, then introduced himself. Rachel ran home and told her father, who hurried back to warmly welcome his sister's son. (Genesis 29:1–14)

- After a while Laban put Jacob to work and eventually offered to pay him. Jacob said he would work seven years with no pay if Laban would give him Rachel for his wife. Laban agreed. (Genesis 29:15–20)

- At the end of seven years, Laban tricked Jacob by giving him Leah, the older sister, instead of Rachel. Laban agreed to let Jacob marry Rachel the following week if Jacob would promise to work another seven years for her. Jacob agreed and ended up with two wives. (Genesis 29:21–30)

- Jacob loved Rachel, but she was unable to have children, whereas Leah gave birth to four sons. A rivalry arose between them, and they even involved their two maids in bearing Jacob's sons. Jacob eventually had six sons with Leah, two with her maid, two with Rachel's maid, and two with Rachel. (Genesis 29:31–30:21)

- Finally God blessed Rachel with a son. Then Jacob asked Laban to release him so he could take his family back home. Laban convinced him to stay and agreed to pay him by letting him keep all the spotted and speckled sheep and goats and every dark-colored lamb in Laban's flocks. Laban thought Jacob would end up with a small flock of sheep, but God made Jacob's flock grow very large. (Genesis 30:22–43)

- Laban's sons complained that Jacob was getting rich by taking what belonged to their father. Laban was also growing hostile toward Jacob. God told Jacob to leave and go back to his home. (Genesis 31:1–3)

- Jacob discussed leaving with Rachel and Leah. They agreed, since Laban had been cheating Jacob for years and the two women had no hope of any inheritance from their father. They left secretly while Laban was away from home. Nobody knew that Rachel had stolen her father's household idols and hidden them in her camel's saddle-bags. (Genesis 31:4–21)

- When Laban discovered that Jacob had left, he went after him. On the way, God warned Laban to be careful what he said to Jacob. When he caught up with them, Laban asked, "Why did you flee away secretly . . . and not tell me?" (verse 27 NKJV). He claimed that he would have given them a big farewell party. Then he asked for his idols. Jacob knew nothing about the idols, so Laban searched for them but couldn't find them. (Genesis 31:22–42)

- Jacob and Laban made a covenant and set up a boundary they both agreed to respect. The next morning Laban returned to his home. (Genesis 31:43–55)

Study Questions

1. How was Laban's greeting to Jacob on his arrival different from his farewell when Jacob left? What changed his attitude?

2. Why do you think God allowed Jacob to be cheated and mistreated by his uncle so many times?

3. What was the reason for the dissension between Jacob's wives?

4. How did God help Jacob prosper in spite of Laban's cheating?

5. How did Jacob know when to leave Laban and where to go?

Genesis 32–36 Jacob Returns to the Promised Land

Chapter Highlights:
- Jacob Prepares to Meet Esau
- Jacob Wrestles with God
- Jacob and Esau Meet
- Jacob Returns to Bethel

Let's Get Started

As Jacob led his family toward home, he nervously prepared himself to meet his estranged brother Esau. In twenty years Jacob hadn't heard from his family. What would he find? How should he plan to meet Esau? How could he protect his family if Esau was still seeking revenge? He tested the waters by sending advance greetings to Esau, only to learn from his messengers that Esau was coming to meet him with an army of four hundred men! In panic, Jacob divided his family and flocks and herds into two camps, hoping that if Esau attacked one group, the other could escape.

Jacob prayed earnestly to God. Then he prepared to send a gift to Esau, a lavish gift of animals that would be valuable in his culture.

That night Jacob wrestled with an unseen man, God in human form. In the encounter, Jacob's name was changed to Israel.

Returning to the Promised Land was heartwarming, but it did not protect Jacob from disappointment and sorrow with his family. At Bethel he built an altar to God and rid his family of foreign gods. God confirmed his covenant with Jacob. Rachel died giving birth to Benjamin. Isaac died and was buried by Jacob and Esau. The section closes with Esau's genealogy.

Jacob Prepares to Meet Esau

The last memory Jacob had of Esau was a terrifying one: Esau had promised to kill him. Now, as he prepared to meet his estranged brother, his heart quivered with fear.

the big picture

Genesis 32:1–21

As Jacob proceeded on his journey, God's angels met him. He called the place Mahanaim [see Appendix B], saying, "This is God's camp" (verse 2 NKJV).

go to

visions
Luke 1:11;
Acts 10:9–17

angels
Genesis 18:1–2;
32:24;
Daniel 8:15

He sent messengers ahead to let Esau know that he was coming. On their return, they informed Jacob that Esau was coming to meet him and had four hundred men with him. Fearing an attack, Jacob divided the people and the animals into two groups, hoping that if Esau attacked one group, the other could escape.

Then Jacob prayed, reminding God of his promises and asking for his protection. Jacob then sent a procession of animals to Esau as gifts, hoping to pacify him and thus avoid a conflict.

Met by Angels

When Jacob had left home twenty years before, God revealed in a vision a stairway reaching from earth to heaven with angels ascending and descending. Jacob named the place Bethel (Genesis 28:10–22).

what others say

Billy Graham

Abraham, Lot, Jacob and others had no difficulty recognizing angels when God allowed them to manifest themselves in physical form. Note, for example, Jacob's instant recognition of angels in Genesis 32:1–2.[1]

Norman Geisler and Thomas A. Howe

People sometimes "see" or "hear" things in their visions, but not with their naked physical senses. When someone saw angels with the naked eye, or had some physical contact with them, it was not a vision but an actual appearance of an angel in the physical world. During these appearances the angels temporarily assumed a visible form after which they returned to their normal invisible state.[2]

GOD AT WORK

Now as Jacob returned home, God's angels met him (32:1–2). There is no record of conversation on this occasion, but certainly the sight of a camp or army of angels must have reminded him of the covenant promises God had given him at Bethel when angels were present.

Putting Out Feelers

Jacob sent messengers to find Esau and inform him of Jacob's homecoming and specifically to find favor in his eyes (Genesis 32:5).

He had not forgotten that when he had left home, Esau had resolved to kill him.

The messengers returned with the terrifying news that Esau was on his way to meet him and had four hundred men with him. "Jacob was greatly afraid and distressed" (Genesis 32:7 NKJV).

Preparing for the Worst

Fearing an attack, Jacob divided his people and the animals into two groups, hoping that if one group were attacked by Esau's men, the other group could escape.

Alone, he prayed to the God of Abraham and Isaac, reminding him of his promise to make him prosperous and saying he was not worthy "of all the mercies and of all the truth" God had shown him (Genesis 32:10 NKJV). He asked God to keep him and all in his party safe from an attack from Esau.

Jacob sends servants with a carefully planned and lavish parade of gifts:

- 200 female goats
- 20 male goats
- 200 ewes
- 20 rams
- 30 female camels with their young
- 40 cows
- 10 bulls
- 20 female donkeys
- 10 male donkeys

They were to arrive with space between each herd. Jacob's intent was to pacify Esau and, hopefully, avoid the attack he so feared.

Jacob Wrestles with God

Jacob had been impressed by the appearance of angels as he embarked on his journey homeward (Genesis 32:1), but their presence did not remove the fear that gripped his heart. God visited Jacob's tent and provided him a life-changing experience.

the big picture

Genesis 32:22–32

That night Jacob was alone. He had sent his wives and children across the ford of the Jabbok River [see Appendix B] while he stayed on the other side. During the night a man wrestled with him, and when he could not win, he forced Jacob's hip so that it was wrenched from its socket. The man changed Jacob's name to Israel, saying, "You have struggled with God and with men, and have prevailed" (verse 28 NKJV). The man refused to give his name, but Jacob named the place Peniel [see Appendix B], saying that he had seen God face-to-face, and yet his life had been spared.

A Night Attacker

Jacob stayed alone the night before he would meet Esau. Undoubtedly he expected to use the time to prepare his mind for what could be an ugly confrontation with his twin brother. For their protection, he had sent his wives, maidservants, and eleven sons across the river Jabbok.

A man appeared and wrestled with Jacob in the darkness. As dawn approached and Jacob appeared to have the upper hand, the man dislocated Jacob's hip so that it was wrenched from its socket (Genesis 32:25). Then the man told Jacob, "Let Me go, for the day breaks" (verse 26 NKJV). But Jacob replied that he would not do so unless the man blessed him. The man did not answer directly. Instead, he asked, "What is your name?" (verse 27 NKJV). When Jacob replied, the man said, "Your name shall no longer be called Jacob, but Israel; for you have struggled with God and with men, and have prevailed" (verse 28 NKJV).

Jacob asked the man's name. As a reply, he responded by blessing Jacob. "Jacob called the name of the place Peniel: 'For I have seen God face to face, and my life is preserved'" (32:30 NKJV).

The man left, but as Jacob limped because of his hip, he had a constant reminder that he had wrestled with God.

what others say

Samuel J. Schultz

His name was changed from "Jacob" to "Israel." Thereafter Jacob was not the deceiver; instead he was subjected to deception and grief by his own sons.[3]

Jacob's new name Israel became the name of all the people covered by God's covenant, not just in Jacob's immediate family, but eventually in the tribes that grew from his sons and in the nation they became.

Jacob and Esau Meet

The face-to-face meeting could not be postponed or avoided. Esau was coming to meet Jacob. Would God answer Jacob's prayer for protection?

the big picture

Genesis 33

Jacob could see Esau approaching with his band of four hundred men. He went to meet him, bowing down to the ground as he approached. Esau ran toward him, embraced him, and kissed him, and they both wept. Then Jacob introduced Esau to his family. He explained that he had sent the droves of animals in an effort to find favor with Esau. Because God had blessed Jacob, he insisted that Esau keep the gifts, though Esau said he had plenty. Esau wanted to travel with Jacob and his party, but Jacob sent him on ahead. Then Jacob settled in Shechem [see Appendix B], buying a plot of land for his tent. He set up an altar, calling it El Elohe Israel.

Jacob looked in the distance and could see that Esau was approaching with his band of four hundred men. He quickly lined up his family, placing Rachel and Joseph in the safest place at the rear. Leaving the group, he went forward to meet Esau, bowing down to the ground seven times.

Esau disregarded the homage being paid him and ran to Jacob, embraced him, throwing his arms around Jacob's neck and kissing him. Both men wept. Esau asked about the women and children that were standing a little way off. Jacob answered that they were "the children whom God has graciously given your servant" (Genesis 33:5 NKJV). He then introduced Esau to his wives and children.

Esau asked about the droves of animals that had been presented to him. Esau had become wealthy and influential, but Jacob insisted that he accept the animals. He wanted to share with Esau some of the blessings God had given him. God's blessings did not mean to Esau what they did to Jacob. He probably didn't understand that Jacob was revealing his heart when he said, "If I have now found favor in your sight, then receive my present from my hand, inasmuch as I have seen your face as though I had seen the face of God, and you were pleased with me" (33:10 NKJV). In response, Esau accepted the gifts. But I'm Still Wary Esau graciously offered to accompany Jacob as they moved south to his home at Mount Seir (see Appendix B). Jacob begged off, however, giving the excuse that his party was unable to move at the pace Esau could. His party included young children and animals that had their young. Esau then offered to leave some of his men to assist in the travel, but Jacob again did not accept, saying that just finding favor with Esau was enough.

Esau started out for his home in Mount Seir, assuming that Jacob would be coming along behind him. Instead, Jacob went first to Succoth and then to Shechem, where he bought a piece of property, and he pitched his tent. Then he set up an altar and called it El Elohe Israel, which meant "El is the God of Israel."

what others say

Gene Getz

In essence, Jacob was saying, "The God of Israel is an 'El' "—that is, a strong God, a mighty One, a God who keeps his promises. Jacob was back in the land, and he wanted everyone to know it was the God of his fathers who brought him safely back.[4]

apply it

Jacob could not bring himself to live in close contact with Esau. In spite of the warm welcome Esau had given him, he seemed to fear future conflict. How often do we avoid people because we do not trust the Lord to help us work for true reconciliation and harmony?

Dinah Is Defiled in Shechem

the big picture

Genesis 34

Jacob's family had settled within sight of the city of Shechem (33:18). When Dinah, Leah's daughter, went into the city to visit women there, she was raped. What transpired after that brought sorrow to Jacob and disgrace to his family.

God had told Jacob to go back to the land of his fathers and his relatives (Genesis 31:3). He had crossed the border to that land and, without seeking God's direction, decided to settle in Shechem instead of proceeding farther.

Low-Blow Vengeance

Jacob settled in at Shechem, even buying a piece of land there. But was this where God wanted him to be?

Dinah, Leah's daughter, went to visit women who lived in the city. There she was raped by Shechem, son of Hamor, the ruler of that area, who then asked his father to secure her for his wife. Hamor made his way to Jacob's camp, eager to build an open relationship between Shechem and Jacob's camp and, more specifically, prepare to negotiate his son's marriage to Dinah. He was probably pleased, because it would be to their advantage to have an alliance with Jacob's wealthy family.

Jacob and his sons, who were well aware of what had transpired during Dinah's visit, made a condition for her marriage to Shechem: all males in the city must be circumcised. This seemed reasonable to Hamor and his son Shechem, so they went to recruit the support of the men of the city. The men agreed, and every male in the city was circumcised.

Three days later, before healing was complete, Dinah's brothers Simeon and Levi "came boldly upon the city and killed all the males," including Hamor and Shechem (Genesis 34:25–26 NKJV). Dinah's brothers rescued her from Shechem's house and left. They were followed by more brothers, who looted the city, carrying off its wealth, including women and children.

Jacob confronted Simeon and Levi with the horror of what they had done. They replied, "Should he treat our sister like a harlot?" (34:31 NKJV).

But Jacob was frightened—and rightly so. Other Canaanites in the area would surely learn what had happened and come to retaliate on behalf of the people of Shechem. Jacob and his whole family could be wiped out.

Bad things may happen to anyone. Even good people are victimized or are affected by disaster. How a person responds to the difficulty shows his or her true character.

go to

foreign gods
Joshua 24:14–15;
1 Samuel 7:3–4

foreign gods
false deities worshiped, replacing the true God

purify
preparing to meet God with wholehearted commitment to him

Jacob Returns to Bethel

Had Jacob forgotten what had happened at Bethel twenty years before when he was running from Esau? At Bethel God had promised to bring him back to the land and to protect him. It was time to go back to the place where Jacob had made his vow to make the Lord his God (Genesis 28:10–22).

the big picture

Genesis 35:1–15

God spoke to Jacob and told him to move to Bethel and settle there. He should build an altar and recall what God had said to him when he was fleeing from Esau. Jacob told his family to get rid of their foreign gods and prepare themselves to meet with God, who had faithfully kept his word to Jacob. At Bethel he built an altar and set up a stone pillar as a sacred remembrance of the place where God had confirmed the covenant with him.

Time for a Spiritual Return

Time spent in Shechem was disastrous, while it also revealed a spiritual vacuum in the hearts of Jacob's family. In mercy, God stepped into the picture. He told Jacob, "Go up to Bethel and dwell there; and make an altar there to God, who appeared to you when you fled from the face of Esau your brother" (Genesis 35:1 NKJV).

Jacob recognized that he had come to a turning point in his life. He told everyone in his household, "Put away the **foreign gods** that are among you, **purify** yourselves, and change your garments. Then let us arise and go up to Bethel; and I will make an altar there to God, who answered me in the day of my distress and has been with me in the way which I have gone" (35:2–3 NKJV).

The family complied. They gave Jacob their foreign gods and their earrings, which were associated with the idols in some way. These he buried under the oak trees at Shechem. Then they set out for Bethel, which was fifteen miles south.

As they moved along the route, they did not encounter any resistance. News of the massacre at Shechem had spread and the people feared Jacob and his sons.

what others say

W. Glyn Evans

When Jacob floundered, God said, "Arise, go up to Bethel, and dwell there" (Genesis 35:1 KJV). Why Bethel? That was where he first met the Lord and covenanted to walk with him.[5]

Two Decades of Blessing

The last time Jacob had been at Bethel, he had been alone, fleeing for his life from Esau, who was angry with him for taking the blessing (Genesis 27:41–28:9). While he slept, he had a dream in which he saw a stairway that stretched from earth to heaven. Angels ascended and descended it. Above it stood the Lord, who confirmed the covenant he had made with Abraham and Isaac.

When Jacob awoke, he made a vow that if God would be with him and bring him back safely, then the Lord would be his God. He set up a stone as a pillar of remembrance of his vow. We need to remember the promises we have made to God.

Now, twenty years later, Jacob returned with evidence of God's good hand of blessing. He built an altar and called the place El Bethel, meaning "The God of Bethel," because God had revealed himself to Jacob at that place.

God appeared to Jacob again, confirming that his name had been changed to Israel. He renewed the covenant, adding this time that kings would be among his descendants.

Jacob set up a stone pillar, as he had done twenty years previously, and poured out a drink offering and oil on it.

While they were in Bethel, Deborah, Jacob's mother's nurse, died and was buried. It appears Rebekah had died and the nurse had attached herself to Jacob's household. Rebekah had sent Jacob away for "a few days" (Genesis 27:44 NKJV), but they never saw each other again.

what others say

Bill T. Arnold

The story of Jacob has been one of struggles, struggles between Jacob and Esau, between Jacob and Laban, and between Jacob and God. At long last, Jacob returns to Bethel to find peace with God, though peace with his family remained elusive.[6]

go to

cried out
Genesis 30:1

prayed
Genesis 30:23–24

Rachel and Isaac Die

God had been shaping Jacob's character through many difficult experiences. His deceptive, manipulative nature had been softened. Now his heart is tenderized with painful partings.

> **the big picture**
>
> **Genesis 35:16–29**
>
> As the party traveled, Rachel began to give birth to a son. She lived only long enough to give him a name. Jacob buried her and set up a pillar to mark her tomb. Moving on, he came to Hebron [see Appendix B] and was with Isaac when he died at the age of 180 years. His sons Esau and Jacob buried him.

Painful Parting

While Jacob moved his family farther south, Rachel began to give birth, and complications came. Rachel's midwife tried to encourage her by telling her that she was giving birth to a son. But Rachel lived only long enough to name her son Ben-Oni, which means "son of my sorrow." Then she died. Jacob named him Benjamin, instead, which means "son of the right hand" or "son of honor or good fortune." Rachel was buried near Bethlehem, and Jacob set up a pillar to mark her tomb.

Years before, Rachel had cried out in anguish that she would die if she could not have a son. Then when Joseph was born, she prayed for a second son. Her prayer was answered, but she died giving birth to Benjamin.

That Jacob mourned the loss of his favorite wife is shown many years later when in his old age he was preparing to bless his sons. He recalled that he had buried her with great sorrow (Genesis 48:7).

Disgrace

Jacob had been disgraced by his sons at Shechem, and now came more disgrace. Jacob's oldest son Reuben slept with Bilhah. She was Rachel's maidservant, and as one of Jacob's secondary wives, she was mother of two of Reuben's half brothers, Dan and Naphtali. This was a sexual sin, but there was another aspect to his sinning with

Bilhah. Since it was a custom that the wives of a deceased leader became wives of his successor, it seemed that Reuben was taking over as the head of the family. Reuben was not punished for his sin immediately, but many years later when Jacob was blessing his sons, he refused to give Reuben his rights as the firstborn, but passed over him to give them to Joseph.

Yet Another Parting

At last Jacob came home to his father at Hebron. Isaac was 180 years old when he died. Esau and Jacob buried him. We do not have a record that the two brothers ever saw each other again.

Esau's Descendants

the big picture

Genesis 36

Esau had three wives, two from the people of Canaan and one distantly related to his family through Ishmael. He flourished in the hill country of Seir, living a distance from Jacob so that their flocks and herds could enjoy the space needed. The names of his sons and daughters are faithfully recorded, as are the chiefs and kings from among his many descendants.

Esau had set his heart on the here and now. It seemed that God's promises to Abraham and Isaac meant nothing to him. God gives us a picture of Esau's family, then turns the page. The rest of the story lies in Jacob's family; through them the promises would be fulfilled.

Be Careful What You Ask For (You Might Get It)

Esau gave up the birthright and missed out on the covenant blessings which would have made him a spiritual leader. He had shrugged that off with indifference to its true value. He wanted satisfaction immediately, and he got it. He became rich in offspring and rich in worldly goods.

apply it

The old saying was fulfilled for Esau: Beware what you set your heart on, for you will surely get it! The warning is for all of us. When we focus all our attention on earthly values, we miss out on heavenly, eternal values.

Chapter Wrap-Up

- As Jacob headed for home, he thought about meeting Esau again. Would Esau still want to kill him? How could Jacob protect his family? He sent greetings to Esau and learned that Esau was coming to meet him with an army of four hundred men. Jacob divided his people and animals into two groups, hoping that one group could escape if the other were attacked. He also sent many gifts of animals to Esau to put him in an accepting mood. (Genesis 32:1–8)

- Jacob prayed, asking God to keep all of them safe. (Genesis 32:9–12)

- The night before he was to meet Esau, Jacob stayed alone, having sent his family and maidservants across the river. During the night, a visitor came and wrestled with Jacob until dawn. He dislocated Jacob's hip, then said, "Let Me go, for the day breaks" (verse 26 NKJV). Jacob said he would not until the man blessed him. Then the man told him his new name would be Israel. Jacob realized that he had wrestled with God. After that, Jacob walked with a limp, a reminder that he had wrestled with God. (Genesis 32:13–32)

- When Esau approached with his four hundred men, Jacob placed Rachel and Joseph at the back of the group for safety, then he went to meet Esau, bowing to the ground seven times. (Genesis 33:1–3)

- Esau ran to Jacob and hugged and kissed him. Both brothers wept. Then Jacob introduced Esau to his family. Esau said he didn't need the animals Jacob had sent, but Jacob insisted he keep them. Jacob wanted to share some of God's blessings with his brother. (Genesis 33:4–11)

- Esau offered to accompany Jacob home or send some men along to help him, but Jacob declined since he wasn't planning to go all the way to Mount Seir, where Esau lived. Jacob went instead to Succoth, then to Shechem. (Genesis 33:12–20)

- After Jacob's family settled near Shechem, his daughter Dinah went to town for a visit. She was raped by the son of Hamor, the ruler of the area, who then decided he wanted her for his wife. Hamor went to negotiate with Jacob for his son's bride. Jacob and his sons agreed on the condition that all the males in the city be circumcised. Hamor agreed and the circumcisions took place. Three days later, Dinah's brothers Simeon and Levi attacked the city, killing every male in it, then took Dinah home. Other brothers followed to loot the city and take captives of women and children. (Genesis 34)

- God mercifully told Jacob to move to Bethel. Jacob finally took some spiritual leadership in his family, telling them to get rid of their foreign gods and purify themselves, and go with him to Bethel where he would build an altar to God. The family complied, and Jacob buried the idols before they set out for Bethel. (Genesis 35:1–5)
- At Bethel God appeared to Jacob and renewed his covenant. Jacob again set up a stone as a pillar and poured oil on it. (Genesis 35:6–15)
- When the family moved again, Rachel died giving birth to Benjamin. She was buried near Bethlehem. (Genesis 35:16–20)
- Jacob's oldest son Reuben slept with Rachel's maid Bilhah. She was one of Jacob's secondary wives, so this was an insult to Jacob as well as a sexual sin. Reuben wasn't punished then, but years later, when Jacob blessed his sons, he gave Reuben's rights as the firstborn to Joseph. (Genesis 35:21–26)
- Jacob finally saw his father Isaac again at Hebron. When Isaac died at the age of 180, Jacob and Esau buried him. (Genesis 35:27–29)
- Esau, who had despised his birthright, missed out on God's covenant blessings, but he became a rich man not interested in spiritual things. (Genesis 36)

Study Questions

1. Jacob asked God to protect him, but how did his actions show his lack of faith?

2. What was the significance of Jacob's new name, Israel?

3. What can we learn about forgiveness from Esau's example?

4. What do the incidents of Dinah's brothers seeking revenge for her and Reuben's sin with Bilhah tell us about the spiritual condition of Jacob's family?

5. What finally made Jacob realize that he needed to be a spiritual leader to his family?

Part Five
God and Joseph

Genesis 37–38 Joseph and His Family

Chapter Highlights:
- **Joseph's Dreams**
- **Twelve Sons, One Favorite**
- **Joseph Sold by His Brothers**
- **Judah and Tamar**

Let's Get Started

To this point, the Bible account of Jacob's life has focused on his relationship with his immediate family and then with his father-in-law Laban and with his wives. The story now shifts to Jacob's children and their relationships, and especially the account of Joseph, Jacob's favored son.

That Joseph was indeed the favored son caused enormous problems. The favoritism shown by Isaac to Esau and Rebekah to Jacob was repeated in Jacob's family with disastrous results. Bad feelings escalated as Joseph told his older brothers about two dreams he had. The brothers resented Joseph and their hatred grew until they callously sold him to traders to be a slave in Egypt.

The account of what happened to Joseph is interrupted by a sorry story of Judah and his family.

Though it's not a pretty picture, God was working out his plan. All twelve sons were in the covenant line as offspring of Jacob. They became known as the sons of Israel (Jacob's new name given him by God). In time, their descendants, as people of the covenant, were known as Israelites.

As the human key to fulfilling his plans, God chose Joseph. We find that through his story of pain and loss, God was working for Joseph's good and for the good of all Israelites, and ultimately for all the world.

Joseph's Dreams

Very early in life, children exhibit personality and character traits that distinguish them for the rest of their lives. Jacob surely observed this in his twelve sons. The heart of one of his boys, Joseph, was especially open to God.

the big picture

Genesis 37:1–11

One day Joseph, Jacob's favorite son, was tending the flocks with his brothers and brought home a bad report of his siblings. So Jacob showed his partiality to Joseph by making him a beautiful coat. The brothers were so jealous that they hated Joseph. One day Joseph told his brothers about two dreams he had had. Discerning the dreams as revealing that he was superior to them, his brothers hated him even more. When Joseph told his father about the dreams, Jacob reproved him mildly, but mulled the matter over in his mind.

Twelve Sons, One Favorite

Jacob had twelve sons and one, Joseph, was his favorite. This made for trouble among the brothers. They each had duties, and Joseph's was to help his older brothers in the fields with the sheep. But when Joseph observed them doing something wicked, he reported their conduct to his father.

Now it was no secret that Joseph was the favored son. In fact, Jacob made him a richly ornamented robe. This coat or tunic has commonly been described as a coat of many colors. Whatever its color, it was a robe that reached to the ankles and had long sleeves. The brothers, taking this gift of the robe as a clear indication that Jacob loved Joseph more than any of them, hated their brother and would not be civil to him. They probably communicated ill feelings toward Jacob as well.

The robe that Jacob gave Joseph was no garment for working on a range, but rather was worn by a gentleman not used to hard work outdoors.

what others say

Gene Getz

Jacob never intended for this coat to be functional. Rather, it represented Joseph's favored position in the family. It was symbolic of the fact that Jacob was letting everyone know that he was planning to treat Joseph as his firstborn with all the rights and privileges—namely, that he was entitled to a double portion of the inheritance and he would be the one who would carry on the leadership of the family.[1]

I Have a Dream

Joseph had a dream which he innocently related to his brothers. The dream was about a common agricultural activity. They were binding sheaves of grain in the field. Suddenly Joseph's sheaf rose and stood upright while his brothers' sheaves gathered around Joseph's and bowed down.

Furious, the brothers asked if he intended to rule over them. They hated Joseph even more because of the dream.

go to

entertaining angels
Hebrews 13:2

I Have Another Dream

Joseph dreamed again, and again he related it to his brothers. This time the sun and the moon and eleven stars were bowing down to him. When he told Jacob about it, Jacob asked, "What is this dream that you have dreamed? Shall your mother and I and your brothers indeed come to bow down to the earth before you?" (Genesis 37:10 NKJV). The brothers responded with jealousy that would poison their hearts, but his father, after mildly reproving him, pondered the matter.

Joseph Sold by His Brothers

Jealousy and anger were like untreated wounds that festered in the hearts of Joseph's brothers. Every day they spoke unkindly about him and to him. Then one day they seized an opportunity to do him great harm.

the big picture

Genesis 37:12–36

The brothers took the flocks to Shechem to graze. After a time, Jacob sent Joseph to see if all was well. When Joseph arrived, the brothers seized the opportunity to throw him in a well, intending to kill him. Instead, Reuben rescued him from death, only to have him sold to a caravan of Ishmaelites who were headed to Egypt. The brothers dipped Joseph's robe in the blood of a goat and showed it to Jacob. Assuming that some ferocious animal had devoured him, Jacob mourned Joseph's death for many days.

Here Comes the Dreamer

cistern
a reservoir for holding water

Ishmaelites
descendants of Abraham by Hagar

Midianites
descendants of Abraham by Keturah

myrrh
fragrant gum from a plant, used for perfume

The brothers went back to Shechem, the scene of their terrible sin against the men of that city (Genesis 34). Then another horrible event happened.

The brothers had moved the flocks to graze at Shechem. Jacob was concerned, so he sent Joseph to check on them and bring word back to him. When Joseph arrived at Shechem, a man directed him twenty miles north to Dothan (see Appendix B), where they had moved. When the brothers saw him approaching, they came up with an idea. They decided to kill him and throw him into a cistern. They would simply tell Jacob that "some wild beast has devoured him" (Genesis 37:20 NKJV).

Reuben was absent when they agreed to the plan. As the eldest, he felt somewhat responsible for Joseph, so he suggested instead of killing him, they throw him in the cistern and leave him there. Reuben secretly planned to rescue Joseph and take him back to Jacob.

what others say

Charles R. Swindoll

It's interesting to note that Jacob's sons returned to the area called Shechem to pasture their animals. This was the very place where their sister, Dinah, had been raped and where they had killed all the men and raided their homes and property. When Jacob realized where they had gone, he probably thought, "Because of what they did to the people of Shechem, my boys may be in danger." So he ordered Joseph to go and check on his brothers and report back.[2]

Sold for Twenty Shekels of Silver

When Joseph arrived, they stripped him of his richly ornamented robe, which they despised. Then they threw him in a **cistern** that had no water in it. They were eating when they observed a caravan of **Ishmaelites** (also called **Midianites**) approaching. Their camels had spices, balm, and **myrrh** which they were delivering to Egypt.

Judah made a proposal. There would be no gain to them if they killed Joseph. However, if they sold him, they would avoid murder and profit by the money received from the traders.

They executed their plan (see Appendix A). The merchants paid twenty shekels of silver and the brothers were rid of the spoiled brat and his dreams. Joseph was on his way to Egypt.

It's hard to imagine the sense of horror that must have gripped Joseph as he gradually discovered the enormity of his brothers' sin against him. As the caravan carried him step-by-step away from his father, step-by-step closer to slavery, anguish must have overwhelmed the teenage boy.

When Reuben discovered what they had done, he became anxious. What would they tell their father? They took Joseph's robe, killed a goat, and dipped the robe in its blood. When they showed the bloodstained robe to Jacob, they let him draw his own conclusion. Joseph had been killed and devoured by a wild beast!

Jacob tore his clothes, put on **sackcloth**, and mourned for his son many days. All his children tried to comfort him, but he refused to be comforted. He would mourn for his son until he went to his grave.

Meanwhile, the merchants sold Joseph in Egypt to Potiphar, the **pharaoh**'s captain of the guard.

go to

waiting
Psalm 27:13–14; 130:5–6

sackcloth
a cloth like burlap, made of goat's or camel's hair, worn as a sign of mourning

pharaoh
powerful ruler in Egypt, equivalent to a king

what others say

Donald Joy

We sometimes imagine that we would love to dance with wisdom, to have great insights, to be a persuasive teacher. But we rarely have a corresponding appetite for pain. Yet pain is the crucible from which insight and wisdom emerge.[3]

Oswald Chambers

Always remember that God's control is behind everything. His care encircles every incident and event of our lives. This means that we can maintain an attitude of perfect trust in him and an eagerness to ask God for aid in our daily living.[4]

Dr. Larry Richards

An ancient trade route led past Dothan; a highway linking Egypt with Damascus and the north. It would not be unusual for a caravan of Arab traders to pass by the place where Joseph was sold by his brothers. Egyptian lists of house slaves mention many with Semitic names. Another authentic touch is the fact that twenty pieces of silver was the standard price for a slave in the earth's second millennium B.C. (see Leviticus 27:5).[5]

go to

levirate marriage
Deuteronomy 25:5–10

levirate marriage
obligation of a brother-in-law to keep a family line going

signet and cord
a seal hanging from a cord about its owner's neck

staff
wooden stick with distinctive carving at the top

Judah and Tamar

God includes an account of Judah's daughter-in-law which provides insight into the understanding Jacob's family had in God's covenant with Abraham.

> **the big picture**
>
> **Genesis 38**
>
> Judah married a Canaanite woman and had four sons. He violated custom in Tamar, his daughter-in-law, and behaved dishonorably with her. He finally acknowledged his wrong.

He Asked for It!

Judah, fourth son of Leah, brought disgrace on himself as a result of making wrong decisions.

Judah left his family and married a Canaanite woman. He had four sons. Judah arranged for his eldest son, Er, to marry Tamar.

But Er was wicked, and the Lord slew him. Er left no son to carry on his name. Following custom, Judah asked his second son Onan to take Tamar and perform his duty by producing offspring for his brother Er. This responsibility was known as **levirate marriage**. But Onan refused to produce a son who would carry on the name of his father and eventually inherit his father's estate. God slew him also.

Judah sent Tamar to live as a widow in her father's household until his third son Shelah matured. But when Shelah was old enough to produce a son with Tamar, Judah neglected to fulfill his obligation.

In the meantime, Judah's wife died. After a period of grieving, Judah hired a prostitute, unaware that it was Tamar, his daughter-in-law, dressed not as a widow but as a prostitute. He agreed to pay for his visit by sending her a goat. But she asked for his **signet and cord** and his **staff** as a pledge. Judah returned home, and so did Tamar. She resumed wearing her widow's clothes.

Meanwhile, Judah wanted his pledge back, so sent a friend to find the woman. The friend made inquiries and learned that there was no prostitute in that area. Judah wanted to avoid being embarrassed, so decided to let the prostitute keep the pledge.

Three months later, Judah learned that Tamar was pregnant as a result of being a prostitute. Judah wanted to enforce the law immediately. She should be exposed and burned to death.

death
Leviticus 21:9;
Deuteronomy 22:24

As the law was being enforced, Tamar sent a message to Judah. She had become pregnant by the man who owned the seal, cord, and staff the messenger bore. Immediately recognizing the objects as his own, Judah admitted that Tamar had been more righteous than he, since he had not given her to his third son Shelah.

what others say

Kathy Collard Miller

Tamar probably understood and believed God's promise that the Messiah will come through Judah. She didn't want the family line to end. Since Shelah wasn't going to marry, she needed to marry Judah. Tamar took action to keep the family line going. Although Tamar's desire to see God's law fulfilled is commendable, she forces it to happen in the wrong way.[6]

Bill T. Arnold

The Tamar episode gives a graphic insight into Judah's character. He is a callous and rapacious individual. He had been the brother who realized that murdering Joseph was pointless when they could gain a profit by selling him (Genesis 37:26–27). In Genesis 38, he fails to express any grief or show mourning for the loss of his two sons, and succinctly orders to have Tamar burned for her crime. Yet later in Genesis, Judah is a changed man.[7]

Judah did not act in ignorance. He brought shame on himself by the wrong decisions he made. However, God did not write him off. He showed grace to Judah and worked out his sovereign plan even through Judah's wrong choices. Tamar the Canaanite is specifically mentioned in the genealogy of Jesus (Matthew 1:3) and their son Perez was an ancestor of King David (Matthew 1:6).

God's grace and mercy extend to us as well. No matter who we are or what we have done, "God demonstrates His own love toward us, in that while we were still sinners, Christ died for us" (Romans 5:8 NKJV).

what others say

Peggy Lynch

A heart that has confessed and forsaken sin will be declared righteous by God through Christ Jesus. Both Tamar and

Judah found God's forgiveness and saw him work out his good purposes through their lives. Only God can bring blessing from disaster, deceit, and disillusionment. Only God knows the heart of a person.[8]

Chapter Wrap-Up

- Of Jacob's twelve sons, Joseph was his favorite. He made this obvious when he gave Joseph a special coat. His brothers became jealous and hated Joseph. (Genesis 37:1–14)

- Joseph had two unusual dreams and told his family about them. In the first dream, their sheaves of grain bowed down to Joseph's sheaf. In the second, the sun, moon, and eleven stars bowed down to him. The family interpreted this to mean that Joseph thought his family would one day bow down to him. This made his brothers hate him even more. (Genesis 37:5–11)

- Joseph's brothers went with their flocks to Shechem. Jacob sent Joseph to check on them. When the brothers, now at Dothan, saw Joseph coming, they decided to kill him. Reuben suggested that instead, they throw Joseph in a cistern and just leave him there. Reuben planned to sneak back later and rescue Joseph. (Genesis 37:12–22)

- When Joseph arrived, the brothers stripped him of his special coat and threw him into a cistern. Later, a caravan of Ishmaelites came by, bound for trading in Egypt. Judah suggested that they sell Joseph to these traders. The brothers agreed, all but Reuben who was not there. The Ishmaelites bought Joseph for twenty shekels of silver and took him away. (Genesis 37:23–28)

- When Reuben returned, he became anxious about how they would explain Joseph's absence to their father. The brothers decided to kill a goat and dip Joseph's coat in its blood. They did this, and Jacob assumed a wild animal had killed his favorite son. Jacob mourned for many days and would not be comforted. (Genesis 37:29–35)

- The Ishmaelites took Joseph to Egypt and sold him to Potiphar, Pharaoh's captain of the guard. (Genesis 37:36)

- Judah left his family and married a Canaanite woman with whom he had four sons. (Genesis 38:1–5)

- Judah arranged for his son Er to marry a woman named Tamar. Er was so wicked the Lord let him die. This left Tamar a widow with no children. Judah asked his second son Onan to produce children with Tamar to carry on his brother's name, according to custom. Onan refused and God caused him to die also. Judah sent Tamar back to her family until his third son would be old enough to have a son with her. But when the time came, Judah did not follow through on this responsibility. (Genesis 38:6–11)

- Judah's wife died and he hired a prostitute for himself, not realizing that it was Tamar in disguise. She asked him for a pledge that he would pay her—his signet and its cord and his staff. He gave them to her. When he tried to contact the prostitute to get his pledge back, he couldn't find her. Three months later, when Judah learned that Tamar was pregnant from being a prostitute, he was going to have her put to death. Tamar then sent him back his pledge to prove that Judah was the man who had made her pregnant. (Genesis 38:12–26)

- Tamar was not killed. Instead, she gave birth to twins, one of whom was in the line of King David and Jesus. (Genesis 38:27–30; Matthew 1:3)

Study Questions

1. How did Jacob's obvious favoritism (like his father's) cause dissension in his family?

2. How did God care for Joseph in the midst of his brothers' hatred?

3. In Genesis 35, Jacob seemed to be taking spiritual leadership in his family. Judging by Genesis 37–38, what effect did this have on his sons?

4. What can we learn about God's grace from Judah's story?

5. What often happens when we, like Judah, choose to spend our time with ungodly people?

Genesis 39–41 Joseph in Egypt

Chapter Highlights:
- **Joseph in Potiphar's House—and in Prison**
- **Joseph Interprets Dreams**
- **Joseph in Charge of Egypt**
- **Joseph's Food Pantries**

Let's Get Started

Joseph didn't get what he deserved. As a matter of fact, God does not give us a record of any sin in Joseph's life—or any fault, even. Hated by his jealous brothers, Joseph had been sold as a slave and found himself in Potiphar's house in Egypt. How God changed his circumstances—from being a slave in an official's house to being unfairly imprisoned, and then suddenly made a ruler in Egypt, second only to the pharaoh. That's the exciting story we discover in Genesis 39–41.

The key to Joseph's unexpected elevation lies in the fact that God was with him. An almost nameless slave was purchased by Potiphar, a high official serving Pharaoh. It soon became evident to Potiphar that Joseph was unusually gifted—everything he was assigned to do was successful. As he assigned more and more responsibility to Joseph, he saw more and more success. In time, he put Joseph in charge of all his affairs, except the food he ate.

Then disaster struck. Joseph was falsely accused of rape by Potiphar's wife and was thrown into prison. Success even followed Joseph there. Before long, he was given responsibility to manage the prison. From there, he went to the palace, where he was elevated to being second in command to Pharaoh himself. And at each step of the way the Lord was working out his plan for Joseph.

Joseph in Potiphar's House—and in Prison

Jacob started out on his long journeys with the promises of God ringing in his ears (Genesis 28:15; 31:3). Joseph had no word from God as the Ishmaelite caravan carried him from Canaan down to Egypt (see Appendix B), no word when he was sold as a slave, no word when he became successful in Potiphar's estate, and no word when he was thrown into prison. Still, God was with him.

go to

mealtimes
Genesis 43:32

the big picture

Genesis 39

Joseph was purchased from the Ishmaelites by Potiphar, captain of Pharaoh's guard. Potiphar soon noticed that God had blessed Joseph in an unusual way, so he put him in charge of his whole household and possessions. Potiphar's wife noticed how attractive Joseph was and privately insisted that he have sex with her. He refused. In her humiliation, she made a false report to her husband, saying that Joseph raped her. Burning with anger, Potiphar sent Joseph to prison. There the Lord continued to give Joseph success in all that he did.

What Is It About That Slave?

Joseph, the seventeen-year-old favored son of a wealthy, God-blessed man, was suddenly a slave. His brothers had sold him to merchants who took him to Egypt.

Potiphar purchased Joseph from the Ishmaelite traders and took him to work in his home. Potiphar was captain of the guard to the pharaoh, or his chief steward. It wasn't long before Potiphar noticed that God was with Joseph, giving him unusual ability as an administrator. Everything Joseph did prospered. So Potiphar put Joseph in charge of all his household and all that he owned, including his fields. He became a business administrator for Potiphar, and God made the affairs of the household and property run so smoothly that the only decision Potiphar had to make every day was what he wanted to eat.

what others say

J. Vernon McGee

This fine-looking young man, 17 years old, would be a prize as a slave in the market. He was bought by Potiphar who was a captain of the guard. Potiphar was in the military, he had his office in the Pentagon of that day, and he was part of the brass, a prominent official.[1]

Victor P. Hamilton

The only thing Potiphar does not delegate to Joseph is the preparation of his food, perhaps because of a general Egyptian concern that non-Egyptians were unaware of how properly to prepare food, or more likely, because of ritual separation at mealtimes.[2]

The Innocent Heartthrob

Potiphar's wife was not blind to Joseph's well-built body and handsome face. After a while she began to harass him, asking him to sleep with her. Joseph refused, not wanting to betray the trust Potiphar had placed in him and, even more, not wanting to sin against God. Day after day she kept up her campaign to seduce him. Day after day he refused.

Then one day when Joseph was in the house tending to his duties while other servants were absent, Potiphar's wife grabbed him by his cloak and again tried to seduce him. Leaving his cloak in her grasp, he ran out of the house.

> **what others say**
>
> **Charles R. Swindoll**
>
> Joseph was a dedicated, well-disciplined believer, but he was smart enough to realize he couldn't tease lust without being whipped. When it came time for a hasty exit, the son of Jacob preferred to leave his jacket behind rather than hesitate and leave his hide.[3]

I'll Get My Revenge!

Potiphar's wife was humiliated by Joseph's repeated rejection of her. But as she held his cloak in her hand she recognized that she had a means of taking revenge on him.

First, she called her household servants to her and told a trumped-up story: "See, he has brought in to us a Hebrew to mock us. He came in to me to lie with me, and I cried out with a loud voice. And it happened, when he heard that I lifted my voice and cried out, that he left his garment with me, and fled and went outside" (Genesis 39:14–15 NKJV). We do not know how the servants responded, but she informed them so they would support her story if anyone questioned it.

When Potiphar came home, she repeated her vicious lies. She referred to her husband's most trusted assistant as "the Hebrew servant," a term with negative racial overtones. Then she repeated the tale she had earlier told her household servants and showed his robe as evidence. She ended with "Your servant did to me after this manner" (39:19 NKJV).

Potiphar was so furious that he did not even ask Joseph for his side of the story. He "put him into the prison, a place where the king's prisoners were confined" (39:20 NKJV).

What Am I Doing Here?

God had blessed Joseph in Potiphar's house, but now he was in prison. What happened? Proof that God had not abandoned him came as the prison warden's heart was warmed and he showed kindness. Joseph had favor in his eyes. The warden gave Joseph a position of responsibility over the prison. As with Potiphar, the warden did not have to supervise Joseph's work because everything went well under his supervision.

what others say

David A. Seamands

There is a scriptural way to deal with all these hurts from our past. God's way goes far beyond forgiving and surrendering resentment. God takes sins, failures, and hurts that happened earlier in your life and wraps His loving purposes around them to change them.[4]

Oswald Chambers

The rarest asset to a godly life is to be practically conscientious in every situation. "But the Lord was with Joseph . . . and gave him favor in the sight of the keeper of the prison" (v. 21). Joseph's adaptability was superb.[5]

something to ponder

Joseph could have been consumed by the way he had been treated, first by his brothers and then by Potiphar. The hurts could have festered in his heart until he became bitter. Instead, though, Joseph found healing. He saw beyond his scars and allowed God to bless and prosper him even in challenging, unpleasant situations.

Joseph Interprets Dreams

Joseph made himself available for whatever task came his way. God gave him success in his prison duties. Beyond that, when two prisoners from the palace confided in him, he responded with humility and grace, little knowing the far-reaching effects his actions would have.

the big picture

Genesis 40

Two of the pharaoh's staff were imprisoned: the cupbearer and the baker. Each man had a disturbing dream. Giving credit to God, Joseph interpreted the dreams, and each was fulfilled exactly as Joseph had said.

Two New Inmates

God had spoken to Abraham, Isaac, and Jacob. He had not spoken to Joseph. How would Joseph know God was with him?

Joseph was in the prison where the pharaoh's prisoners were confined. One day two of the pharaoh's staff offended him. Angrily, the pharaoh sent both men to prison, where they were put under Joseph's supervision.

After some time, both men had dreams which disturbed them deeply. Noting their depressed spirits, Joseph asked what was troubling them. They confided that they both had dreams but had nobody to go to who could interpret their meaning.

Joseph asked with a humble heart, "Do not interpretations belong to God?" (Genesis 40:8 NKJV). Then he graciously invited them to tell him their dreams. He would trust God for their interpretation.

go to

interpretation
Daniel 2

cupbearer
a high official in Pharaoh's court

what others say

Elisabeth Elliot

Grace is a marvelous but elusive word. "Unmerited favor" is the definition most of us know. It means self-giving, too, and springs from the person's own being without condition or consideration of whether the object is deserving.[8]

The Cupbearer's Dream

Pharaoh's **cupbearer** related his dream. He saw a vine with three branches that budded, blossomed, and developed clusters that ripened into grapes. In the dream the cupbearer squeezed the juice of the grapes into Pharaoh's cup and then handed the cup to Pharaoh.

The Interpretation

Joseph interpreted the dream to mean that within three days Pharaoh would restore him to his position. He would once again hand Pharaoh his cup.

Then Joseph made a personal request. Would he please remember Joseph by mentioning him to Pharaoh and plead for his release? "I was stolen away from the land of the Hebrews; and also I have done nothing here that they should put me into the dungeon" (Genesis 40:15 NKJV).

what others say

Gene Getz

> Joseph knew he was innocent and that this was God's divine moment for him to explain his predicament and ask for help. And I'm glad he did, for it indicates there's a time to defend ourselves against false accusations—even though God is the ultimate vindicator. There's also a time to ask someone to put in a good word for us even though we are trusting God with all our hearts to help us and to defend us.[7]

The Chief Baker's Dream

Encouraged by the positive interpretation of the cupbearer's dream, the chief baker told about his dream. On his head were three baskets of bread. The top basket contained a variety of baked goods for Pharaoh, which birds were eating. Since birds were sacred in Egypt and therefore were protected, the chief baker needed to be diligent in keeping them from helping themselves to his baked goods. In his dream, he was allowing them to consume food that was supposed to go to the pharaoh's table.

The Interpretation

Joseph then interpreted the dream: within three days Pharaoh would behead the baker and hang him. The birds would consume the baker's flesh.

The Dreams Come True

Pharaoh's birthday came three days later, and he gave a feast for all his officials to celebrate the occasion. He restored the chief cupbearer to his former position, but he hanged the baker, exactly as Joseph had predicted.

"The chief butler did not remember Joseph, but forgot him" (Genesis 40:23 NKJV).

Lord
Psalm 146:3, 5–6

what others say

Warren Wiersbe

After his release and restoration, the cupbearer not only said nothing to Pharaoh about Joseph, but also he forgot Joseph completely! So much for turning to people for help instead of waiting on the Lord.[8]

It was commonly believed that dreams had real significance and often contained hints of the future. The interpretation of dreams was considered an art.

Once the cupbearer was restored to his duties with Pharaoh, Joseph must have had high hopes that he would soon be summoned to the palace and have his unfair prison sentence removed. But he was enrolled in God's school. The subject was learning to do what God wanted. The test assigned was waiting, waiting, waiting. For two long years Joseph waited, longing for release, but receiving no shred of hope.

Joseph Interprets Dreams of Pharaoh

Joseph was available for whatever God wanted him to do. He was also prepared for whatever God planned for him. While conducting his duties in the prison, Joseph received a summons to go to Pharaoh's palace.

the big picture

Genesis 41:1–40

Pharaoh was disturbed by a dream. When he fell asleep again, he had a second equally disturbing dream. When the magicians and wise men were unable to interpret the dream, the cupbearer remembered Joseph. Summoned to the palace, Joseph interpreted Pharaoh's dreams as God's message to prepare for a famine that was coming. Joseph recommended a plan of action that would save the Egyptians from starvation. Seeing the wisdom in Joseph's plan, Pharaoh elevated him to be in charge of affairs. Joseph's position was second only to the pharaoh himself.

One Strange Dream

Joseph was in prison two more years, forgotten by his family, forgotten by the cupbearer, but not forgotten by God. God was in charge of events. Neither Joseph nor the forgetful cupbearer were able to change God's timetable.

Pharaoh dreamed that he was standing by the Nile River. Out of the water came seven sleek, fat cows that grazed among the reeds by the riverbank. Then came seven more cows. These were gaunt and ugly. They ate up the seven fat cows.

Another Strange Dream

Pharaoh woke up, then fell asleep again and had a second dream. One single stalk of grain bore seven healthy, good heads. Then came seven other heads of grain that sprouted thin and were scorched by the east wind. The seven thin heads swallowed up the seven healthy, full heads.

Then Pharaoh woke up from the dream.

Trouble in the Palace

Morning found the pharaoh deeply disturbed. He called for all the magicians and wise men of Egypt, but none of them could tell the ruler what his dreams meant, even though they were supposed to be specialists in dream interpretation.

Then the cupbearer remembered Joseph. He told Pharaoh how Joseph had interpreted both his and the baker's dreams, "and it came to pass, just as he interpreted for us, so it happened" (Genesis 41:13 NKJV).

A Summons from the Palace

Pharaoh lost no time in sending for Joseph. In the prison, Joseph quickly shaved and changed his clothes, then appeared before the ruler of Egypt.

Pharaoh related his dilemma and challenged Joseph to interpret his dreams as he had interpreted the dreams of the cupbearer and baker.

Joseph answered, "It is not in me; God will give Pharaoh an answer of peace" (Genesis 41:16 NKJV).

Egyptian men did not wear beards, as did the sons of Abraham. Joseph had to shave before appearing before Pharaoh.

Joseph had waited for this moment for two long years. Here was his opportunity to sell himself to Pharaoh. But Joseph did not take advantage of his chance. Instead, he spoke humbly and truthfully. He could not interpret the dreams, but God could—not one of the many gods the Egyptians worshiped, but the true God of heaven and earth.

Pharaoh Tells His Dreams

Pharaoh described to Joseph the first dream of the seven healthy cows that were consumed by the scrawny, very ugly, lean cows. Even after eating the healthy cows, the lean cows looked just as ugly as before.

Then he described the second dream in which a single stalk bore seven heads of full, good heads of grain. Then seven other heads sprouted—withered, thin, and scorched by the east wind. The thin heads swallowed up the seven good heads.

None of the Egyptian magicians could interpret these strange dreams.

God Gives Joseph the Interpretation

Joseph explained that the two dreams really had one message that God was revealing to Pharaoh. The seven good cows were seven years and the seven good heads of grain were seven years. The seven lean, ugly cows were seven years and so were the seven worthless heads of grain. They represented seven years of famine.

God was showing Pharaoh what he was about to do. After seven years of great abundance throughout Egypt, seven years of famine would follow.

Joseph Makes a Recommendation

Joseph then gave Pharaoh his recommendation: "Select a discerning and wise man, and set him over the land of Egypt" (Genesis

signet ring
ring with a royal symbol engraved on it. When used to sign a document, the ring was impressed into clay or wax and pressed on the document as an official stamp.

41:33 NKJV). Joseph went on to recommend precisely how the food should be stored during the years of abundance and then distributed during the years of famine.

Joseph Receives a Promotion

Pharaoh and all his officials could see that Joseph's recommendation had great merit. Pharaoh then commended Joseph for his genius, discernment, and wisdom, and elevated him to be in charge of the palace with all his people submitting to Joseph's orders. Joseph would be second in command in the whole nation of Egypt, under Pharaoh.

Joseph in Charge of Egypt

Pharaoh had been let down by his magicians and wise men. He quickly recognized that in Joseph were the traits he needed: true wisdom and more—the Spirit of God on his life. He took action immediately.

the big picture

Genesis 41:41–57

Pharaoh gave Joseph his signet ring and gave him a new wardrobe. He gave Joseph an Egyptian name, Zaphnath-Paaneah and the daughter of a priest to be his wife.

Joseph at thirty years of age entered into Pharaoh's service. During the seven years of abundance, Joseph collected the abundant harvests and stored them in cities. Then, seven years later when famine spread over the whole country, Joseph opened the storehouses and made food available to all Egyptians and surrounding countries.

From Prisoner to Potentate

Joseph woke up that morning in prison and retired that night as second in command in Egypt!

Joseph had dressed in prison garb in the morning. By night he was wearing royal robes with Pharaoh's personal **signet ring** on his finger (see Appendix A). Pharaoh had given him a new name and a wife. Joseph's status had changed from prisoner to being second in command to Pharaoh himself.

what others say

W. Glyn Evans

Sometimes we have too narrow a view of deliverance. We often look upon it as extrication from circumstances. But in God's eyes, deliverance is in the circumstance itself. When Joseph tried to escape from the temptress, Potiphar's wife, he landed in prison (Genesis 39). Where was God's deliverance? God had promised to make him a prince, but he became a prisoner! Not only was there no deliverance, his circumstances were getting worse! However, Joseph's string of degrading experiences ended while in prison. He interpreted Pharaoh's dream and, in gratitude, the king elevated him to a position of power and honor next to his own throne (Genesis 41:40). The prince had finally arrived! Joseph's entire life shows how God's deliverance of his children is intertwined with the painful circumstances in which they find themselves.[9]

Joseph's Operation "Food for All"

During the seven years of bountiful crops, Joseph set up a strategic command to garner all excess food for storage in cities. The abundant harvests yielded so much food that Joseph finally stopped keeping records of the stockpiles in his granaries.

During this time of plenty, Joseph had two sons. The first was named Manasseh, "for God has made me forget all my toil and all my father's house" (Genesis 41:51 NKJV). The second son he named Ephraim, "for God has caused me to be fruitful in the land of my affliction" (verse 52 NKJV).

what others say

V. Gilbert Beers

Most granaries were buildings with beehive-shaped domes, divided into a series of rooms. Grain was poured into each room from the top, and taken out through a small door near the bottom.[10]

Joseph's Food Pantries

After seven years of bountiful crops, the seven years of famine began. When food ran short, the people protested to Pharaoh. He sent them to Joseph. At the right time, Joseph opened the storehouses and sold grain to the Egyptians. Because the famine was severe in all the world, Joseph also sold food to people from nearby lands who came for food.

go to

dreams
Genesis 37:1–11

sold to slavery
Genesis 37:12–27

promoted
Genesis 39:1–6

accused
Genesis 39:7–18

imprisoned
Genesis 39:19–23

forgotten
Genesis 40:1–15, 23; 41:9

something to ponder

Insights from a Songwriter

Many years later, a songwriter put music to Joseph's painful but triumphant experience:

PSALM 105:16–22
[God] called for a famine in the land;
He destroyed all the provision of bread.
He sent a man before them—
Joseph—who was sold as a slave.
They hurt his feet with fetters,
He was laid in irons.
Until the time that his word came to pass,
The word of the LORD tested him.
The king sent and released him,
The ruler of the people let him go free.
He made him lord of his house,
And ruler of all his possessions,
To bind his princes at his pleasure,
And teach his elders wisdom. (NKJV)

Joseph could not see how God was working behind the scenes to accomplish his plan. He did not know that the famine that was coming to Egypt would also reach Canaan and would be the motivating force that would bring his brothers to him. He had no idea that God was working to make his dreams of long ago come true, that his brothers would some day actually bow before him.

It would be enough that Joseph put his trust in God day after day, whether he was mistreated and sold to slavery by his brothers, promoted by Potiphar, falsely accused by Potiphar's wife, unfairly imprisoned by Potiphar, or forgotten by Pharaoh's cupbearer.

Chapter Wrap-Up

- In Egypt, Joseph became a slave in the house of Potiphar. When it became obvious that God was with him, Joseph was soon trusted to be in charge of the whole household. (Genesis 39:1–6)

- When Potiphar's wife continually tempted Joseph to sleep with her, he resisted. She finally got revenge by falsely accusing him and, though he was innocent, he was put in prison. (Genesis 39:7–20)

- In prison, God continued to be with Joseph, giving him favor with the warden, who gave Joseph a responsible position over the prison. (Genesis 39:21–23)

- Pharaoh's cupbearer and baker, in prison with Joseph, had strange dreams which he interpreted with God's help. The cupbearer's dream revealed that he would soon be back at his job. Joseph asked the cupbearer to speak to Pharaoh about him. The baker's dream revealed that he would soon be executed. Both dreams came true, but the cupbearer forgot about Joseph. (Genesis 40)

- Some time later, Pharaoh had strange dreams about seven thin cows eating fat ones and seven thin stalks of grain swallowing fat ones. No one could be found to explain the meaning of these dreams to Pharaoh until the cupbearer remembered Joseph. (Genesis 41:1–13)

- Joseph, giving God credit for the interpretations, told Pharaoh that his dreams meant that after seven years of abundant crops, Egypt would have seven years of famine. (Genesis 41:14–32)

- Joseph advised Pharaoh to find a wise man and put him in charge of storing food from the good years to use during the famine. Pharaoh chose Joseph. He became second in command over the whole nation of Egypt and was given royal robes, Pharaoh's ring on his finger, a wife, and a new name. (Genesis 41:33–49)

- Joseph's stockpiling efforts were so successful that they lost count of the amount of food placed in reserve. Joseph had two sons. He gave both of them names that glorified God for his goodness to Joseph. (Genesis 41:50–52)

- When the seven good years were over and the famine began, Pharaoh sent the people to Joseph, who then opened the storehouses and sold grain to them—and even to people from other lands. (Genesis 41:53–57)

Study Questions

1. How did God show that he was with Joseph?

2. What can we learn from Joseph about the importance of a good attitude in every situation?

3. How did Joseph give God credit before Pharaoh and his people?

4. Why do you think God continued to bless and help Joseph throughout his life in Egypt?

5. Why was Joseph so well qualified to be in charge of Egypt's famine relief plan? Had he any training for the job?

Genesis 42–50 Joseph and His Brothers

Chapter Highlights:
- Joseph's Brothers
- Twelve Sons, Eleven Prophecies
- Devoted Son, Devoted Brother

Let's Get Started

Joseph's painful experience of being sold by his brothers and sent into slavery in Egypt may have seemed like a terrible mistake. Even his promotion to power and prominence in Egypt seemed to have nothing to do with the covenant God had made with Abraham, Isaac, and Jacob. Also, we have no record that God spoke audibly to Joseph during this time. Has Joseph been sidelined from God's covenant?

In the closing chapters of Genesis, we learn that God had been working out his purposes all along. We see how he used the famine to bring Joseph's family to Egypt for a very special reason. These chapters also give us a beautiful picture of God's great heart expressed through Joseph. Instead of finding bitterness and revenge in Joseph, we see the power of forgiveness and love that overlooks the past and extends itself to unite a family.

Joseph's Brothers Appear in Egypt

For Joseph, it was a long time coming, but God was ready to bring him and his family together. God used a famine in Canaan to have Jacob send his sons to buy grain in Egypt. The story unfolds.

the big picture

Genesis 42

There was a famine in Egypt, but their storehouses were filled with grain. Jacob sent his sons there to buy grain. Joseph recognized his ten older brothers when they bowed down to him as governor of the land. Joseph, speaking through an interpreter, dealt harshly with them. He accused them of being spies, and when they protested their innocence, he insisted that they prove their honesty by bringing the youngest brother to him. To ensure their return, he kept Simeon as hostage. The brothers gave Jacob their report: the lord over the land had spoken harshly to them and accused them of being spies. He kept

Simeon until they would bring Benjamin back with them. When they showed Jacob that the payment for the grain had been returned, he was alarmed. He could not bear to think of letting Benjamin go to Egypt, since the lord of the land was so demanding.

What Did We Do to Deserve This?

The famine in Egypt was severe also in Canaan. When word reached Jacob that food was available in Egypt, he took action.

As the famine threatened starvation, Jacob spoke to his sons,

"Why do you look at one another? . . . I have heard that there is grain in Egypt; go down to that place and buy for us there, that we may live and not die" (Genesis 42:1–2 NKJV).

Joseph's ten older brothers went to Egypt (see Appendix A). Jacob kept Benjamin back because he feared some harm might come to him. When the brothers arrived in Egypt, they went to the governor of the land, who was in charge of selling grain. They bowed down to him as an appropriate show of respect. Joseph immediately recognized them, but he concealed his identity. Speaking harshly to them, he asked where they came from. Seeing them bowing before him, he recalled the dreams he had told them about some twenty years before.

"You are spies! You have come to see the nakedness of the land!" he accused (42:9 NKJV). Alarmed, the brothers protested. They had come to buy food. They claimed to be sons of one man. They were honest, innocent men, not spies.

Joseph pretended not to believe them. He accused them again of being spies. The brothers tried to clarify their identity. They were ten of twelve sons of one man who lived in Canaan. The youngest son was with their father; the other was "no more" (42:13 NKJV). Again Joseph accused them of being spies, but this time he offered a test. They could prove their honesty by bringing their youngest brother to Egypt. They should go back to Canaan to bring the youngest brother. In the meantime, he would keep Simeon in prison.

what others say

Charles R. Swindoll

I have often wondered whether, perhaps, Joseph had been looking for them all along. As the people of other countries poured into Egypt seeking food, he may have wondered whether someday his own family might appear before him.

Finally, there they stood—and the account tells us "he recognized them, but he disguised himself." There's a play on words here in the Hebrew. They were recognized, but he made himself unrecognizable (disguised himself).[1]

go to

guilt
Psalm 32:3–5

We Know What We Did to Deserve This

After three days, Joseph relented. He would let the brothers return home with the grain, but they still must bring the youngest brother back.

Unaware that Joseph could understand their language, the brothers began to talk among themselves: "We are truly guilty concerning our brother, for we saw the anguish of his soul when he pleaded with us, and we would not hear; therefore this distress has come upon us" (Genesis 42:21 NKJV).

Reuben spoke up: "Did I not speak to you, saying, 'Do not sin against the boy'; and you would not listen? Therefore behold, his blood is now required of us" (42:22 NKJV).

Joseph heard every word they were saying and his heart was deeply touched as his brothers admitted their guilt. He had to turn away to conceal his tears. But he spoke in the guise of the harsh Egyptian governor. He ordered Simeon to be taken from them and bound as a prisoner.

What's Going On Here?

The brothers went on their way back to Canaan carrying the grain they had purchased—and heavy hearts. Their problem with the governor of Egypt intensified when they discovered that the silver they had paid for the grain appeared mysteriously in their sacks of grain. Immediately they sensed that this was not just a coincidence. They asked, "What is this that God has done to us?" (Genesis 42:28 NKJV).

go to

Rachel
Genesis 35:24

Joseph
Genesis 37:31–35

What Do We Tell Father?

When they returned home, they reported to Jacob all that had happened:

- The lord of the land had accused them of being spies.
- In order to prove their innocence, the lord of the land required them to return with their youngest brother.
- The lord of the land had kept Simeon as hostage until they complied with his demand.
- They made the frightening discovery that every man's payment of grain had been placed in the sacks of grain.

Jacob's Heartbreak

Jacob was distraught. In the heat of emotion he said, "You have bereaved me: Joseph is no more, Simeon is no more, and you want to take Benjamin. All these things are against me" (Genesis 42:36 NKJV).

Reuben took a bold step. He even offered the lives of his own sons if he did not bring Benjamin back with him. But Jacob could not bear the thought of losing Benjamin. His beloved wife Rachel had given him two sons. Joseph was gone. He would not allow Benjamin out of his sight.

what others say

Gene Getz

Over twenty years after Joseph had supposedly been killed by a wild animal, Jacob was still hurting deeply over what he thought was Joseph's cruel death. He didn't want to lose the one that had taken Joseph's place in terms of affection and love.[2]

Joseph Tests His Brothers

Joseph waited, wondering if his brothers would return or if they would callously abandon Simeon, who had been left in Egypt. Then one day the brothers returned—with Benjamin!

the big picture

Genesis 43–45

The famine continued without any sign of relief. Jacob sent his sons to go back to Egypt for more grain. They returned with Benjamin, gifts for the lord of the land, and a double payment of the grain they had purchased on the first trip.

Joseph hosted a feast for his brothers, releasing Simeon for the occasion. He asked them about their father, but when he was introduced to Benjamin, he was overcome with emotion and left the room.

When the brothers were ready to return to Canaan, Joseph again gave orders for the money to be placed in their sacks. In addition, he ordered his silver cup to be placed in Benjamin's sack. When Joseph's servant found the cup, the brothers returned to Joseph. Judah told all to the lord of the land, revealing his deep concern for their father Jacob. Joseph revealed his true identify, assuring his brothers that he had only goodwill toward them. He urged them to bring Jacob back with them to live in Egypt.

Facing Their Worst Fears

The famine continued. As the grain diminished, Jacob knew there was no postponing it. He must send his sons back to Egypt for food. Judah confronted Jacob with the unavoidable fact that there would be no food for them if Benjamin did not accompany them. Jacob was in anguish. Why had his sons ever mentioned that they had a younger brother? Why, then, did the ruler of Egypt demand that they bring him on their return?

When Judah promised to guarantee Benjamin's safety, Jacob reluctantly agreed to the plan. He ordered that double the money be returned to the ruler of Egypt as payment for the first purchase of grain. In addition, he sent gifts of balm, honey, spices, myrrh, pistachio nuts, and almonds. He expressed his heart yearnings when he asked God to give his sons mercy so that he would allow Simeon and Benjamin to come back to him. However, anticipating sorrow, he added, "If I am bereaved, I am bereaved!" (Genesis 43:14 NKJV).

what others say

Henry M. Morris

It is interesting to note also that, since there were ten brothers involved in these two purchases, in effect there were

pieces of silver
Genesis 37:28

> twenty bundles of money involved. It seems possible that the brothers themselves may have noted the ironical connection between the facts that they had sold their brother for twenty pieces of silver into Egypt, and that now they were having to pay into the treasuries of Egypt not merely twenty pieces of money but twenty bundles of money.[3]

Invitation to Dinner

The brothers traveled to Egypt as quickly as they could, taking Benjamin, the gifts, and double the money they owed. When they presented themselves to Joseph, his eyes sought out Benjamin. He ordered his steward to take the men to his house, slaughter an animal, and prepare a meal to be served at noon.

The brothers were frightened to be taken to the home of the governor. They concluded that the governor was setting up an occasion to attack them and seize them as slaves.

> **what others say**
>
> **Charles R. Swindoll**
>
> Notice what Joseph's brothers feared: "He may seek occasion against us and fall upon us, and take us for slaves." They had sold their own brother into slavery, and now that was what they feared for themselves. Paralyzed by guilt, they feared the worst, when Joseph dominated by grace, was planning the best.[4]

May We Explain?

The brothers decided to be proactive. They approached the steward and explained how they had found the money in the sacks of grain. To prove their honesty, they said they had brought additional money.

The steward gave an amazing response, "Peace be with you, do not be afraid. Your God and the God of your father has given you treasure in your sacks; I had your money" (Genesis 43:23 NKJV).

Then he brought Simeon out to them.

The Governor's Reception

The steward took the men into Joseph's home, gave them water to wash their feet, and provided fodder for their donkeys. While they waited for Joseph to come, they arranged their gifts, hoping to make a good impression on him.

When Joseph did arrive, they presented their gifts and bowed down before him. He made inquiries about their aged father before he gave his attention to Benjamin. Just seeing his younger brother affected him so deeply he had to hurry from the room to weep in private. When he had washed his face and was under control again, he told his servants to serve the meal.

As an Egyptian, he could not eat with Hebrews, so he was seated separately from them. As the brothers were seated at their table, they noted that he had designated their places so that they sat in order of their ages. This amazed them. Then when portions of food were served, Benjamin received five times as much as the other brothers.

The Governor's Silver Cup

When it was time for the brothers to return home, Joseph ordered that their sacks be filled with grain and that their silver be returned in the top of each man's sack. In addition, the governor's silver cup was to be placed in Benjamin's sack.

Early in the morning, the brothers began their return journey.

what others say

V. Gilbert Beers

Gold was quite common in the land of Egypt, but silver was considered a more precious metal because it was harder to come by. Joseph's personal drinking cup was made of silver. But this kind of cup was used for more than just drinking. The cup was called a "divination" cup. Skilled craftsmen engraved symbols, spells, and religious phrases on the cup. Often the owner's name was also inscribed on the cup. When drinking from it, all of the liquid had to be drained from the cup in order to repel evil and bring the god's blessings.[5]

go to

tore their clothes
Job 1:20

selling
Genesis 37:26–28

divination
seeking information by supernatural means

The Governor's Accusation

Joseph then sent his men after them to accuse them of stealing his cup. Protesting their innocence, the brothers reasoned that they would never do a thing like that. They had shown their honesty by returning the silver found in their sacks on their first trip. They even went so far as to say, "With whomever of your servants it is found, let him die, and we also will be my lord's slaves" (Genesis 44:9 NKJV). The steward amended the punishment to, "He with whom it is found shall be my slave, and you shall be blameless" (verse 10 NKJV). The brothers allowed Joseph's servant to inspect the sacks. He began with the sack of the oldest and moved down according to the brothers' ages. Finally, he opened Benjamin's and found the cup.

In great distress, the brothers tore their clothes. Then the group returned to Joseph. He spoke very harshly to them, asking them what they had done and didn't they know he could find out their theft by **divination**.

Judah spoke for the group: "What shall we say to my lord…?" (44:16 NKJV). Judah's compassion for his father proved that his heart had changed.

"What shall we speak? Or how shall we clear ourselves? God has found out the iniquity of your servants; here we are, my lord's slaves, both we and he also with whom the cup was found" (44:16 NKJV). But Joseph held to his position that he would keep Benjamin only and let the rest go home in peace.

Judah then begged Joseph to spare their father grief by letting him be prisoner instead of Benjamin. He rehearsed his account of Jacob's sorrow and his need to have Benjamin near him, because his "life is bound up in the lad's life" (44:30 NKJV). Judah showed such compassion for his father that Joseph could see he had experienced a true change of heart. Since Judah had initiated selling Joseph, it was especially important to know that he had changed. The brothers had passed the test Joseph had given them.

what others say

Charles Caldwell Ryrie

It is unlikely that Joseph used divination; rather, this statement (made in order to attach special significance to the cup) was part of the situation Joseph contrived in order to test his brothers. Would they seize on this opportunity to get rid of Benjamin, or had their hearts indeed been changed so that they would stand with him?[6]

When Brother Blesses Brother

Joseph suddenly had the room cleared of all his servants. He wept so loudly that his servants heard and quickly spread the news to Pharaoh's palace. When he was able to speak, he revealed his true identity as their brother. They could not respond to him; they were frozen with terror.

Joseph spoke kindly to them and asked them to draw close to him. He said, "I am Joseph your brother, whom you sold into Egypt. But now, do not therefore be grieved or angry with yourselves because you sold me here; for God sent me before you to preserve life" (Genesis 45:4–5 NKJV). He went on to explain that there had been two years of famine, and there would be five more years. God had sent him ahead of the family to save their lives. "So now it was not you who sent me here, but God; and He has made me a father to Pharaoh, and lord of all his house, and a ruler throughout all the land of Egypt" (45:8 NKJV).

what others say

David A. Seamands

Early in my ministry I discovered that the experience of grace is the most therapeutic factor in emotional and spiritual healing. A doctor who works in a mental hospital in Tennessee put it this way: "Half of my patients could go home in a week if they knew they were forgiven."[7]

Good Things Are Ahead

Joseph urged his brothers, "Hurry and go up to my father, and say to him, 'Thus says your son Joseph: "God has made me lord of all Egypt; come down to me, do not tarry"'" (Genesis 45:9 NKJV).

He promised that the whole family could live in the region of Goshen (see Appendix B)—they, their children, and grandchildren, their flocks, and herds—everything they owned would be provided for.

He threw his arms around Benjamin, and both brothers wept. He kissed all his brothers and wept over them. Afterward his brothers felt safe enough to talk with him.

Pharaoh heard of the joyful reunion and encouraged Joseph to make provision for the brothers as they traveled. He sent carts to carry the people and even said they should not bother to bring their belongings "for the best of all the land of Egypt is yours" (45:20 NKJV).

Joseph supplied the carts and food for the journey. In addition, he gave each man new clothing, but to Benjamin he gave three hundred shekels of silver and five sets of clothes. He sent his father ten donkeys loaded with good things of Egypt and ten more donkeys with grain, bread, and other food for his journey.

As the brothers started to return home, Joseph cautioned them, "See that you do not become troubled along the way" (45:24 NKJV).

On arriving home, the brothers jubilantly reported that Joseph was still alive—and was ruler of all Egypt! "Jacob's heart stood still, because he did not believe them" (45:26 NKJV), until they had shown him all the gifts and provisions Joseph had sent. When he saw the Egyptian carts, Jacob finally took in the good news, and his spirit was revived.

what others say

Hannah Whitall Smith

It is no matter who starts our trial, whether man, or devil, or even our own foolish selves, if God permits it to reach us, he has by this permission made the trial his own, and will turn it for us into a chariot of love which will carry our souls to a place of blessing that we could not have reached in any other way.... Joseph was sold into Egypt by the wickedness of his brethren, but God made their wickedness the chariot that carried Joseph to his place of triumph over the Egyptians.[8]

Joseph's Family Moves to Egypt

It seemed almost overwhelming for Jacob to deal with the emotions that surged through him: surprise and joy to know that Joseph was alive, aching yearning to see him again, pain at his sons' past deception, hunger to link all this excitement with God and the covenant promises, and a certain fear as he made this move from the Promised Land.

It's hard to imagine who had the greater joy: Joseph in Egypt as he anticipated receiving his family, or the family in Canaan making hasty preparations for the move to Egypt.

go to

Abraham
Genesis 12:10–20; 20

Isaac
Genesis 26:1–11

the big picture

Genesis 46–47

Jacob set off for Egypt, eager to meet Joseph. God met him in a vision, giving him a sense that God was directing the events and promising to bring Jacob's descendants back to the land. Joseph's family lived in peace and prosperity, growing stronger and more prosperous. In time, Joseph took family members to meet Pharaoh. His brothers met Pharaoh, and his father Jacob blessed Pharaoh. Though the famine tightened its grip on Egypt, Joseph's family prospered. The people of Egypt gradually gave all the rights to Pharaoh—first the livestock, then the property. Joseph instituted a form of taxation on crops that grew after the famine. The people praised Joseph and complied with the taxation.

Jacob pulled up his roots in Canaan, the land God had promised to give him. He was going to Egypt. Did he remember the troubles his grandfather Abraham had had when he went to Egypt in a time of famine? And again when he left Canaan to stay in Gerar? And the problems his father Isaac had had when he left Canaan, again in a time of famine?

Jacob stopped at Beersheba to offer sacrifices to the God of his father Isaac. "God spoke to Israel in the visions of the night, and said, 'Jacob, Jacob!' And he said, 'Here I am.' So He said, 'I am God, the God of your father; do not fear to go down to Egypt, for I will make of you a great nation there. I will go down with you to Egypt, and I will also surely bring you up again; and Joseph will put his hand on your eyes'" (Genesis 46:2–4 NKJV).

With a lighter heart, Jacob left Beersheba with a party of seventy riding in the carts Pharaoh had insisted that Jacob provide for their comfort. Included in the caravan was a multitude of livestock and possessions.

As the group approached Egypt, Jacob sent Judah in advance to ask Joseph for directions to Goshen. When they arrived in the area, Joseph was there to meet his father. He "fell on his neck and wept on his neck a good while" (46:29 NKJV).

Then Jacob told Joseph, "Now let me die, since I have seen your face, because you are still alive" (46:30 NKJV). His years of mourning for his favorite son were lifted in that joyful reunion.

what others say

Max Lucado

Judgment is God's job. To assume otherwise is to assume God can't do it.

Revenge is irreverent. When we strike back we are saying, "I know vengeance is yours, God, but I just didn't think you'd punish enough. I thought I'd better take this situation into my own hands. You have a tendency to be a little soft."

Joseph understands that. Rather than get even, he reveals his identity and has his father and the rest of the family brought to Egypt. He grants them safety and provides them a place to live. They live in harmony for seventeen years.[9]

Let's Use Our Words Wisely

Knowing that the Egyptians looked down on shepherds, Joseph tried to prepare his family to present themselves honestly but honorably to the Egyptians. They would be asked by Pharaoh about their occupation. He counseled them to answer that they had tended livestock all their lives, as their fathers had. The Egyptians would not want them as close neighbors, but would be happy to have them settle in Goshen, a part of Egypt that was particularly suited to grazing livestock.

Shepherd to the Stars

Joseph visited Pharaoh and reported the arrival of his family. When he introduced five of his brothers to Pharaoh, the question came exactly as Joseph had predicted. The brothers answered appropriately and requested the pharaoh's permission to live in Goshen. This was granted to the extent that Pharaoh told Joseph that if any of his family had unusual skill in working with livestock, he should put them in charge of Pharaoh's own livestock.

Meet My Father

Joseph presented his father to Pharaoh. The Egyptian leader asked his age. Jacob replied, "The days of the years of my pilgrimage are one hundred and thirty years; few and evil have been the days of the years of my life, and they have not attained to the days of the years of the life of my fathers in the days of their pilgrimage" (Genesis 47:9 NKJV).

Then Jacob blessed Pharaoh and left.

Joseph settled his family in the best part of the land, as Pharaoh had directed. He provided for their needs and saw to it that they had the food they needed for each member of the family.

The Famine Goes On

The famine was relentless. No food grew in Egypt or Canaan. The citizens paid for the food that had been stored, but finally their money was used up. Joseph told them that if they would bring their livestock instead of money, he would exchange their livestock for food. They followed this plan until Pharaoh owned all the horses, flocks, herds, and donkeys in the land. Then they ran out of livestock.

To help the hungry people, Joseph proposed that they let him buy their land in exchange for food. His plan worked. Joseph bought all the land in Egypt for Pharaoh, and in this way Joseph reduced the people to servitude and "moved them into the cities, from one end of the borders of Egypt to the other end" (Genesis 47:21 NKJV).

Now that Pharaoh owned most of the land, Joseph distributed seed to be planted as the famine relented. The plan was that when a crop was reaped, the people would give one-fifth of it to Pharaoh. The other four-fifths they could keep as seed and as food for themselves.

The people had no objection. They applauded Joseph for saving their lives and were willing to be servants to Pharaoh.

Meanwhile, Back in Goshen...

In Goshen, Joseph's family prospered and grew in number. Jacob, who had been willing to die once he had seen Joseph again, actually lived seventeen years after moving to Egypt.

At age 147, he knew he would not have long to live. He called Joseph to him and asked him to swear solemnly to honor his last request: Do not bury me in Egypt but take my body back to the purchased site where Isaac, Rebekah, and Leah are buried. Joseph made a solemn promise to honor his father's request.

Jacob's Final Word

the big picture

Genesis 48–49

The time had come for Joseph to bring his two sons, Manasseh and Ephraim, to meet his father. Jacob gave them a blessing as his own adopted sons and, thus, gave them a valid inheritance in Canaan, the land God had promised.

Jacob then blessed his twelve sons individually, inspired by God to tell in advance what would transpire in the lives of their offspring. Then Jacob died.

Indelibly impressed on Jacob's heart was his experience in receiving the blessing from his father Isaac. Now, as his life was drawing to its end, Jacob prepared to bless his sons. It was an important responsibility, for his words would have an effect on each son's future.

Grandpa Jacob Rallies

Jacob knew he would soon die, and he had serious responsibilities to fulfill before that day arrived.

Joseph took his two sons, Manasseh and Ephraim, to visit Jacob. It was a very special meeting. Jacob, who was now unwell, "strengthened himself and sat up on the bed" (Genesis 48:2 NKJV). Jacob rehearsed the covenant blessings God had given him at Luz (Genesis 35:9–15), promises God made to Jacob, his children, and his children's children—some already being fulfilled as Jacob's family was prospering and multiplying in Goshen, though that was only a temporary home. The land God had promised to give them was Canaan.

Jacob then turned from a review of the past to look to the future. He addressed the place Joseph's two Egyptian-born sons had in the covenant. He had given this some serious thought. Just as God gave Jacob the strength to fulfill all necessary responsibilities, so will he give us strength.

Joseph Receives the Birthright

Jacob gave the birthright to Joseph by changing the status of Ephraim and Manasseh from grandsons to sons. In this way, Jacob gave a double portion of the inheritance to Joseph. His sons, Ephraim and Manasseh, would co-inherit with their uncles.

As for any other sons Joseph might have, they would receive their inheritance as offspring of Ephraim and Manasseh.

In giving the blessing to Joseph's son, Jacob recalled his grief in the death of Joseph's mother, Rachel. She was Jacob's beloved wife.

In receiving the double blessing, Joseph was silent. Unlike Jacob, who had deceived his father to get the blessing, Joseph had left the future with God. And that was wise. For God tells us, "By faith Jacob, when he was dying, blessed each of the sons of Joseph, and worshiped, leaning on the top of his staff" (Hebrews 11:21 NKJV). Joseph did not need to manipulate or deceive to receive God's blessing.

key point

Grandpa's Blessing

Jacob then looked personally at Joseph's sons. He was almost blind, so he asked Joseph to bring the sons close. Jacob addressed Joseph, "I had not thought to see your face; but in fact, God has also shown me your offspring!" (Genesis 48:11 NKJV).

It was such a moving moment that Joseph removed his sons from Jacob's knees and bowed down to the ground. Then he guided his sons to come close to Jacob: Ephraim at Jacob's left hand and Manasseh at his right hand. Jacob reached out his right hand and placed it on Ephraim's head, even though he was the younger, and crossing his hands, he placed his left hand on Manasseh's head, even though he was the firstborn.

Then he gave his blessing on the sons. But Joseph was not pleased. He saw that his father had transposed his hands on the boys' heads, mixing the firstborn with the second born. But Jacob refused him. He had not made a mistake. He had received insight from the Lord that the younger would be greater than the firstborn, much as Jacob, the younger, had become greater than Esau, the firstborn.

go to

rights as firstborn
1 Chronicles 5:1–2

A Private Word

Jacob had an intimate conversation with Joseph, his most beloved son. He spoke of his approaching death and confided that he deeply desired that his body be taken back to the land of Abraham and Isaac—the land of promise. Jacob specifically gave Joseph a plot of land, "one portion above your brothers, which I took from the hand of the Amorite with my sword and my bow" (Genesis 48:22 NKJV). Though we do not find other references to that conquest, it is interesting that Joseph was later buried in Shechem (Joshua 24:32) rather than the family burial cave at Machpelah, where Abraham and Isaac were buried and where Jacob would later be laid to rest.

Twelve Sons, Eleven Prophecies

Jacob was growing old and feeble, but his mind was alert and his heart was vibrant. It was time to bless each of his sons. His words caused each to look back and to look ahead.

the big picture

Genesis 49

Jacob gathered his sons around him in order to give his final words to them. He spoke of each son by name, telling something about their character and foretelling something about their future in the land God had promised to give them. He concluded the meeting by giving directions for his burial, and then he died.

Jacob's Final Words to His Sons

Jacob called all his sons to gather around his bed. He spoke with amazing discernment, showing insight into their characters and telling what would happen in the future.

Though feeble and almost completely blind, Jacob spoke with clarity and force.

Reuben (Genesis 49:3–4): As firstborn, he would have expected to receive the birthright, but the double portion of blessing had already been given to Joseph's sons (Genesis 48). The rights as firstborn were denied him because he had disgraced himself when he defiled his father's bed with his adultery with Bilhah, one of his father's secondary wives (Genesis 35:22). Reuben's sin impacted generations to come. Reuben did not qualify for a position of leadership in the family because he was "unstable as water" (Genesis 49:4 NKJV).

Simeon and Levi (Genesis 49:5–7): Jacob described these sons as cruel and violent with both human and animal life. He was referring to their massacre of the men of Shechem in retaliation for one man raping their sister Dinah (Genesis 34:25–29). The descendants of both Simeon and Levi were scattered, so they did not receive an area when the land was portioned out to the tribes.

The descendants of Simeon disintegrated as a tribe and lived in the territory given to Judah. The descendants of Levi would be given the honor of serving as the **priestly tribe** living in forty-eight places scattered throughout the land.

Judah (Genesis 49:8–12): Jacob had good words for Judah's future. He did not refer to Judah's wrongdoing in taking part in selling Joseph and then deceiving his father about Joseph's fate, or his treatment of his daughter-in-law (Genesis 37–38). Jacob spoke of Judah's tribe having the respect and praise of his brothers. Kings would be among his descendants. "The scepter shall not depart from Judah . . . until Shiloh comes; and to Him shall be the obedience of the people" (49:10 NKJV). Jacob was foretelling that a ruler would come from Judah's line and be the Messiah. Jesus came from the tribe of Judah. When Jesus returns, he will be acknowledged as King by all people. The area of Canaan assigned to Judah's tribe would be fertile.

Zebulun (Genesis 49:13): Jacob then departed from addressing his sons in their birth order. Zebulun was the tenth son, the sixth and last son by Leah. Zebulun's tribe would be involved with ships, even though its area would not border the Mediterranean Sea. They would do business with their neighbors, the Phoenicians, whose country did border the sea.

Issachar (Genesis 49:14–15): Speaking of the future, Jacob said that Issachar's descendants would bow "his shoulder to bear a burden, and [become] a band of slaves" (verse 15 NKJV). (In fact, the tribe was located in the plain of Esdraelon and was subject to armies that invaded the land from time to time.)

Dan (Genesis 49:16–18): Jacob called on Dan to provide justice for his people, even though he was destined to behave as "a serpent

go to

impacted generations
Exodus 20:5

Jesus
Matthew 1:2–3, 16

priestly tribe
generations later, priest of the tabernacle and the temple were descendants of Levi

by the way, a viper by the path" (verse 17 NKJV) by being the first tribe to become seriously involved in the practice of **idolatry**, a sin God hated. Jacob interrupted speaking to his sons to raise his prayer to the Lord for deliverance.

Gad (Genesis 49:19): Jacob described Gad as being attacked and attacking in return. The tribe of Gad was assigned the area next to the people of Ammon who frequently made border raids.

Asher (Genesis 49:20): The tribe of Asher would live in the northwest part of the land, a fertile area that provided abundant crops.

Naphtali (Genesis 49:21): Settling to the east of Asher, the tribe of Naphtali was characterized as free mountain dwellers.

Joseph (Genesis 49:22–26): Jacob spoke in greater detail of Joseph than any of the other sons, for the most significant blessing was bestowed on him and his two sons. Jacob spoke of Joseph's fruitfulness in spite of being attacked with "bitterness" and "hostility" by his brothers and by Potiphar's wife. He was promised victory because he was blessed by God himself, God who would make him prosper. Jacob spoke of his blessings on Joseph as "the crown of the head of him who was separate from his brothers" (verse 26 NKJV). In the history of Joseph's sons are accounts of victorious leaders. From the tribe of Ephraim came Joshua, Deborah, and Samuel. From the tribe of Manasseh came Gideon and Jephthah.

Benjamin (Genesis 49:27): Benjamin, son of Jacob's beloved Rachel, was given his name which means "son of the right hand" or "son of honor or good fortune." But Jacob was brief in speaking of his destiny and described Benjamin's tribe as violent. History records violent individuals from his tribe. For example, King Saul, from the tribe of Benjamin, was ruthless in his attempts to assassinate David.

go to

a sin God hated
Judges 18:30

name
Genesis 35:18

King Saul
1 Samuel 9:1–2

attempts to assassinate David
1 Samuel 19:10; 22:17; 23:7–8; 24:2

idolatry
worshiping local pagan gods rather than the real God

what others say

Andrew Murray

"I have waited for Thy salvation, O Lord!" (Genesis 49:18 KJV) It is not easy to say exactly in what sense Jacob used these words, in the midst of his prophecies in regard to the future of his sons. But they do certainly indicate that both for himself and for them his expectation was from God alone. It was God's salvation he waited for; a salvation which God had promised and which God himself alone could work out. He knew himself and his sons to be under God's charge. Jehovah the Everlasting God would show in them what his saving power is and does.[10]

patriarchs
chief ancestors

Carry Me Back to Ol' Canaan

Jacob had blessed each of his sons "according to his own blessing" (Genesis 49:28 NKJV). That task accomplished, he turned to the one remaining matter to be discussed. Though he had spoken privately to Joseph about his burial, he wanted all his sons to know of his wishes to be buried back in Canaan, where Abraham and Sarah, Jacob and Rebekah, and Leah had been laid to rest.

God had blessed and prospered Jacob and his whole family in the seventeen years they had lived in Goshen, but Jacob knew it was a temporary location. By faith he knew their permanent land was in Canaan, the land God had first promised to give Abraham, and then confirmed that promise to Isaac and to Jacob. It was extremely important to Jacob that he not be buried in Egypt but in Canaan.

Having given his last word, Jacob "drew his feet up into the bed and breathed his last, and was gathered to his people" (49:33 NKJV).

Devoted Son, Devoted Brother

It was the end of an age, for with the death of Jacob, Joseph's family buried the last of the **patriarchs**. Now it was a time of celebration to honor the memory of grand old Jacob and a time to clarify and cement relationships within his family.

the big picture

Genesis 50

Joseph mourned his father's death and honored him with a formal expression of mourning. Then he led a large funeral procession to Canaan, where they mourned again. Finally, Joseph and his brothers carried Jacob's body to the cave in the field of Machpelah, where they laid his body to rest. Back in Egypt, the brothers, who still lived with guilt over their treatment of Joseph, began to fear that he would take revenge on them. Joseph assured them that while they did intend to harm him, God had turned their action into good and had enabled him to save many lives. He told them not to be afraid but to trust him to provide for them. Joseph lived to be 110 years old. Then, as Jacob had done, he asked his brothers to promise that they would carry his bones to Canaan, the land he believed God had given them.

The Passing of a Patriarch

embalm
treatment of a corpse to preserve from decay

threshing floor
flat, open space used to dry grain for threshing

grace
a kindly and favorable attitude that reflects God's compassion and gracious goodwill

Joseph's brothers had viewed their father Jacob as a buffer between them and Joseph. What would happen when Jacob was no longer there?

Joseph mourned his father's death forty days. It seems that Pharaoh honored Jacob by having a formal seventy-day period of mourning for a person of prominence—a tribute to Joseph who had saved the nation from starvation. Because Jacob's burial would not be immediate, Joseph directed the Egyptian physicians to **embalm** Jacob. Then after receiving Pharaoh's permission to bury his father in Canaan, Joseph led a very large funeral entourage that included family members and a great number of Egyptian officials: all Pharaoh's officials, the dignitaries of Pharaoh's court and Egypt. They were carried in chariots with horsemen.

The group stopped at a **threshing floor** near the Jordan River and spent seven days mourning Jacob, "with a great and very solemn lamentation" (Genesis 50:10 NKJV). The Canaanites observed this unusual event and called the place Abel Mizraim, which means "mourning of Egypt." At the end of this week of grievous mourning, Jacob's body was carried on its final part of the journey to the cave of Machpelah, where it was laid to rest as Jacob had requested.

what others say

Dr. Larry Richards

Why would Jacob want to be buried in Canaan? Jacob's request was an affirmation of faith. God had promised that his descendants would inherit Canaan. In choosing to be buried with his father and grandfather in Canaan, Jacob affirmed his conviction that his descendants would return and God's promises would be fulfilled.[11]

Guilt That Breeds Fear

The family portrait was beautiful. Jacob's sons and their families were smiling, but behind the picture-perfect scene, an ugly fog clouded the glowing countenances.

On their return to Egypt, the brothers began to worry that Joseph would now seek revenge for the wrongs they had done to him. Though Joseph had shown them only kindness and God's **grace**, their guilt had never been put to rest. Now that Jacob was no longer with them, their fears grew, and at last they were willing to acknowledge their true guilt. Afraid to face him, they sent a message begging his forgiveness.

good
Romans 8:28

It is interesting that they based their appeal on Jacob's dying instructions—something they may have fabricated, since Jacob never made reference to what they had actually done to Joseph.

Did they keep their secret from him to the end? Knowing Joseph's devotion to their father, they aimed to touch a tender spot by saying, "Before your father died he commanded, saying, 'Thus you shall say to Joseph: "I beg you, please forgive the trespass of your brothers and their sin; for they did evil to you."' Now, please, forgive the trespass of the servants of the God of your father" (Genesis 50:16–17 NKJV).

Joseph wept, then reassured them that they had no reason to fear him. He had forgiven them years before. While they had intended harm, God had used their actions for good. Again he told them not to be afraid. Then he assured them that he would continue to take care of them.

what others say

James Montgomery Boice

What gave Joseph the grace to make this remarkable reply? There is only one answer: Joseph knew God. In particular, he knew two things about God. He knew that God is sovereign—that nothing ever comes into the life of any one of his children that he has not approved first; there are no accidents. And he knew that God is good—therefore, the things that come into our lives by God's sovereignty are for our benefit (and for others') and not for our harm.[12]

A Final Expression of Faith

Joseph lived to be 110. He lived to see his two sons grow up, marry, and have children. As he held his grandchildren in his arms, he must have basked in the blessings God had given him. Wrenched from his family as a teenager and suffering the lonely years in Egypt, God gave him years of close family relationships which must have helped erase some of the pain.

Before Joseph died, he told his family that when God led them

go to

good
Romans 8:28

back to Canaan, they were to take his bones from Egypt to the Promised Land. All the glory of being a VIP in Egypt was nothing compared to the blessing of being part of God's covenant promises that would eventually bring blessing to the whole world.

what others say

Oswald Chambers

Faith, before it is real, must be tried. As we dispose ourselves to believe, we see God all the time, not in spasms. We see his arm behind all the facts in individual life and in history.[13]

something to ponder

Why these tears? Joseph was highest in command under Pharaoh. He had shown amazing leadership skills in preparing for the famine and in managing the food distribution program for the many people whose lives depended on him. He had shown sterling moral character, had been resilient under incredible mistreatment by his family and the false accusation of Potiphar's wife. He had all these strengths, yet he wept. In fact, the Bible account tells of seven times when he wept—more times than for any other Old Testament character.

- ***Genesis 42:24:*** Joseph wept when Reuben reminded his brothers that they were now being called by God to give an accounting for Joseph's blood.
- ***Genesis 43:30:*** On seeing Benjamin, his younger brother, he was deeply moved and went to a private room to weep. Another translation reads, "Joseph made haste; for his bowels did yearn upon his brother: and he sought where to weep; and he entered into his chamber, and wept there" (Genesis 43:30 KJV).
- ***Genesis 45:2:*** He wept loudly just before he made himself known to his brothers.
- ***Genesis 45:14:*** He wept as he embraced Benjamin.
- ***Genesis 45:15:*** He wept as he kissed all his other brothers.
- ***Genesis 50:1:*** On Jacob's death, he threw himself on his father and wept over him and kissed him.
- ***Genesis 50:17:*** He wept when he received his brothers' request for forgiveness.

What do these accounts tell us about Joseph?

what others say

Gene Getz

What we know of Joseph's tears reflects, not just his humanity, but his heart attitude. Here was a man who had more power, prestige, and authority than any man in the world. And yet he never lost his ability to be tender, to show compassion, and to feel deeply. He was definitely a man's man—but a gentle man! He certainly demonstrated that "big boys do cry"![14]

David A. Seamands

In biblical days, the word *bowels* was used exactly as we use gut level now. Much more than mere emotions, it also included attitudes and actions and deeds, and was an all-pervasive way of thinking, feeling, doing, and relating. It meant that the whole personality was affected, right down to the deepest levels.[15]

Chapter Wrap-Up

- The famine in Egypt extended to Canaan where Jacob's family was threatened with starvation. Jacob sent his ten older sons to Egypt to buy grain. They went to the governor and bowed down to him, not recognizing that he was their brother Joseph. (Genesis 42:1–6)

- Joseph recognized his brothers but concealed his own identity. He spoke harshly to them and accused them of spying. He insisted that if they wanted grain, one of them must return to Canaan and bring back their youngest brother, while the rest stayed in prison in Egypt. Three days later, Joseph relented and told his brothers they could have grain, but they must bring their youngest brother back next time. He kept Simeon as a prisoner, but let the others go back to Canaan. (Genesis 42:7–24)

- On the way home, the brothers discovered that their payment for the grain had been put in their grain sacks. This confused them. When they got home and told Jacob everything, he refused to let them go back to Egypt with Benjamin. (Genesis 42:25–38)

- When the grain was almost gone, Jacob realized he would have to let his sons return to Egypt with Benjamin. Judah pledged to keep the youngest brother safe. Jacob sent double the money to pay for the first purchase of grain as well as the second. He also sent gifts to the Egyptian governor. (Genesis 43:1–14)

- When the brothers arrived in Egypt, Joseph had a special feast prepared for them. The brothers explained to Joseph's steward about their money being returned in their grain sacks. He assured them that everything was all right. Then he released Simeon. (Genesis 43:15–24)

- The brothers offered their gifts to Joseph. He questioned them about their father, then seeing Benjamin, he quickly left the room to weep. When Joseph returned, the meal was served. The brothers were amazed to see that their seating had been arranged in order of their ages. (Genesis 43:25–34)

- When the brothers prepared to leave, Joseph had their money once again put in the grain sacks and his own silver cup was added to Benjamin's sack. (Genesis 44:1–2)

- On their way home, the brothers were stopped by Joseph's men and accused of stealing his cup. When it was found in Benjamin's sack, they were taken back to Joseph, who spoke harshly to them. He said he would keep Benjamin, but the others could return home. Judah begged to take Benjamin's place, and Joseph saw that his brothers had indeed changed. (Genesis 44:3–34)

- Joseph sent away his servants and revealed himself to his brothers. He reminded them how they had treated him, but told them he forgave them, because God had intended it all for good. (Genesis 45:1–8)

- Joseph urged his brothers to return home and bring back their father and their families to live in Egypt. He sent them back with new clothes, money for Benjamin, and gifts for his father. (Genesis 45:9–24)

- Jacob was stunned by the news that Joseph was alive and well. He agreed to move to Egypt. On the way, God spoke to him to assure him that Egypt was where God wanted him to be. (Genesis 45:25–46:28)

- Joseph greeted his father with tears and open arms. He introduced his family to Pharaoh, who agreed that they should live in Goshen, a good place for raising sheep. (Genesis 46:29–47:12)

- The famine continued until the Egyptian people had no money to buy grain. Joseph let them trade horses and livestock and finally land for grain. He also instituted a program of giving Pharaoh one-fifth of all future crops when the famine was over. (Genesis 47:13–26)
- Jacob asked Joseph to see that he was buried in Canaan, where his parents and his first wife were buried. Then Jacob blessed Joseph's two sons and gave Joseph the birthright. Finally, Jacob blessed each of his sons. When he died, Joseph took him to Canaan and buried him. (Genesis 47:27–49:33)
- After their father's death, Joseph's brothers were afraid Joseph might seek revenge for what they had done to him. Joseph assured them that he held no grudges and would continue to take care of them. (Genesis 50:1–21)
- Joseph died at the age of 110. Before he died, he told his family he wanted his bones taken to Canaan when his people returned there someday. (Genesis 50:22–26)

Study Questions

1. How did Joseph's boyhood dreams come true when his brothers came to Egypt to buy food?
2. Why do you think Joseph dragged out the meetings with his brothers for so long and played tricks on them before revealing his identity?
3. Why was Joseph able to freely forgive his brothers for what they had done to him?
4. How did God reassure Jacob about going to Egypt?
5. Why was it so important to Joseph that his bones be taken to Canaan when his people returned there?

Appendix A—Time Line

Undated	*Creation*
	The Fall
	The Flood
	Tower of Babel *Domestication of animals* *Invention of writing* *Development of metal* *Invention of musical instruments* *Pyramids built in Egypt*
2165 BC	*Abraham born*
2090 BC	*Abraham enters Canaan*
2065 BC	*Isaac born*
2005 BC	*Jacob born*
1915 BC	*Joseph born*
1898 BC	*Joseph sold to Egypt*
1885 BC	*Joseph made second in command*
1860 BC	*Joseph's family comes to Egypt*

Appendix B – Map

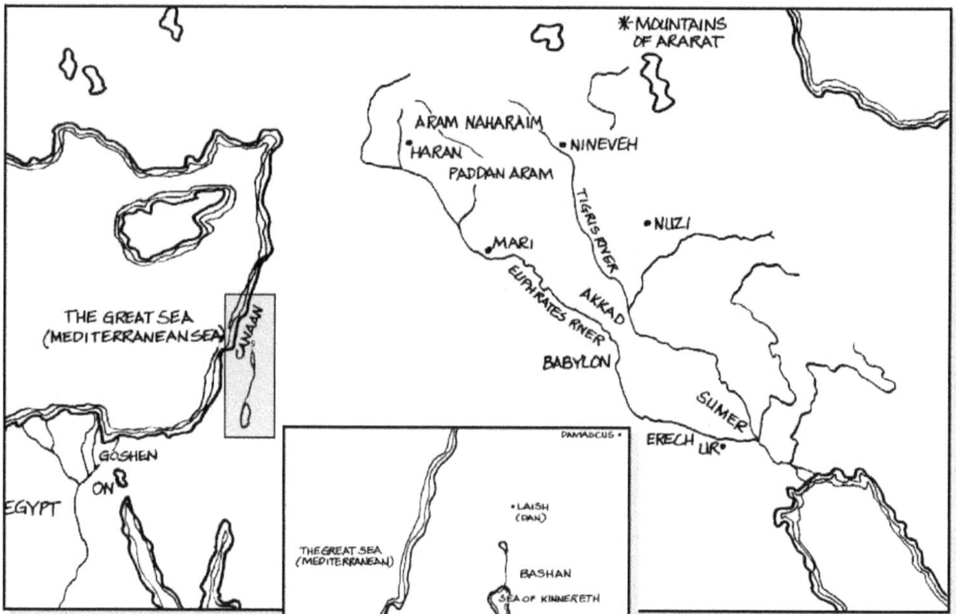

Enlargement of inset

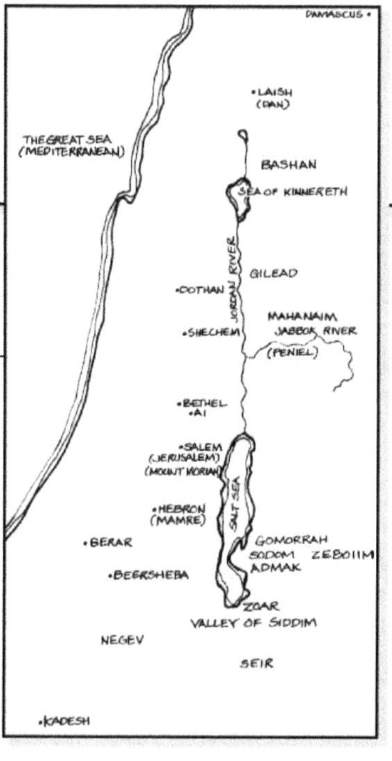

Appendix C – The Answers

CHAPTER 1: GENESIS 1—THE BEGINNING

1. God existed before he created the universe. He has power to speak, to bring order out of chaos, and to create. He is the God of power, order, incredible variety, and beauty. He set in motion natural laws that govern the universe. He made man and woman in his image—with the capacity to know him and communicate with him. They could think, feel, choose, and bring him pleasure. (Genesis 1)
2. The heavens display God's glory, power, and immensity. He is knowable, yet far beyond our capacity to understand and measure. (Genesis 1:14–19; Job 11:7–8)
3. God made all parts of the universe, including a large number of living creatures, by speaking. In creating humans, God spoke with himself, saying, "Let us make man." He made only one man and one woman, molding them in his image by giving them unique qualities of personhood. He gave the man and woman the role of ruling over all creatures. (Genesis 1:26–31)
4. God gave man the responsibility of filling the earth by reproducing. They were to subdue the earth by ruling over all living creatures, and they were to enjoy the vegetation God created for their food. (Genesis 1:28–30)

CHAPTER 2: GENESIS 2—THE CROWN OF CREATION

1. God created an orderly universe, teeming with life, each kind capable of reproducing itself. He made vegetation to provide food for man's enjoyment with the exception of one tree, the fruit of which he said man should not eat: The Tree of the Knowledge of Good and Evil. He brought the animals and birds for man to name. Knowing that man had no suitable companion, he made woman from one of man's ribs. (Genesis 2)
2. On the seventh day, God rested from his work. Creation was complete and everything was good. He blessed that day and made it holy. (Genesis 2:1–3)
3. God designated the seventh day, the Sabbath, as a special day in which man rested from his work and honored God. (Exodus 16:23)
4. Work is part of God's plan for man's well-being. Man was to rule over God's Creation, to take care of it. Through his work man could enjoy God's Creation and honor his maker. (Genesis 2:15)
5. God saw that it was not good for man to be alone. He intended woman to be a "helper suitable for him." Man and woman were intended to become one flesh, viewed by God as one unit, separated from parents or other family members. (Genesis 2:18, 20–24)

CHAPTER 3: GENESIS 3—TROUBLE IN THE GARDEN

1. The serpent questioned God's goodness when he asked, "Did God really say, 'You must not eat from any tree in the garden'?" In responding, the woman fell into the trap of altering what God had said. Then the serpent called God a liar by denying the penalty of eating from the tree. Satan uses the same methods today. (Genesis 3:1–5)
2. Like Eve, we are tempted to question God's goodness and to desire to disobey God and be independent of him. (1 John 2:16)
3. The first man and woman, ashamed to know they were naked, feared God and tried to hide from him. (Genesis 3:7–8)
4. Jesus Christ came to "crush the head" of Satan. He did this in his death on the cross. (Genesis 3:14–15; 1 Corinthians 15:20–28)
5. The woman's consequences were pain in childbirth and disequilibrium in her relationship with her husband. The man's consequences included painful toil and hard work in taking care of the earth. Both would suffer the consequence of

physical death (Genesis 3:16–19). For us, the consequences are the same, for we all sin. (Romans 3:23; 5:12)

CHAPTER 4: GENESIS 4–5—THE FIRST FAMILY

1. Cain brought an offering from the produce he had cultivated. Abel brought an offering from his flocks, which God accepted. Abel's offering pleased God because he presented it with faith in his heart. (Genesis 4:1–5; Hebrews 11:4)
2. God gave Cain opportunity to bring an offering that would be acceptable. After Cain killed Abel, God cursed the ground so it would not produce for Cain and made him a restless wanderer. However, he showed mercy by putting a mark on Cain so that nobody would kill him. (Genesis 4:6–16)
3. Cain fled from God's presence while his brother Seth called on the name of the Lord. (Genesis 4:16, 25–26)
4. Walking with God is a privilege for which men and women were created, a privilege which was lost through sin, but restored for all who have faith and earnestly seek God. (Genesis 3:8; 5:24; Hebrews 11:5–6)

CHAPTER 5: GENESIS 6–7—NOAH AND THE FLOOD

1. The people in Noah's day lived longer than people do today. This gave them added years to practice evil and to pass their godless values to new generations. They did not have the Word of God in written form, and there was only one godly man to be a model of faith. Ways in which people were the same as people today: they were preoccupied with earthly interests—eating, drinking, and marrying. (Genesis 6:1–10; Matthew 24:37–39; Luke 17:26–27)
2. God chose to save Noah and his family because Noah alone was righteous. (Genesis 6:8–10)
3. Noah had no understanding of what the Flood would be or of what kind of vessel he would need. God gave him specific directions for building the Ark for both his safety and the safety of the creatures that would be on board. (Genesis 6:14–16)
4. Noah proved his faith in God by obeying all his instructions. In the same way, today we show our faith by obeying God. (Genesis 6:22; Hebrews 11:7; John 14:23–24)
5. God is faithful to keep his promises, whether of judgment or of blessing. (Joshua 24:14–16; 2 Peter 3:9)

CHAPTER 6: GENESIS 8–9—A FRESH BEGINNING

1. God waited 120 years before sending the Flood. During this time, Noah's faith was tested as he built the Ark and preached to his unrepentant neighbors. He was on the Ark one year and 17 days before God told him to disembark. Waiting is difficult, but God's timing is not according to earthly schedules. (Genesis 8:13–17)
2. God kept them safe and healthy so they could multiply and fill the earth. (Genesis 8:15–17; 9:1)
3. God had kept his promises to Noah. As Noah left the Ark, his heart overflowed with praise and desire to worship God. (Genesis 8:15–22)
4. The rainbow is a reminder of God's covenant never again to destroy all life by a Flood. (Genesis 9:8–17)
5. Noah's drunkenness illustrates the fact that no person is beyond sin, apart from God's grace. (Genesis 9:18–29; Ephesians 2:8–10)

CHAPTER 7: GENESIS 10–11—BIRTH OF NATIONS

1. As with the first man and woman in the Garden, God has given each person the responsibility to make choices. He permits the ungodly to prosper, giving them time to repent and turn to him. He also can use their accomplishments to fulfill his plans. (Genesis 10:8–12)
2. Nimrod rebelled against God's command to multiply and fill the earth. He determined to lead his followers to make a name for themselves and to build a city with a tower that would challenge God. People today are still trying to fulfill their ambitions apart from God. (Genesis 11:1–4)
3. God confused the languages so that the tower had to be abandoned. He was protecting people from the concentration of evil that had led to the Flood in Noah's day. (Genesis 11:5–9)
4. God is sovereign. Though men were living without regard for him, God was preparing to call a man, Abram, to fulfill his plan for the world. (Genesis 11:27–32)

CHAPTER 8: GENESIS 12—ABRAM

1. God called Abram from a family of idol worshipers. God promised to show Abram a new land, but at seventy-five years of age, Abram could have felt too old for such a venture. God promised to make him into a great nation, but Abram had no children. (Genesis 12:1–3)
2. Abram obeyed God's call, not because it made sense or was "a good deal" for him, but because he believed God. (Genesis 12:4–5)

3. When Abram arrived in Canaan, God promised to give that land to his descendants. Abram responded by building an altar to the Lord as an act of worship. (Genesis 12:6–9)
4. Abram feared that the people would kill him in order to take his beautiful wife Sarai. To protect himself, Abram and Sarai agreed that she would claim to be Abram's sister. (Genesis 12:10–14)
5. God protected Sarai in Pharaoh's palace by inflicting Pharaoh and his household with diseases until he released Sarai. God overruled Abram's wrongdoing and even used it to increase Abram's wealth (Genesis 12:14–20). God showed compassion to Abram. (Psalm 86:15–17)

CHAPTER 9: GENESIS 13–14—ABRAM AND LOT

1. Abram put peacemaking with Lot ahead of striving for what was rightfully his. (Genesis 13:1–13; 1 Peter 3:10–12)
2. Abram was the loser in the immediate situation, but long range, he was far ahead. While Lot enjoyed good grazing land for his herds, God was blessing Abram and was promising to give him the whole land. (Genesis 13:14–15)
3. When Lot was carried away as a captive of enemy kings, Abram set out to rescue him, responding as if Lot had never wronged him. He forgave and forgot the earlier offense. (Genesis 14:1–17)
4. Abram gave Melchizedek one-tenth of the goods he recovered from his raid on the enemy kings. (Genesis 14:18–20; Hebrews 7:1–10)
5. What skills or power Abram had were gifts from God, so when he won such a stunning victory over the enemy kings, Abram gave God the credit for the victory and refused to accept a reward from the king of Sodom. (Genesis 14:22–24)

CHAPTER 10: GENESIS 15—GOD'S COVENANT

1. After Abram had turned down the reward offered by the king of Sodom, God spoke to him saying, "I am your exceedingly great reward." By putting God first, Abram made himself available to receive God's protection and blessing. (Genesis 15:1)
2. Today God speaks to us through the Bible and through the Holy Spirit. (Hebrews 4:12; 2 Timothy 3:16–17; John 14:26)
3. God gives us great and precious promises to encourage us in becoming mature believers. (2 Peter 1:3–11)
4. All believers are connected to Abram because everyone who has faith is blessed along with Abram. (Galatians 3:6–9)
5. Abram's part in God's covenant with him was simple faith. Similarly, our part in God's covenant of salvation is simple faith. (Genesis 15:6; Ephesians 2:4–10)

CHAPTER 11: GENESIS 16—HAGAR AND ISHMAEL

1. God had promised to give Abram a son, but after years of waiting, Sarai still could not conceive. Rather than wait for God to work out his plan, Sarai persuaded Abram to take Hagar, her maidservant, and father a child through her. Abram and Sarai came up with their solution rather than waiting for God to work things out. (Genesis 16:1–4)
2. Once she was pregnant, Hagar began to despise Sarai, who, in turn, tried to make Abram responsible for dealing with Hagar. Abram put the problem back into Sarai's hands. This caused the conflict to escalate so that Hagar fled. Though Abram missed the opportunity to be the peacemaker, God used it to speak to Hagar. (Genesis 16:4–11)
3. Nobody is beyond God's knowledge. Though Hagar was not part of God's plan for Abram, God saw her and gave direction for her and her unborn son, even giving him his name. (Genesis 16:7–12)
4. Hagar realized that God saw her, knew her misery, and had plans for her unborn son. (Genesis 16:13–14)
5. God is sovereign. He will work out his plans in his time and in his own way. He can even use our mistakes to accomplish his plans. (Genesis 16)

CHAPTER 12: GENESIS 17—GOD'S COVENANT CONFIRMED

1. God identified himself as El Shaddai, God Almighty, the One who has power to make and keep his promises. (Genesis 17:1–8)
2. Abram's name meant "father" or "exalted father," implying he was a father of children. God changed his name to Abraham, which meant "father of a multitude" or "father of nations." This name change was part of God's everlasting covenant with Abraham and his descendants. (Genesis 17:1–8)
3. "Circumcision of the heart" means believing God, setting oneself apart for him and, in light of that commitment, living to love and serve him wholeheartedly. (Deuteronomy 10:16; Romans 2:28–29; 4:9–12)
4. God changed Sarai's name to Sarah, making her the mother of nations. He included her by name as part of his everlasting promise to Abraham. (Genesis 17:15–16)

5. Abraham obeyed God immediately by circumcising every male in his household. (Genesis 17:23–27)

CHAPTER 13: GENESIS 18–19—JUDGMENT ON SIN

1. Abraham laughed with amazement that at one hundred years of age he could have a son with Sarah, who was ninety. Sarah, on the other hand, laughed with unbelief that such an event could occur. (Genesis 17:17; 18:9–15)
2. In a sense, Abraham was testing how merciful God would be. (Genesis 18:16–33)
3. Lot sat at the gateway of the city, the role of a leader. He was willing to give his daughters to the evil men who were demanding to have the angels. His sons-in-law thought he was joking when he came to warn them. The angels had to pull Lot, his wife, and his daughters from the city. (Genesis 18:1–22)
4. God does not arbitrarily send judgment on evil people. He gives time for repentance, but judgment will come. (2 Peter 2:6–9)
5. In spite of repeated warnings that Christ will come again, many people are so preoccupied with their lives that they do not fear judgment. (2 Peter 2:6–9)

CHAPTER 14: GENESIS 20—ABRAHAM AND ABIMELECH

1. Abraham made excuses for deceiving Abimelech about Sarah. He thought there was no fear of God in Gerar and that men would kill him to have Sarah. He also excused his own lie because Sarah was in fact his half sister. (Genesis 20:11–13)
2. God showed his righteousness and mercy when he intervened to keep Abimelech from taking Sarah. He spoke to Abimelech in a dream, warning him. He also "closed every womb" in Abimelech's household. (Genesis 20:3–7, 17)
3. Abraham was a great man of faith, but he was a man. No person is beyond temptation.
4. We need to live by God's standards in all our interactions with people who do not know God. There is no contact that does not matter.

CHAPTER 15: GENESIS 21—REORDERING LIFE

1. God Almighty overruled human limitations in the birth of Isaac. He enabled Sarah to give birth at the precise time he had promised. (Genesis 21:1–3)
2. God planned for Ishmael and Isaac to establish separate peoples. Sarah's antagonism toward Hagar and Ishmael furthered God's plan to remove Ishmael from the household. (Genesis 21:8–13)
3. Hostility would have grown between Sarah and Hagar. Abraham, because of his love for Ishmael, might have been tempted to give Ishmael some of the wealth that God had intended for Isaac.
4. God saved Ishmael from death in the wilderness and promised to make him into a great nation. (Genesis 21:11–21)

CHAPTER 16: GENESIS 22–23—A HEARTRENDING TEST

1. Isaac was Abraham's dearly loved, long-awaited son, and he was the visible evidence of God's covenant with him. All Abraham's hope for God's blessing was wrapped up in Isaac. (Genesis 22:1–3)
2. God's command tested Abraham's understanding of God's character. God created life, making people in his image. He had already provided for man's need to make a sacrifice for sin by prescribing the sacrifice of an animal. After the Flood, God said he would demand an accounting of anyone who killed another human being. God also expressed his abhorrence of sacrificing children to the pagan deity Molech.
3. Abraham's faith was tested to the depths, but he did not fail. He told his servants that he and Isaac would return. He also assured Isaac that God would provide the lamb for the burnt offering. He believed God could raise Isaac from the dead. (Genesis 22:4, 8; Hebrews 11:17–19)
4. God never tempts us to do evil, but he tests us to strengthen us through what we learn from the testing. (James 1:12–14)
5. By burying Sarah in a cave he purchased, Abraham showed his belief that Canaan was the land God had given him and his descendants. (Genesis 23)

CHAPTER 17: GENESIS 24—ISAAC AND REBEKAH

1. Abraham wanted Isaac to marry a woman who would know God and bear a son who would carry out God's covenant promise. A Canaanite woman would not acknowledge the true God. (Genesis 24:1–4)
2. Abraham's chief servant embarked on a difficult errand. How would he find the right woman? What if she refused to come back with him? He prayed for specific guidance, and God answered, leaving no question about Rebekah (Genesis 24:5–61). When we pray for God's plan to be fulfilled, we can trust God to answer. (1 John 5:14–15)

3. Rebekah showed courtesy to the stranger at the well. Then, in volunteering to draw water for his camels, she showed extraordinary thoughtfulness, high motivation for work, and unusual energy and endurance. (Genesis 24:15–21)
4. Rebekah's kindness and helpfulness were given with no expectation of reward. She acted out of her own character and was surprised to be amply rewarded. (Genesis 24:22)
5. God revealed his will to the servant by fulfilling the sign exactly as the servant had requested (Genesis 24:42–54). Today God guides mostly through Scripture and the counsel of godly people.

CHAPTER 18: GENESIS 25–26—GOD'S COVENANT IS PASSED ON

1. God provides details of Abraham's descendants through his sons by Keturah as well as through Ishmael. Then he turns to a detailed account of Isaac's family, since the covenant promises were being fulfilled through Isaac. (Genesis 25:1–18)
2. Esau is described as godless because he sold something of great spiritual value for one single meal. Though he later regretted his decision, he could not reverse it. (Genesis 25:29–34; Hebrews 12:16–17)
3. Even before Esau and Jacob were born, God had said Jacob would inherit the covenant promise. Jacob wanted that inheritance, but did not look to God to fulfill his promise. Instead, he took it from Esau when it was to his advantage to do so. (Genesis 25:23–34)
4. Parents who do not let God help them overcome their weaknesses may pass them on to their children. Twice Abraham had feared for his life and called Sarah his sister. Isaac yielded to the same temptation. (Genesis 26:7–11)
5. God blesses peacemakers. People who trust God can look to him to meet their needs. (Genesis 26:26–33)

CHAPTER 19: GENESIS 27–28—GOD'S BLESSING FOR JACOB

1. Isaac prepared to give Esau the blessing, though he had known since before Esau and Jacob were born that God had chosen Jacob to have it. Rebekah directed Jacob in a scheme to trick Isaac into giving Jacob the blessing. Esau was determined to get the blessing, which he had sold with his birthright. (Genesis 27)
2. We reap the consequences when we deliberately go against what we know God plans. After Jacob had to run for his life, he never saw his mother again.
3. God carried out his plan for Jacob, in spite of the faulty actions of all family members.
4. As Jacob journeyed to his relatives to escape Esau's death threat, God appeared to him in a dream, restating the covenant blessing and promising to watch over him and bring him back to the land. (Genesis 28:10–15)
5. When Jacob woke up, he realized that God had spoken to him. After setting up a pillar and pouring oil on it, Jacob made a vow that if God would be with him and bring him back, he would honor God and give him one-tenth of all his possessions. (Genesis 28:16–22)

CHAPTER 20: GENESIS 29–31—JACOB IN PADDAN ARAM

1. Laban welcomed Jacob into his home, embracing him with a kiss and saying "You are my own flesh and blood." Twenty years later, when Jacob left, Laban and Jacob made a heap of stones to mark their separation. Laban did not kiss Jacob. He resented God's blessing on Jacob. (Genesis 29:13–14; 31:43–59)
2. God used Laban's cheating and mistreatment of Jacob to discipline him and refine his character.
3. Jacob's wives competed. Leah bore him sons, but Rachel had his love. In competing, both wives gave Jacob their maids to produce more sons. (Genesis 29:14–30:26)
4. God prospered Jacob's herds and built his wealth in spite of Laban's deceit and cheating. (Genesis 30:25–43)
5. Jacob became aware of Laban's hostility but did not leave until the Lord told him to return to Canaan. (Genesis 31:1–2)

CHAPTER 21: GENESIS 32–36: JACOB RETURNS TO THE PROMISED LAND

1. While Jacob was asking God to protect him from Esau's four hundred men, he took steps to protect his family and herds. He divided them into two groups and sent gifts of animals to pacify Esau. Then as Esau approached, he divided his wives and children to minimize loss if Esau was hostile. (Genesis 32:7–8, 13–16; 33:1–2).
2. Jacob's name meant "supplanter" or "deceitful." Israel meant "he fights and overcomes with God."
3. Esau welcomed Jacob with a tearful embrace and appeared to have forgotten his anger, but neither man spoke of forgiveness. While the relationship was congenial, Jacob did not fully trust Esau. The brothers never did spend lengthy time together. (Genesis 33:1–17)
4. Jacob was not a spiritual leader in his family. Even when his sons slaughtered the men of Shechem,

Jacob expressed more concern for his safety than for their sin. (Genesis 34; 35:21–22) When Reuben slept with Jacob's concubine Bilhah, Jacob did not confront him. (Genesis 35:22)

5. God spoke to Jacob and told him to return to Bethel, the place of Jacob's encounter with God when he was escaping Esau's anger twenty years before (Genesis 28:10–22). Jacob required his family to get rid of their foreign gods and prepare to meet with God. At Bethel God renewed his covenant with Jacob. (Genesis 35:1–15)

CHAPTER 22: GENESIS 37–38—JOSEPH AND HIS FAMILY

1. Joseph, firstborn son of beloved Rachel, was clearly Jacob's favorite son. By giving Joseph a special coat, Jacob aroused in his other sons deep feelings of jealousy and hatred toward Joseph. (Genesis 37:1–4)
2. God gave Joseph two dreams that Joseph and his family understood had significance for his future. While the dreams only infuriated the brothers, they gave Joseph hope. (Genesis 37:5–11)
3. Though Jacob had met with God at Bethel, and there God had renewed his covenant with Jacob and his descendants, his sons did not regard God in their behavior. (Genesis 35:1–14; 37–38)
4. God showed grace to Tamar, who had been disgraced by Judah. He showed grace to Judah and worked out his sovereign plan in spite of Judah's wrongdoing. Tamar is included in the genealogy of Jesus. (Matthew 1:3)
5. God warns of the danger of being influenced by ungodly people. They can bring temptations that lead us away from God. (Psalm 1; Proverbs 1:8–19; 13:20)

CHAPTER 23: GENESIS 39–41—JOSEPH IN EGYPT

1. God was with Joseph, giving success to everything he did. He gave Joseph strength to resist the enticement of Potiphar's wife. In prison, God gave Joseph wisdom to interpret the dreams of Pharaoh's cupbearer and baker. Then, in the palace, he gave Joseph wisdom to interpret Pharaoh's dreams. That put Joseph in favor with Pharaoh so that Joseph became second in command in Egypt. (Genesis 39–41)
2. Joseph did not allow bitterness to take root in his heart, and thus he was ready for God to fulfill his plans for him. Throughout the difficulties and injustices, Joseph grew in character. God was preparing him for a leadership role.
3. Joseph immediately told Pharaoh that he could not interpret his dream, but that God would give the answer. Joseph then told Pharaoh that the dreams were God's way of telling what he was going to do. Pharaoh acknowledged that God's Spirit was in Joseph. (Genesis 41:16, 25, 28, 32, 38–39)
4. God was with Joseph in a special way because Joseph's heart was pure and open to God, even in times when he could have been bitter and in despair.
5. Though Joseph had received no training in administering resources on a national scale, he was qualified to take charge of Egypt's famine relief plan because he knew how to receive wisdom from God, and God continued to prosper his work.

CHAPTER 24: GENESIS 42–50—JOSEPH AND HIS BROTHERS

1. Without knowing who the Egyptian official really was, the brothers bowed before him, just as Joseph's dreams had indicated. (Genesis 37:5–11; 42:1–9)
2. Joseph tested his brothers to see if their hearts had changed. (Genesis 42–44)
3. Joseph was able to forgive his brothers because he knew that God had taken what they had meant for harm and used it for good. (Genesis 50:15–21)
4. As Jacob set out for Egypt, God spoke to him, telling him not to fear going there, for God would make his family into a nation in Egypt and would bring them back to the Promised Land. (Genesis 50:1–4)
5. When Joseph asked that his bones be carried from Egypt to Canaan, he was affirming his belief that some day God would take his family out of Egypt to give them the Promised Land. (Genesis 50:24–25)

Appendix D – The Experts

Allen, Ronald B.—Professor of Bible Exposition at Dallas Theological Seminary.

Anderson, Leith—Senior pastor of Wooddale Church, and a popular speaker.

Arnold, Bill T.—Professor of Old Testament and Semitic languages at Asbury Theological Seminary.

Arthur, Kay—Well-known Bible teacher, best-selling author, and the founder of Precept Ministries.

Atkinson, David—Fellow and chaplain of Corpus Christi College, Oxford, and author of Bible study books.

Beers, V. Gilbert—Prolific writer of Bible background and children's books, curriculum developer, and editor.

Bilezikian, Gilbert—One of the cofounders of Willow Creek Community Church and a professor of biblical studies at Wheaton College.

Boice, James Montgomery—Senior pastor of Philadelphia's Tenth Presbyterian Church, radio speaker and writer of Bible study books.

Bridges, Jerry—On the staff of Navigators Community Ministries Group with a Bible-teaching ministry, and author of best-selling books.

Carmichael, Amy—Founder of the Dohnavur Fellowship in India, author of many books about the ministry and books of poems and devotionals.

Chambers, Oswald—A Bible teacher, conference leader, and YMCA chaplain. His writing, compiled after his death by his widow, is available in devotional books, including the popular *My Utmost for His Highest.*

Dawson, Gerrit Scott—Senior minister of First Presbyterian Church in Lenoir, North Carolina, and author of devotional studies.

Duck, Daymond R.—This best-selling author of *The Book of Revelation—The Smart Guide to the Bible*™ and *The Book of Daniel—The Smart Guide to the Bible*™. Teaches about Bible prophecies on radio and television.

Elliot, Elisabeth—Public speaker, best-selling author, and speaker on the radio program *Gateway to Joy.*

Evans, W. Glyn—Minister-at-large for the Conservative Baptist Association of New England. Has been a pastor, professor, and writer.

Fortosis, Stephen—College professor and writer.

Foster, Richard J.—Best-selling author, founder of Renovare, an organization dedicated to church renewal, and professor of Spiritual Formation at Azusa Pacific University.

Geisler, Norman—Dean of the Southern Evangelical Seminary in Charlotte, North Carolina, and author or coauthor of over thirty books.

Getz, Gene—Senior pastor of Fellowship Bible Church, radio commentator, and writer.

Graham, Billy—World-famous evangelist and best-selling author of several books.

Ham, Ken—Director and Founder of Answers in Genesis (in the United States) and the Creation Science Foundation ministry (in Australia).

Hamilton, Victor P.—Professor of religion at Asbury College, Wilmore, Kentucky.

Hayford, Jack W.—Pastor of The Church On The Way in Van Nuys, California, teacher, composer, author of many books, and Senior Editor of the *Spirit Filled Life Bible.*

Howe, Thomas A.—Associate Professor of Bible and Biblical Languages at the Southern Evangelical Seminary in Charlotte, North Carolina.

Hybels, Bill—Senior pastor of Willow Creek Community Church and the author of many books.

Joy, Donald—Professor of Human Development and Christian Education at Asbury Theological Seminary in Wilmore, Kentucky.

Kidner, Derek—Former warden of Tyndale House, Cambridge, and author of Bible commentaries.

Lewis, C. S.—Teacher of English Literature and Language and Professor of Medieval and Renaissance English Literature, and best-selling author of books of theology, science fiction, and juvenile fantasies, "The Chronicles of Narnia."

Lotz, Anne Graham—Daughter of Billy and Ruth Bell Graham, and founder of AnGel Ministries for which she speaks, provides audiotapes, books, and devotional study aids.

Lucado, Max—Pastor, speaker, and author of numerous best-selling books.

McGee, J. Vernon—Former host of the popular *Through the Bible* radio program.

Mehl, Ron—Pastor and author of best-selling books.

Meyer, F. B.—British Bible teacher whose writing has enriched readers for more than one hundred years.

Miller, Kathy Collard—Writer and speaker about issues facing women, including how to heal and grow a marriage. She has written or compiled over thirty books, including the best-selling God's Vitamin C for the Spirit series and *Women of the Bible—The Smart Guide to the Bible*™.

Morris, Henry M.—President of the Institute for Creation Research.

Ogilvie, Lloyd—Former Senior Pastor of the First Presbyterian Church of Hollywood, now Chaplain of the Senate, writer, radio and television broadcaster.

Ortlund, Ray—Speaker on Haven broadcasts, has worldwide ministry with his wife Anne with Renewal Ministries, Newport Beach, CA.

Packer, J. I.—Professor of Systematic and Historic Theology at Regent College in Vancouver, British Columbia.

Peterson, Eugene H.—Pastor of Christ Our King United Presbyterian Church in Bel Air, writer.

Piper, John—Senior pastor of Bethlehem Baptist Church in Minneapolis and a best-selling author.

Richards, Larry—One of today's well-known biblical writers, with over 175 books to his credit including works on Christian education, biblical and theological study, devotional and enrichment topics, and study Bibles.

Ryrie, Charles Caldwell—A theologian, Professor of Systematic Theology at Dallas Theological Seminary, author of theological books and the notes for *The Ryrie Study Bible.*

Sailhamer, John H.—Professor of Hebrew Scriptures at Western Seminary, Portland, Oregon, and author of Bible commentaries.

Schaeffer, Edith—Cofounder of L'Abri Fellowship with her husband, Dr. Francis Schaeffer, well-known Christian speaker, counselor, and writer.

Schultz, Samuel J.—Former professor emeritus of Bible and Theology at Wheaton College, Wheaton, Illinois, and an author.

Seamands, David A.—Former missionary and pastor, now Professor of Pastoral Ministries at Asbury Theological Seminary in Wilmore, Kentucky.

Skilling, Tom—Chief meteorologist at Chicago's WGNTTV, and the writer of "Ask Tom Why," a weather-related column in the *Chicago Tribune.*

Smith, Hannah Whitall—A writer and Bible teacher, best known for her book, *The Christian's Secret of a Happy Life*, first published in 1875.

Sproul, R. C.—Theologian, pastor, teacher, chair man of the board of Ligonier Ministries, writer of best-selling books.

Swindoll, Charles R.—President of Dallas Theological Seminary, host of the nationally syndicated radio program *Insight for Living*, and author of more than twenty-five books.

Tobias, Cynthia Ulrich—Founder and president of Learning Styles Unlimited, Inc., and a popular author and speaker.

Tozer, A. W.—Pastor, longtime editor of *The Alliance Weekly* (now called *Alliance Life*, the official magazine of The Christian and Missionary Alliance), and author of many books.

Wiersbe, Warren—One of the evangelical world's most-respected Bible teachers, and author of more than one hundred books.

Willard, Dallas—Professor at the University of Southern California's School of Philosophy, and author of best-selling books.

Endnotes

CHAPTER 1: GENESIS 1—THE BEGINNING

1. C. S. Lewis, *The Quotable Lewis* (Wheaton: Tyndale House Publishers, 1989), 33.
2. Anne Graham Lotz, *God's Story* (Nashville: Word Publishing, 1997), xxiv.
3. V. Gilbert Beers, *God's Pioneers* (Grand Rapids: The Zondervan Corporation, 1980), 13.
4. Bruce Malone, Creation Science Evangelism, http://www.drdino.com/articles.php?spec=8.
5. Lawrence O. Richards, *It Couldn't Just Happen* (Nashville: Word Publishing, 1989), 11–12.
6. Michael Behe, biochemist quoted in *New Man*, Mar/Apr 2003, page 31 and Issue #43, May 2003, *Current Thoughts & Trends,* online archives.
7. David Hall, "Covering the Past," *Tabletalk*, July 2001 (Vol. 25, No. 7, p. 8–10 and Issue #25, November 2001, *Current Thoughts & Trends*, online archives.
8. Arno Froese, "World Focus," *Midnight Call*, June 2005, 41.
9. Lee Strobel, *The Case for a Creator, Student Edition* (Grand Rapids, MI: Zondervan, 2004), 31.
10. Lotz, *God's Story*, 254.
11. Todd Strandberg, "This Old Planet," raptureready.com/rr-planet.html.
12. Henry M. Morris, *The Genesis Record* (Grand Rapids: Baker Book House, 1976), 63.
13. Henry Hengeveld: *Banner*, April 24, 2000 (Vol. 135, No. 9), page 24–25 and Issue #11, September 2000, *Current Thoughts & Trends,* online archives.
14. George F. Will, "The Gospel from Science," *Newsweek*, November 9, 1998, 88.
15. Lawrence O. Richards, *The Teacher's Commentary* (Colorado Springs: Chariot Victor, 1987), 28.
16. Rick Warren, *The Purpose-Driven Life* (Grand Rapids, MI: Zondevan, 2002), 63.
17. J. Vernon McGee, *Genesis 1–15* (Nashville: Thomas Nelson Publishers, 1991), 75.
18. James Montgomery Boice, *Genesis, Volume 1: Creation and Fall* (Grand Rapids: Baker Books, 1998), 86.

CHAPTER 2: GENESIS 2—THE CROWN OF CREATION

1. John Piper, *Let the Nations Be Glad* (Grand Rapids: Baker Book House, 1993), 14.
2. Tom Skilling, "Ask Tom Why," *Chicago Tribune* (January 9, 1999).
3. Bill Hybels, *Laws of the Heart* (Colorado Springs: Chariot Victor, 1985), 51.
4. Ron Mehl, *The Ten(der) Commandments* (Sisters, OR: Multnomah Publishers, 1998), 109–110.
5. Ronald B. Allen, *The Majesty of Man* (Sisters, OR: Multnomah Press, 1984), 199
6. Isaac Newton, quoted by Dr. Paul Brand and Philip Yancey, *Fearfully and Wonderfully Made* (Grand Rapids: Zondervan, 1980), 161.
7. Paul Brand with Philip Yancey, *Fearfully and Wonderfully Made* (Grand Rapids: Zondervan, 1980), 161.
8. Jack Hayford, General Editor, *Spirit-Filled Life Bible, New King James Version* (Nashville: Thomas Nelson, 1991), 7.
9. Wiersbe, *Be Basic*, 39.
10. Morris, *The Genesis Record*, 90.
11. McGee, *Genesis 1–15*, 81.
12. Wiersbe, *Be Basic*, 13.
13. Carl F. H. Henry (quote in *Modern Reformation*, May/June 1999, page 14) and Issue #3, January 2000 *Current Thoughts & Trends* online archives.

14. Victor P. Hamilton, *The Book of Genesis Chapters 1–17* (Grand Rapids: William B. Eerdmans Publishing Company, 1990), 175.
15. Lotz, *God's Story*, 52.
16. Morris, *The Genesis Record*, 100.
17. Richard J. Foster, *Seeking the Kingdom* (New York: HarperSanFrancisco, 1995), 107.
18. Elisabeth Elliot, *The Path of Loneliness* (Nashville: Thomas Nelson, 1988), 15.
19. Edith Schaeffer, *Lifelines* (Wheaton: Crossway Books, 1982), 144.
20. Lloyd Ogilvie, *Enjoying God* (Nashville: Word Publishing, 1989), 3.

CHAPTER 3: GENESIS 3—TROUBLE IN THE GARDEN

1. Wiersbe, *Be Basic*, 60.
2. Hamilton, *The Book of Genesis Chapters 1–17*, 190.
3. David A. Seamands, *Freedom from the Performance Trap* (Colorado Springs: Chariot Victor, 1988), 60–61.
4. Elliot, *Keep a Quiet Heart* (Ann Arbor: Servant Publications, 1995), 45.
5. Wiersbe, *Be Basic*, 64.
6. Gilbert Bilezikian, *Christianity 101* (Grand Rapids: Zondervan, 1993), 131.
7. R. C. Sproul, *Now That's a Good Question* (Wheaton: Tyndale House Publishers, Inc., 1996), 475.
8. Liz Curtis Higgs, *Bad Girls of the Bible* (Colorado Springs, CO: Waterbrook Press, 1999) 38-39.
9. Elliot, *A Lamp to My Feet* (Ann Arbor: Servant Publications, 1985), 45–46.
10. Richards, *Illustrated Bible Handbook* (Nashville: Thomas Nelson Publishers, 1997), 31.
11. Allen, *The Majesty of Man*, 106.

CHAPTER 4: GENESIS 4–5—THE FIRST FAMILY

1. McGee, *Genesis 1–15*, 103.
2. Mehl, *The Ten(der) Commandments*, 157.
3. Schaeffer, *Lifelines*, 122.
4. Lotz, *God's Story*, 101.
5. Wiersbe, *Be Basic*, 78.
6. Norman Geisler and Thomas Howe, *When Critics Ask* (Grand Rapids: Baker Books, 1992), 38.
7. W. Glyn Evans, *Don't Quit Until You Taste the Honey* (Nashville: Broadman Press, 1993), 99.
8. J. I. Packer, *Knowing God* (Downers Grove: InterVarsity Press, 1973), 99.

CHAPTER 5: GENESIS 6–7: NOAH AND THE FLOOD

1. Hamilton, *The Book of Genesis Chapters 1–17*, 173.
2. R. C. Sproul, *Almighty Over All* (Grand Rapids, Baker Books, 1999), 70.
3. Hamilton, *The Book of Genesis Chapters 1–17*, 184.
4. Boice, *Genesis, Volume 1*, 328.
5. Ibid., 327.
6. Beers, *God's Pioneers*, 51.
7. Amy Carmichael, *Whispers of His Power* (Fort Washington: Christian Literature Crusade, 1982), 45.
8. Lawrence O. Richards, *The Revell Bible Dictionary* (New York: Wynwood Press, 1990), 140.
9. Elliot, "Joy to the World," *The Elisabeth Elliot Newsletter* (November/December 1996): 2.
10. Victor P. Hamilton, *The Book of Genesis Chapters 1–17*, 288.
11. McGee, *Genesis 1–15*, 132.
12. Duck, *The Book of Daniel—The Smart Guide to the Bible*(tm) series (Nashville, TN: Thomas Nelson Publishers, 2006). .
13. John H. Sailhamer, *Biblical Archaeology* (Grand Rapids: Zondervan Publishing House, 1998), 27.
14. Richards, *The Revell Bible Dictionary*, 390.

CHAPTER 6: GENESIS 8–9—A FRESH BEGINNING

1. Schultz, *The Old Testament Speaks*, 16.
2. McGee, *Genesis 1–15*, 138.
3. Matthew Henry, *Matthew Henry's Commentary on the Whole Bible* (USA: Hendrickson Publishers, 1991) 27.4.
4. Richards, *Illustrated Bible Handbook*, 40.
5. Boice, *Genesis, Volume 1*, 372.
6. Dallas Willard, *The Divine Conspiracy* (New York: HarperSanFrancisco, 1998), 243.
7. Wiersbe, Be Basic, 117.
8. Kay Arthur, *Our Covenant God* (Colorado Springs: WaterBrook Press, 1999), 22.

9. Atkinson, *The Message of Genesis 1–11*, 164.
10. Walvoord and Zuck, *The Bible Knowledge Commentary*, 41.
11. Atkinson, *The Message of Genesis 1–11*, 178.

CHAPTER 7: GENESIS 10–11—BIRTH OF NATIONS

1. David Atkinson, *The Message of Genesis 1–11* (Downers Grove: InterVarsity Press, 1990), 174.
2. Atkinson, *The Message of Genesis 1–11*, 178.
3. Eugene H. Peterson, *A Long Obedience in the Same Direction* (Downers Grove: InterVarsity Press, 1980), 101.
4. Richards, *The Revell Bible Dictionary*, 119.
5. Schultz, *The Old Testament Speaks*, 17.
6. Richards, *The Revell Bible Dictionary*, 1002.

CHAPTER 8: GENESIS 12—ABRAM

1. Gerrit Scott Dawson, *Called By a New Name* (Nashville: Upper Room Books, 1997), 30–31.
2. McGee, *Genesis 1–15*, 169.
3. F. B. Meyer, *The Life of Abraham* (Lynnwood: Emerald Books, 1996), 36.
4. Boice, *Genesis, Volume 2, A New Beginning* (Grand Rapids: Baker Books, 1998), 474.
5. Bill Hybels, *Laws of the Heart*, 100.

CHAPTER 9: GENESIS 13–14—ABRAM AND LOT

1. Schultz, *The Old Testament Speaks*, 33.
2. Boice, *Genesis, Volume 2*, 493.
3. R. C. Sproul, *The Invisible Hand* (Nashville: Word Publishing, 1997), 45.
4. Hayford, *Spirit Filled Life Bible*, 25–26.
5. Walvoord and Zuck, *The Bible Knowledge Commentary*, 54.
6. Bill T. Arnold, *Encountering the Book of Genesis* (Grand Rapids: Baker Books, 1998), 90.

CHAPTER 10: GENESIS 15—GOD'S COVENANT

1. Lloyd Ogilvie, *12 Steps to Living Without Fear* (Nashville: Word Books, 1987), 24.
2. Henry T. Blackaby and Claude V. King, *The Experiencing God Study Bible, The New King James Version* (Nashville: Broadman & Holman Publishers, 1994), 19.
3. Elliot, "Faith for the Unexplained," *The Elisabeth Elliot Newsletter* (September/October 1996): 1.
4. Boice, *Genesis, Volume 2*, 546.
5. Richards, *The Bible Reader's Companion* (Colorado Springs: Chariot Victor, 1991), 35.
6. A. W. Tozer, *The Knowledge of the Holy* (New York: Harper & Brothers, 1961), 67–68.

CHAPTER 11: GENESIS 16—HAGAR AND ISHMAEL

1. Gene A. Getz, *Abraham: Holding Fast to the Will of God* (Nashville: Broadman & Holman Publishers, 1996), 99.
2. Morris, *The Genesis Record*, 329–330.
3. Meyer, *The Life of Abraham*, 99.
4. Kay Arthur, *Lord, I Want to Know You* (Sisters, OR: Multnomah Books, 1992), 37.
5. J. I. Packer, *Knowing God*, 39.

CHAPTER 12: GENESIS 17—GOD'S COVENANT CONFIRMED

1. Richards, *The Revell Bible Dictionary*, 332.
2. Arnold, *Encountering the Book of Genesis*, 97.
3. Dawson, *Called By a New Name*, 75.
4. Kathy Collard Miller, *Women of the Bible—The Smart Guide to the Bible™ series* (Nashville, TN: Thomas Nelson Publishers, 2006).
5. Boice, *Genesis, Volume 2*, 731–732.
6. R. C. Sproul, *Now That's a Good Question*, 253.

CHAPTER 13: GENESIS 18–19—JUDGMENT ON SIN

1. V. Gilbert Beers, *Victor Handbook of Bible Knowledge* (Colorado Springs: Chariot Victor, 1981), 445.
2. Billy Graham, *Angels: God's Secret Agents* (Garden City: Doubleday & Company, Inc., 1975), 33.
3. Hayford, *Spirit Filled Life Biblee*, 31.
4. Charles Caldwell Ryrie, *The Ryrie Study Bible, New American Standard* (Chicago: Moody Press), 35.
5. Lloyd Ogilvie, *Turn Your Struggles into Stepping Stones* (Nashville: Word Publishing, 1993), 65.
6. Charles R. Swindoll, *Growing Strong in the Seasons of Life* (Sisters, OR : Multnomah Press, 1983), 387.

CHAPTER 14: GENESIS 20—ABRAHAM AND ABIMELECH

1. Kidner, *Genesis*, 137.
2. Elliot, "Afraid?" *The Elisabeth Elliot Newsletter* (May/June 1991): 1.

3. Meyer, *The Life of Abraham*, 138.

CHAPTER 15: GENESIS 21—REORDERING LIFE

1. Dallas Willard, *The Divine Conspiracy*, 238–39.
2. Getz, *Abraham*, 159.
3. Stephen Fortosis, *Great Men and Women of the Bible* (Mahwah: Paulist Press, 1996), 14.
4. Kidner, *Genesis*, 141.
5. Hamilton, *The Book of Genesis, Chapters 18–50*, 92.

CHAPTER 16: GENESIS 22–23—A HEARTRENDING TEST

1. Walvoord and Zuck, *The Bible Knowledge Commentary*, 64.
2. Meyer, *The Life of Abraham*, 165.
3. Wiersbe, *Be Obedient* (Colorado Springs: Chariot Victor Publishing, 1991), 109–10.
4. Ryrie, *The Ryrie Study Bible*, 40.

CHAPTER 17: GENESIS 24—ISAAC AND REBEKAH

1. Kidner, *Genesis*, 146.
2. Leith Anderson, *When God Says No* (Minneapolis: Bethany House Publishers, 1996), 154.
3. Wiersbe, *Be Obedient*, 120.
4. Hayford, *The Spirit Filled Life Bible*, 38–39.
5. Meyer, *The Life of Abraham*, 181.
6. Elliot, *A Lamp to My Feet*, 90.
7. Boice, *Genesis, Volume 2*, 720.
8. Foster, *Seeking the Kingdom*, 64.
9. Wiersbe, *Be Obedient*, 123.

CHAPTER 18: GENESIS 25–26—GOD'S COVENANT IS PASSED ON

1. Ray Ortlund, *Anchor* monthly devotional (Costa Mesa, CA: Haven Ministries), Volume 24, Number 10, Day 29.
2. Wiersbe, *Be Obedient*, 134.
3. Morris, *The Genesis Record*, 410.
4. Elliot, *The Path of Loneliness*, 139.
5. Richards, *The 365-Day Devotional Commentary* (Colorado Springs: Chariot Victor, 1990), 26.
6. Cynthia Ulrich Tobias, *The Way They Learn* (Colorado Springs: Focus on the Family Publishing, 1994), 4.
7. Gene Getz, *Jacob* (Nashville: Broadman & Holman Publishers, 1996), 15.
8. Morris, *The Genesis Record*, 416.
9. Wiersbe, *Be Authentic* (Colorado Springs: Chariot Victor, 1997), 16.
10. Kidner, *Genesis*, 154.
11. Donald Joy, *Walk On!* (Colorado Springs: Chariot Victor, 1988), 77.

CHAPTER 19: GENESIS 27–28—GOD'S BLESSING FOR JACOB

1. Boice, *Genesis, Volume 2*, 752.
2. Getz, *Jacob*, 40.
3. Morris, *The Genesis Record*, 433.
4. Boice, *Genesis, Volume 2*, 757.
5. Kidner, *Genesis*, 157.
6. Walvoord and Zuck, *The Bible Knowledge Commentary*, 72.
7. Joy, *Walk On!*, 81.
8. Jerry Bridges, *The Joy of Fearing God* (Colorado Springs: WaterBrook Press, 1997), 35–36.

CHAPTER 20: GENESIS 29–31—JACOB IN PADDAN ARAM

1. Getz, *Jacob*, 75.
2. Ibid., 79.
3. Elliot, "The Proof of Love," *The Elisabeth Elliot Newsletter* (March/April, 1997), 4.
4. Richards, *The 365-Day Devotional Commentary*, 29.
5. Fortosis, *Great Men and Women of the Bible*, 19–20.
6. Schultz, *The Old Testament Speaks*, 36–37.
7. Hamilton, *The Book of Genesis, Chapters 18–50*, 317.

CHAPTER 21: GENESIS 32–36—JACOB RETURNS TO THE PROMISED LAND

1. Graham, *Angels: God's Secret Agents*, 31.
2. Geisler and Howe, *When Critics Ask*, 395.
3. Schultz, *The Old Testament Speaks*, 37.
4. Getz, *Jacob*, 159.
5. Evans, *Don't Quit Until You Taste the Honey*, 49.
6. Arnold, *Encountering the Book of Genesiss*, 137.

CHAPTER 22: GENESIS 37–38—JOSEPH AND HIS FAMILY

1. Getz, *Joseph* (Nashville: Broadman & Holman Publishers, 1996), 23.
2. Charles R. Swindoll, *Joseph* (Nashville: Word Publishing, 1998), 13.

3. Joy, *Walk On!*, 116.
4. Oswald Chambers, *Devotions for a Deeper Life* (Grand Rapids: Francis Asbury Press, 1986), 133.
5. Richards, *The Bible Reader's Companion*, 45.
6. Kathy Collard Miller, *Women of the Bible—The Smart Guide to the Bible*™ series.
7. Arnold, *Encountering the Book of Genesis*, 149.
8. Peggy Lynch, "Seek and Find," a Bible study in *Unveiled* by Francine Rivers (Wheaton, IL: Tyndale House, 2000) 151.

CHAPTER 23: GENESIS 39–41—JOSEPH IN EGYPT

1. McGee, *Genesis, Chapters 34–50* (Nashville: Thomas Nelson Publishers, 1991), 69.
2. Hamilton, *The Book of Genesis Chapters 18–50* (Grand Rapids: William B. Eerdmans Publishing Company, 1995), 460.
3. Charles R. Swindoll, Come Before Winter (Sisters, OR: Multnomah Press, 1985), 33.
4. Seamands, *Healing for Damaged Emotions* (Colorado Springs: Chariot Victor, 1981), 35–36.
5. Oswald Chambers, *Our Portrait in Genesis* (London: Oswald Chambers Publications Association and Marshall, Morgan & Scott, Ltd., 1957), 70–71.
6. Elliot, *Twelve Baskets of Crumbs* (Chappaqua: Christian Herald House, 1976), 65.
7. Getz, *Joseph*, 75.
8. Wiersbe, *Be Authentic* 100.
9. Evans, *Don't Quit Until You Taste the Honey*, 25–26.
10. Beers, *The Victor Handbook of Bible Knowledge*, 80.

CHAPTER 24: GENESIS 42–50—JOSEPH AND HIS BROTHERS

1. Swindoll, *Joseph*, 92.
2. Getz, *Joseph*, 133.
3. Morris, *The Genesis Record*, 606.
4. Swindoll, *Joseph*, 122–123.
5. Beers, *The Victor Handbook of Bible Knowledge*, 83.
6. Ryrie, *The Ryrie Study Bible*, 78.
7. Seamands, *Freedom from the Performance Trap*, 7.
8. Hannah Whitall Smith, *The Unselfishness of God* (Princeton: Littlebrook Publishing, Inc., 1987), 222.
9. Lucado, "Life Lessons with Max Lucado, Book of Genesis," excerpt from *When God Whispers Your Name* (Colorado Springs: Navpress, 1987), 104.
10. Andrew Murray, *Waiting on God* (London: Nisbet & Co. Ltd.), 21.
11. Richards, *The 365-Day Devotional Commentary*, 39.
12. Boice, Genesis, Volume 3, 1254.
13. Chambers, *Our Brilliant Heritage* (London: Oswald Chambers Publications and Marshall, Morgan & Scott, 1929), 118.
14. Getz, *Joseph*, 173.
15. Seamands, *Freedom from the Performance Trap*, 28.

The Genesis Record by Gilbert Morris. © 1976 Baker Book House.

Genesis, 3 Volumes by James Montgomery Boice. © 1998 Baker Book House.

God's Story by Anne Graham Lotz. © Word Publishing, Nashville, TN.

Jacob by Gene A. Getz. © 1996 LifeWay Christian Resources of the Southern Baptist Convention, 127 Ninth Avenue North, Nashville, TN 37234. Published by Broadman & Holman Publishers, Nashville, TN.

Joseph by Charles R. Swindoll. © Word Publishing, Nashville, TN.

Joseph by Gene A. Getz. © 1996 LifeWay Christian Resources of the Southern Baptist Convention, 127 Ninth Avenue North, Nashville, TN 37234. Published by Broadman & Holman Publishers, Nashville, TN.

Keep a Quiet Heart by Elisabeth Elliot. © 1995 by Elisabeth Elliot. Published by Servant Publications, Box 8617, Ann Arbor, MI 48107.

A Lamp for My Feet by Elisabeth Elliot. © 1985 by Elisabeth Elliot. Published by Servant Publications, Box 8617, Ann Arbor, MI 48107.

The Life of Abraham by F. B. Meyers. © 1996 Emerald Books, P.O. Box 635, Lynnwood, WA 98026.

The Message of Genesis 1–11 (BST) by David J. Atkinson. © 1990 by David J. Atkinson. Used with permission from InterVarsity Press, P.O. Box 1400, Downers Grove, IL 60515.

A Path Through Suffering by Elisabeth Elliot. © 1985 by Elisabeth Elliot. Published by Servant Publications, Box 8617, Ann Arbor, MI 48107.

The Revell Bible Dictionary by Lawrence O. Richards. © 1990 Baker Book House.

Spirit-Filled Life Bible ed. by Jack Hayford. © 1982, 1991 Thomas Nelson, Inc.

The Teaher's Commentary by Lawrence O. Richards. © 1987 Cook Communications Ministries.

The 365 Day Devosional Commentary by Lawrence O. Richards. © 1990 Cook Communications Ministries.

Index

F

G

H

I

J

O

P

R

S

Printed in the USA
CPSIA information can be obtained
at www.ICGtesting.com
LVHW081911031124
795410LV00001B/2

9 781418 509934